David Rizzio
and Mary
Queen of Scots

Queen Mary's Closet, Holyrood.

David Rizzio and Mary Queen of Scots

Murder at Holyrood

DAVID TWEEDIE

SUTTON PUBLISHING

First published in the United Kingdom in 2006 by
Sutton Publishing Limited

This revised edition first published in 2007 by
Sutton Publishing, an imprint of NPI Media Group Limited
Cirencester Road · Chalford · Stroud · Gloucestershire · GL6 8PE

British Library Cataloguing in Publication Data
A catalogue record for this book is available from the British Library.

ISBN 978-0-7509-4332-1

To my wife, Mary

Typeset in Sabon.
Typesetting and origination by
NPI Media Group Limited.
Printed and bound in England.

Contents

List of Illustrations

Chapter heading motif: the old abbey at Holyrood
Chapter tailpiece motif: the palace of Holyroodhouse

Note on the Text

Spelling and orthography have changed since the sixteenth century. John Knox, for example, referred to 'duck' when he meant 'duke'. Here modern punctuation and capitalisation are provided, and the language updated, so as to make sense to the reader today. Some specific Scots words – for example, 'thole', 'policies' – will also be found. But the quotations keep to the original language as much as possible, especially in Mary's letters.

The New Year is assumed to begin on 1 January, and not on 25 March (Lady Day, the Feast of The Annunciation) and dates are given accordingly.

Any errors are the fault of the author, for which he begs indulgence.

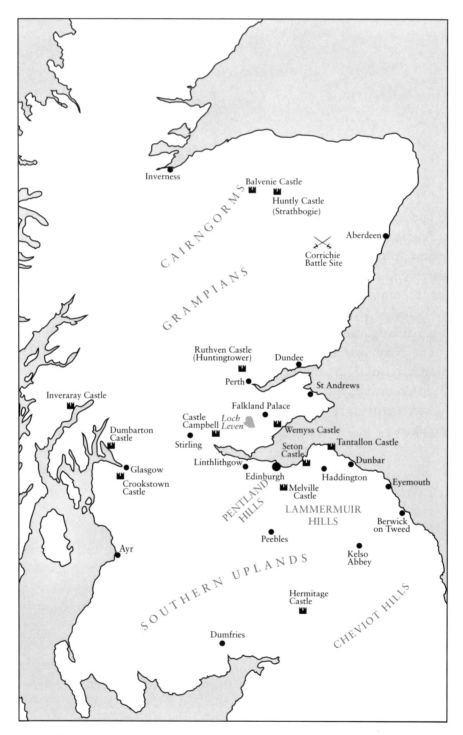

Map of Scotland showing the main places mentioned.

Prologue

For over 200 years an enormous smoky, black, bitumen-based oil painting has hung in the Guildhall at the heart of the old City of London. This dark canvas depicts the murder of David Rizzio in gory Gothic detail. It shows Patrick, Lord Ruthven, wasted with cancer and cased in body armour, holding back the anguished figure of Mary Queen of Scots, as his henchmen ready themselves to stab their prey to death.

Since the picture was first hung in 1793, statesmen, aldermen, monarchs and national heroes, when enjoying the City's hospitality, have lifted their eyes from the turtle soup and liverymen's fare to ponder this work by John Opie. Only two generations ago the Soviet Foreign Minister, Mr Gromyko, cracked a rare joke when he saw the painting, after the then British Prime Minister, Sir Alec Douglas Home, had told him that he was descended from Rizzio's murderers. It must have reminded him of life back home under Marshal Stalin.

This is the story of the victim in that picture.

David Rizzio was Italian. He arrived in Edinburgh in December 1561, where he rose to an influential position at the cosmopolitan Renaissance court of Queen Mary. He became her secretary, her chief minister, so that for a brief moment they ruled the country together, much to the irritation of the English government.

His ascendancy was at its zenith between the autumn of 1565 and the spring of 1566. An intelligent and personable adventurer, he offered a programme of religious toleration at home and friendship with the leading powers abroad. Ill-wishers said that the Queen became his mistress. It was also rumoured that he was to be appointed Lord Chancellor and be given a large estate south of

1

Edinburgh. He certainly lived as a rich man in the style of a great Florentine prince like Cosimo de' Medici.

Yet his regime could not last. The Queen and her minister had made too many powerful enemies. His sense of fun and love of music may have helped him charm his way to the top. But he was too exotic for prim bourgeois Edinburgh, and sadly his quips and jokes failed to work on the newly Protestant Scots, who were just grimly concerned for the security of their religion. Soon the militant Protestants and disaffected barons combined together to revolt against his rule.

On the evening of 9 March 1566 the storm broke. A party of malcontents, led by Ruthven and backed up by at least eighty of his Douglas clansmen, forced their way into the palace of Holyroodhouse, overcame the protests of the gatekeepers and brutally slaughtered the Italian secretary while he was sitting at supper with the Queen. 'Sauvez moi madame, sauvez ma vie! Justizia, Justizia' was his pathetic cry just before he met his end, in his strange mixture of French and Italian.

The attack took place with the acquiescence and in the presence of Mary's jealous, but hopelessly inadequate, husband, Henry Stewart, the Lord Darnley. The conspirators then proceeded to hold her captive. This was an atrocity performed for a political purpose but dressed up as a *crime passionel*. It was also an act of masculine aggression against a defenceless female, symbolised by the grey steel of Ruthven's dagger pressed to Mary's womb as she tried to shield her terrified retainer. She was then six months pregnant by Darnley, or, as some said, by Rizzio, and the risk of miscarriage was high. The impact of his death that cold spring night still resonates. It is at least arguable that, if he had been given more time to consolidate his power and if Mary had shown some of the hard-headed realism of 'her Cousin and Good sister', Queen Elizabeth of England, Scotland might today still be an independent state of nominal Catholic faith.

This book explains why Rizzio so enraged the Scots lords that they planned his murder with such zest. It points to the complicity of Elizabeth and her leading ministers in the conspiracy to do away with him, and it tells why the Reformed congregations around

Europe exulted when they heard of the killing, since with him died the possibility of religious counter-reformation.

But much of his life is still a mystery. He was killed in his prime, before he could pen any justification for his work. There are few papers and little surviving correspondence to illuminate his real personality and policies, which must all be pieced together from what shadowy evidence is available.

The Queen escaped the assassins and took shelter with her ally and future lover, James, Earl of Bothwell, in his castle by the coast. Soon she was able to return to her capital in triumph and plot her revenge. She sent an express messenger to her old friend and spiritual adviser, James Beaton, the absentee Archbishop of Glasgow, who was away in exile in Paris, with a detailed account of the murder.

Rizzio was an attractive older man with a masterful personality, and perhaps became something of a father figure to Mary. Were they really lovers, or maybe he was gay? She certainly liked his company, and found his conversation witty and charming, while his sunny Latin jokes and pleasantries reminded her of happy childhood days by the Loire. And political business often brought them together. His position as her secretary required constant close contact, which inevitably gave rise to yet more gossip and speculation.

In council he argued his case forcibly, and his views counted. A vivid description exists of him debating policy there in his deep and eloquent bass voice. He argued with Mary like a spouse, and, it was reported, 'sometimes he reproved her more sharply than her own husband would do'.[1] If true, this was a fault on his part, which sensible prime ministers in later ages have wisely avoided. It is hard to imagine Disraeli addressing Queen Victoria like a hectoring husband.

The rumour that Mary took him as her lover was, of course, sensational. It did no good to her reputation then, and maybe still damages it today. It soon spread like wildfire throughout the Protestant community, who enjoyed exaggerating the reputation of 'the Scottish Queen' for sexual promiscuity, and whose behaviour could be contrasted with her chaste cousin, Elizabeth, 'the Virgin

Queen'. The reports soon reached the English ambassador in Edinburgh, and lost nothing in the telling. As early as October he had alluded to the reasons for Mary's new hostility to her older brother, which was because 'he understandeth some such secret part (not to be named for reverence sake) that standeth not well with her honour, which he so much detesteth being her brother'.[2]

ONE

Mary's Glittering Court

She was brocht up in joyusitie . . .

(John Knox, 1561)

The early life of Mary Queen of Scots is well chronicled. Ascending the Scots throne at the age of six days on the death of her father, James V, she was sent to the French court as a child of 5 to escape English attention, and there she grew up among the lovely châteaux built by the Valois kings along the banks of the River Loire. Her sheltered upbringing was very different from that of her cousin, Princess Elizabeth of England.

The infant queen spent many happy hours with her mother's family; educated with all the privileges of a princess of France; the little girl was then betrothed to François, the Dauphin of France, and the heir to his father, King Henri II. She was to be yet another link in the chain of the *auld alliance* forged between France and Scotland on the anvil of English aggression. And the wedding in April 1558 when she was aged 15 was an outward celebration of the traditional alliance.[1]

But the untimely death of the young King François II in 1560 forced Mary to accept the invitation of the revolutionary Protestant regime, which was governing Scotland in her name, to come home in the summer of 1561.

Fully to understand the special place of David Rizzio in Mary's story, we must look back a little into her early life.

Mary was born on 8 December 1542, the only legitimate child and heiress to the King of Scots, James V. Her mother was French, a daughter of the noble and influential family of Guise. She had many illegitimate half-brothers and sisters, of whom the most interesting, and influential, was Lord James Stewart.

Queen Mary of England had died lamenting the loss of her stronghold at Calais to a French army, which was commanded by Mary Stewart's formidable uncle, the Duc de Guise. When they learnt of her death on 17 November 1558, the Dauphin and Dauphiness, Mary and François, put in their own claim to the English throne, and were also persuaded by the King of France, Henri II, to insert the royal arms of England within their own quarterings in heraldic assertion of their rights to that crown.

Mary Stewart's claim to the English Crown came from her descent, in the female line, from Henry VII, since she was his great-granddaughter, by her grandmother Margaret Tudor. The lure of this inheritance, as the legitimate offspring of the marriage between the thistle and the rose, was to be a guiding star for most of her life. Her earlier ministers, Lord James Stewart and William Maitland, were always pressing for her to be accepted as heiress to the English throne in default of legitimate issue to Elizabeth. The prospect of English acres, and English gold, was bound to hold a certain appeal to needy Scots lords. For the moment Mary was well content for her agents to argue her cause in London as they saw fit. And Elizabeth, in turn, was only too glad to procrastinate. She claimed to need legal advice on Mary's claim, and said that 'she had ordered some of the best lawyers in England diligently to search out who had the best right, and she heartily wished it might be found to be her good sister, rather than any other'.[2]

But Mary's child husband, by now François II, was frail and sickly, and in consequence it may very well be that he was insufficiently mature to consummate their marriage. Whether this was so or not, his sudden death on 6 December 1560 made her person available for yet another dynastic marriage. The marriage of a ruling prince was always of concern in the politics of Renaissance Europe, and her fate was no different.

This terrible personal disaster meant that there was now no place for her in France. She was forced to return to her native land, to become 'une reine française en Écosse'.[3] She did, however, keep her royal title as a dowager Queen of France, and was a very rich one at that. Already an heiress of Scotland, under the terms of her marriage settlement she was entitled to a life interest in the revenues of the duchy of Touraine in Poitou, which amounted to 60,000 livres a year. This French income, although sometimes erratic in payment, was to be a huge support for the rest of her life.

The Reformation had come to Scotland by the time Mary Queen of Scots landed in Leith out of an early sea mist on the morning of 19 August 1561. But she found the Protestant triumph was not quite as complete as the religious extremists might have hoped. Most of the Highlands and Lowlands still revelled in their unstable and tribal ways, while such central control as there was over the various wild and disparate regions that made up her realm was in the hands of her half-brother Lord James Stewart, and his Protestant faction.

Lord James acquired the earldom of Moray within the year, and was to be referred to as Moray from then on.[4] As a character he was clever, ambitious both for himself and for his gospel; he may well have been right when he thought that he was better qualified to sit on the throne than his legitimate sister.

If he did aspire to the throne of his Stewart fathers, he grew up nonetheless knowing that it would never be his, since, in the expressive Italian of the day, he was *bastardo*.[5] King James V left many illegitimate children, but Moray, now aged 30, was the best of the flock, an intelligent man very much in his prime. The great Protestant Reformer John Knox held him in high opinion, and thought him a 'man whom all the Godly did most reverence'.

Moray was Mary's elder half-brother by eleven years; born in 1531, he was at least two years older than his rival Rizzio. The difficulty was his birth. His mother, Lady Margaret Erskine Douglas, was already married to Robert Douglas of Lochleven at the time of his conception. Lady Margaret was herself a daughter of the Earl of Mar, and took pride in her status as one of the many mistresses of the King. James openly acknowledged the boy, and arranged for him to be granted the revenues of the Priory at St Andrews when only a child of 7. He also petitioned Rome for authority to dispense with the illegitimacy, which might otherwise bar his son's appointment to any more church livings. Lord James, for he took his father's names and was granted the honours of a younger son of a Scots earl, was sent to university at St Andrews. When old enough to fight he served bravely in various border skirmishes against the *auld enemie* in the summer of 1557. By then he appeared to be in every respect a loyal subject to the Queen Regent, Mary of Guise.

But by now he had experienced a religious conversion. All the evidence suggests that his faith was sincere. It was this driving force, combined with his semi-royal status, that gave him such authority over the Protestant militants, who under the banner of their faith had risen in rebellion against Mary of Guise. From now on he worked in coalition with William Maitland of Lethington to argue that the country must follow a Protestant, and therefore a pro-English policy.

Despite his handicap, it is hard to avoid the conclusion he aimed to fill the vacuum left by the death of the Regent, Mary of Guise. For the moment his policy appeared to be to rule in the name of his younger sister, whether she was around or not, just as the Duke of

Northumberland had hoped to rule England with his daughter-in-law, Lady Jane Grey, on the throne as a puppet. He would help her keep the Crown, but only on the condition that she acted, like a Japanese Mikado, as the figurehead for his grouping of Reformers and sympathisers. Since so many of her supporters disagreed, a battle for supremacy became inevitable.

Indeed, at first he appeared to be a dutiful subject to his sister. It was Moray who went to France to invite her home in the spring of 1561, it was Moray who kept the door against the mob at the riot during her first mass, and it was Moray who supplied the strategic skills that led to the downfall of the Gordons in 1562. It was no accident that he then acquired vast lands and estates in the Gordon country by way of reward for his part in the victory, which also brought him ennoblement in his own right as Earl of Moray.

The chief of the Gordons, George, the Earl of Huntly, was one of Moray's staunchest opponents, and Knox was not alone when he discerned the threat he represented. Ensconced in his heartlands deep within his mountain fastness, Huntly had led the opposition to the pro-English policy of Moray's council. He was something of a gambler, and played for high stakes. In the summer of 1561 he tried to persuade Mary to sail direct from Calais and disembark in Aberdeen. There he would muster 20,000 men, so that together they would drive the Protestants into the sea and restore the old faith.

'Huntly says the Queen has only to give the word, and he will have mass celebrated all over the kingdom in spite of the heretics' was how the Duke of Savoy's ambassador, de Moretto, described his conceits to the Spanish ambassador, Quadra, when they met after his return from the Scots court.[6] But such optimism was misplaced in the light of Moray's ambitions to the contrary. And sometimes, when down in Edinburgh, Huntly would even condescend to attend Knox's sermons, where he would show his irritation with the preacher by pulling his bonnet down over his eyes, picking at his nails and muttering 'when these knaves have railed their fill, then they will hold their peace'.[7]

The return of the Queen meant there were now many new excitements and opportunities in Edinburgh, and not only at court. Despite the grumbles and protests of the radical reformers, Mary was determined to keep her private Roman Catholic clerical establishment, which was one of the terms guaranteed by Moray to the Protestant Lords in the agreement for her homecoming from France.

So as a result the traditional Catholic offices could once more be heard in the old abbey church by the palace at Holyrood, even though the Protestant minister at St Giles, John Knox, continued to rail at 'Baal's bleating priests', as he called the clergy who had returned with the Queen.[8] All Saints' Day, 1 November 1561, saw a near riot when the royal mass was celebrated with special ceremony. Knox complained about it bitterly. With the other Protestant ministers, he protested vehemently to the Privy Council and demanded public celebration of the mass be stopped in accordance with the laws enacted by the Reformation Parliament only the year before, but which Mary steadfastly refused to approve.

Just as electric storms trigger displays of northern lights in high latitudes, the brief intervention of David Rizzio into the early councils of Mary served only to illuminate the limits of her power. An immigrant Italian from Piedmont, Rizzio was to end his days as her first minister, dedicated to the ideal of an independent Scotland, in communion with Catholic Europe.

Many years later Mary wrote a long letter to Cosimo de' Medici, the Grand Duke of Tuscany, in which she set down all she knew about her 'special servant', as she fondly called David Rizzio. He was born about 1533, in the small village of Pancalieri, some twenty miles south of Turin, in the duchy of Savoy.

The wealthy republic of Venice, on the other side of the Italian peninsula from Savoy (Piedmont), was reputed to run the best diplomatic service in Europe. Venetian laws said that, while an ambassador must always be a patrician, his secretary might come from inferior stock – that is, from the upper plebeian class. This echoed the Rizzio family background. The Rizzios seem to have originated from the cultured Piedmontese *bourgeoisie*, and were a product of the prosperous local economy, with a tradition of working in the service of the state. Indeed, a generation earlier, one Giovanni Angelo Rizzio, or Riccio, as the name was sometimes spelt, served as first secretary to Francesco Sforza, the Duke of Milan, and this Giovanni corresponded on more than one occasion about King Henry VIII's 'great matter', the divorce from his queen, Catherine of Aragon.[9]

David Rizzio's father taught music and was careful with his savings. We know nothing about his mother. The immediate family included a younger brother, Joseph. His father was sensible enough to see the benefits of a good humanist education, and happy to invest in the future of his children. He encouraged his boy, David, to take up music, and probably sent him on to study at one of the great north Italian universities, Bologna, Ferrara, Padua or Siena. Padua seems the most likely, as it was not too far from Venice. The university already had links with Savoy, and it may be relevant that a Piedmontese 'nation' had been set up there in 1534 to look after the Savoyard students. Using family connections, the older Rizzio then found a place for his son at the court of his sovereign, the Duke of Savoy, which rotated between Chambery and Nice, since Turin itself was under French occupation. To spend time in the household of a great ruler was itself an education, and to be at an Italian ducal court was no bad vantage point to learn the ways of the world and see the arrangements made to comfort and entertain a Renaissance prince.

Suitably polished from his time at court, and well bolstered by his classical learning, the musical youth next came to the attention of the church authorities as a potential candidate for the priesthood. He knew his Latin and was schooled in the humanities. He had a voice and could sing the mass. However, his personal faith was never deep enough to press him forward to take the final vows. Instead he found a patron on this earth. The young man had caught the interest of the Archbishop of Turin, Cardinal Caesar Usdimo, who recognised his promise and took him under his wing.

Cardinal Usdimo came from one of Savoy's leading families, the Cibos. Among the Cibo cousins were the Solartos. This family link gave Rizzio his opportunity. Western Europe then enjoyed a rare moment of peace, and once again travel was possible. Robertino Solarto, the Marquis de Moretto, who headed the house of Cibo, lived near the Rizzios, and in the summer of 1561, Emmanuel Philibert, the Duke of Savoy, chose him to head the mission he was sending to distant Scotland.

The return of the Queen of Scots to her capital had aroused European interest, which was why the Duke of Savoy, no mean general himself, decided to send an experienced agent to assess matters. Not much news about events in this remote northern land trickled back to Italy, though the Grand Duke of Tuscany did own a modern, and rather inaccurate, map of the British Isles by Egnacio Danti, which hung on the walls of the Palazzo Vecchio in Florence.

De Moretto was a veteran diplomat. In time he was to become Savoy's expert on Scotland and would revisit Edinburgh again. The ostensible object of this mission was to persuade the Queen of Scots to be represented at the long-running conference on the reform of the worldwide Catholic Church, which was about to reconvene at Trent. He also brought secret instructions to encourage the young Queen to accept the Spanish candidate, Alfonso d'Este, the Duke of Ferrara, as her next husband, for it was inconceivable she either wanted, or would be allowed, to stay long unmarried. The question of her choice of husband was to be the critical issue for the rest of Rizzio's life.

And so David Rizzio, ambitious, personable, well educated and intelligent, arrived in Edinburgh early in the month of December 1561. He was about 28 years old. Someone, probably Cardinal Usdimo himself, suggested that de Moretto take him along as an attaché or secretary in his entourage. With no call to the church, and keen for a more adventurous life than his father's, he leapt at the prospect of the northern pilgrimage. Italian family ties are strong, and de Moretto was happy to have one of the cardinal's protégés with him on the long journey.

By contemporary standards the embassy of Emmanuel Philibert, Duke of Savoy, to the court of Mary Queen of Scots was quite a modest affair. We do not know the precise numbers involved, but the Duke's ambassador would certainly have travelled with numerous attendants, including a train of cooks, grooms, muleteers, musicians, postilions and other domestic servants.

Their odyssey took them two to three months. To start with they rode slowly across France to Paris, crossed the Channel and continued on post horses up through the midlands of England. It was then about seven days' riding along the muddy and rain-sodden Great North Road, up through small market towns such as Royston and Grantham, until they reached the newly strengthened border fortress at Berwick-upon-Tweed. From there another two short winter days along the coastal paths past the castles at Dunbar and Tantallon brought them to the city gates of Edinburgh.

A letter to Cardinal Borromeo back in Rome gives a rare glimpse of their progress and confirms they passed through London on the way, where they were made much of by the Spanish ambassador, Don Alvaro de la Quadra.[10] It was a busy time for diplomats, as the French minister to Scotland was also in town. Both envoys, with their entourages, were granted the honour of an audience with Queen Elizabeth. For good reasons of his own, her secretary, Sir William Cecil, wished the Frenchman to get to Edinburgh first, so did his best to delay de Moretto's departure: 'The Queen of England . . . kept Morretta here some days ago after the other left, so the latter should arrive, and settle his business first.'[11]

The Spanish ambassador lived at Durham House, in its sprawling grounds near the Strand, between the River Thames and what is today Charing Cross railway station. He did not find it very comfortable and often complained that the house was 'so damp, and close to the water'.[12] Old-fashioned the house might have been, but this had advantages: 'through its being a thoroughfare, it offers great facilities for the secret admission of many different persons.'[13]

The population of Edinburgh was then between twelve and fifteen thousand, and accommodation was under pressure that winter. The return of court life, the demands of the Queen's retainers and the arrival of all the foreign envoys with their staffs meant that such lodgings as were available were expensive and uncomfortable. The English ambassador, for one, was always complaining about the cost of his accommodation.

Mary gave the Duke of Savoy's representative a warm welcome. To start with, de Moretto was put up in the rooms at Holyroodhouse usually used by her half-brother, Lord Robert Stewart, but he was soon invited to share more comfortable quarters with her retainer, George, Lord Seton, at his property outside town.[14] But there was no space for Rizzio beside his master. Money was short. He was poor and hungry in these early days, and was forced to seek shelter for the night elsewhere, bedding down under his cloak on a pile of boxes and old chests, somewhere in the nether regions of the old abbey at Holyrood.

Edinburgh was then something of a diplomatic cockpit. There was much European excitement about the young Queen of Scots, which meant that there were now at least three ministers accredited to her court – from the Queen of England, the King of France and the Duke of Savoy respectively. Indeed a fourth, from Portugal, had only just been and gone. Inevitably there was a certain amount of jockeying for position between them. The Savoyard de Moretto got on reasonably well with de Foix, the French envoy, but this was not the case with the English minister, Thomas Randolph. Randolph and de Moretto had very different instructions and saw through each other's aims soon enough.

They met once on the sandy seaside links outside Edinburgh's port of Leith, where, after a certain amount of polite fencing between them, they chatted away as they admired Mary and her ladies play a winter game, 'running at the ring'. The Italian was diplomatic in his comments about the Queen and her countrymen. He declined to say why he was in Edinburgh, beyond that he was there to congratulate the Queen on her safe return from France and to give her official intimation that her aunt, the Duchess of Savoy, was with child.

David Rizzio's expensive education and his time at a ducal court meant that he was well qualified to serve as the political eyes and ears of his master once they were installed in Scotland. Most chancelleries, in Tudor times as today, held intelligence officers whose job was to file confidential reports back to their home governments. Thomas Randolph, the English ambassador to the court of Mary Queen of Scots, whose papers are such a key source for his life, was particularly skilled in this craft.[15]

Rizzio's enemies later asserted that he was a priest, a Spanish spy or at the very least an agent of the Pope, though there is no precise corroboration this was ever so. However, since Piedmont, or Savoy, was firmly allied to Philip II and in the Spanish camp, the conjecture is not wholly unfounded. There is, however, no conclusive proof that he was anything more than an adventurous individual keen to try his luck in a foreign land.

When a secret mission from the Pope finally arrived in 1562 – that is, six months after that from Savoy – it was led by a Jesuit priest, Father Nicholas de Gouda. He had a difficult sea crossing in a small fishing boat out of Antwerp in the Spanish Netherlands, and was uncomfortably disguised, to confuse the suspicious Fife fishermen, as a Scottish gentleman in court dress, complete with sword, boots and hat, so to some extent Protestant fears about Catholic spies were understandable.

Overall, de Moretto's embassy was not a great success, though he did glean much useful information on local conditions, all duly reported back to the Spanish authorities. He left Edinburgh before the spring broke, but failed to persuade Mary to accept the Spanish candidate for her hand, or to send an envoy to the Council convened to discuss reforms to the Catholic Church, which William Maitland, her secretary, thought inappropriate. Her government was now strongly Protestant, and at this stage she had little say in such policy decisions.

The Queen enjoyed de Moretto's company, especially the news he brought from France, and was sorry see him go. Although she declined to take the princeling from Ferrara as a husband, she sent the Italian minister away with the gift of a fine gold chain, which cost her Treasury £300, and gave him an extra parting present of three valuable horses as well.[16]

In many ways Scotland was then, as it still is today, a foreign land by comparison to England. Even the domestic architecture looked different. Over the border the half-timbered buildings of the south gave way to the grey stone town houses of the merchants, the sturdy towers of the nobility and the straw hovels of the peasants. The latest continental building fashions could also be seen at the royal palaces of Stirling, Holyrood and Falkland, all embellished by the skilled craftsmen sent from France on the orders of King James V and his Queen, Mary of Guise; so to some extent the Italian party felt themselves more at home here, in the lowlands of Scotland, than they had in damp and dirty London by its River Thames.

Edinburgh itself was an old, insanitary, medieval town, clinging to the crest and side of an ancient volcanic hill. The tall town residences of the barons and leading tradesmen adorned the High Street and Canongate, which ran down the Royal Mile from the castle to the old Augustinian abbey buildings at Holyrood, where the monarch kept her court.

Whatever the city's defects, there were many in the Piedmontese party who found its atmosphere more congenial than anything back in northern Italy. David Rizzio was one such, and he decided to stay on. The light might not be as bright as in Nice, the town's wynds and closes were doubtless a little insalubrious, and the weather was certainly colder, but life here in the Scots capital offered better opportunities than anything available by the shores of the Mediterranean.

The country was enjoying a rare moment of peace, with a young and healthy sovereign enthroned under her cloth of state. Trade was good. After long regency, civil war, invasion and insurrection, all the glittering pleasures of court life and urban prosperity were once again on show, however much the Protestant preachers might grumble at the temptations that resulted. Since Mary was essentially French – half French by birth and wholly French by nurture – it is hardly surprising that numerous foreign immigrants, including many French, not a few Italians and even some English, worked away in her service.

Historians have long argued about the Queen of Scots' vices and virtues. She herself was not a little passionate and occasionally naive in her judgements; so very unlike her more worldly-wise cousin, Elizabeth, Queen of England. In 1560 she was only 18 years old, and relatively immature, having been brought up as a virtual orphan within the bosom of her Guise relations and usually sheltered from the worst excesses of the Valois court. She was also very human, but still knew enough about her rival monarch to keep her end up in the regular diplomatic jousts they played together. So, when a little later, in June 1562, she received some correspondence from Elizabeth, she ostentatiously 'put it in her bosom next her skin', and then told the courier as she retrieved the letter, 'if I could put it nearer my heart I would'.[17]

Her ways of thinking put John Knox quite at a loss. He was quite unable to comprehend her attitude, because 'she was brocht up in joyusitie, so termed she her dancing, and other things thereto belonging'.[18] Yet she had many strengths, not least the magical Stewart gift for inspiring loyalty to her person and her cause. Once under her spell, David Rizzio was to become her devoted servant.

With the old Catholic faith restored at the heart of government, a choir was needed once again to sing the anthems required by the liturgical year. Scotland had its own long musical tradition. King James IV had built up the choir at the Chapel Royal, and Mary was keen to copy her grandfather's accomplishments. Large choruses were required to make sure that the sometimes demanding polyphony settings could be heard to the full. The Sistine chapel in Rome, for example, held at least twenty-eight voices, while some of the larger English cathedrals may have had as many as thirty-four in the choir stalls. The regular repertoires of sacred music changed as the calendar demanded, and included such lovely motets as Thomas Tallis's 'Spem in alium', Alessandro Striggio's 'Ecce beatam lucem', or Scotland's own Robert Carver's Mass for Three Voices.

Just before the departure of the Savoyard minister, Rizzio heard through the usual court grapevine that there was a vacancy for a fourth bass voice in the newly re-established Chapel Royal choir. He moved fast and persuaded de Moretto to recommend him for the post, and, since the Queen's Guise uncle, René d'Elbeuf, who stayed on as well to enjoy the excitements of an Edinburgh winter, also supported the envoy's patronage, he got the job. But it seems he had to pay a little for the position. The chorister's place was not particularly grand, but was an investment that soon showed its value, for it brought him directly to the Queen's attention.

Envious gossip said later that Seigneur Davie, as the Scots grew to call him, spent most of his spare cash on that first and vital place in the choir, and, with the inflated rents demanded in the capital, was for some time after unable to afford to move on to better accommodation. His enemies remembered how in these first few weeks he still continued to sleep on the old chests in a back corner of the abbey to save a few bawbees. But it was not for long, as more comfortable lodgings were soon on their way.

Rizzio was about to enjoy a significant change in status. Once he had decided to cast in his lot with the Scottish Queen, it was not long before he was well housed and fed. Luck and talent had brought him to Mary's side. She appreciated his company, took him into her favour and began to give him tangible proofs of her affection. Like a troubadour of old, he possessed the ability to sing *chansons* in his deep attractive voice, organise court masques and choreograph entertainments. Mary, who was more than a little bullied by her elder brother Moray and bereft of parents, husband or lover at her side, recognised his talents and soon came to rely on him. She started to give him lavish presents, which were duly recorded by the dry accountancy of the Lord Treasurer of Scotland's clerks.

A few tantalising pieces of information now begin to appear in the archives, particularly about his finances.[19] They show how quickly he began to enjoy all the trappings of royal approval. Sometime in

December 1562, that is only a year after he had reached Edinburgh, 'David le Chantre', as he was now called by courtier colleagues and menials alike, was given a very expensive present from the Queen. This was a set of eight sumptuous cloth hangings, or tapestries, taken from her stock of beautiful chattels, recently arrived from France; and there was also an extra bed coverlet. They were all designed to emphasise his importance. The Master of the Wardrobe, his friend and fellow *varlet de chambre*, Servais de Conde, made the arrangements. Rizzio used them in his chambers in Holyrood, and would sometimes take them with him when he accompanied Her Grace in her progresses round the country.

Within the next two years he also enjoyed an annual salary of £80 Scots in recompense for his duties as *varlet de chambre*, paid quarterly in arrears. The salary was substantial enough, though it bears contrast with the more generous emoluments of £300 a year paid by the Edinburgh town council to John Knox as the minister of St Giles.

So it seemed for now that Rizzio had made the right decision to stay on in Scotland.

TWO

Religious Frenzy

Professing Christ Jesus, his Holy Evangel . . .
(*Acta Parliamentorum Mariae apud Edinburgh*, August 1560)

As David Rizzio rode into Edinburgh on that winter's day in early December 1561 there were numerous signs of how the land was gripped by religious frenzy. Ranting preachers, psalm-singing officials and desecrated churches evidenced the arrival of the Protestant Reformation. Shrines and wayside images were no more. The old Catholic Church, which for so long had satisfied the spiritual aspirations of the people, was now challenged by a popular revolution that was encouraged by the leading nobles, and spurred on by the exhortations of the new men of God. The mass was illegal. Monasteries and abbeys were no longer at work or prayer.

And the church lands were falling into the hands of acquisitive men who held to new beliefs.

The return of court life to the capital meant that there was now a new divide between the faith of the monarch and that of her people. The Queen's court might glitter, but, said the preachers, it was but a false cosmopolitan glow, at odds with true Protestant spirit.

Well before Mary's homecoming, the settled certainties of past ages had ceased to apply. The Protestant Reformation, which began when Martin Luther nailed his ninety-five questions to the chapel door at Wittenberg Castle in 1517, soon spread throughout northern Europe. In 1560 the Scots Parliament decided that it must follow the example of England, Germany and Scandinavia.

The demand for religious reformation was helped by new technology. The invention of the printing press meant that reading matter passed quickly from devout to sceptic, so that people could ponder for themselves on the truth of the Scriptures.[1] Luther's own writings circulated in enormous quantities.

Rizzio, who had grown up at a time of such intellectual turmoil, was well aware of the spreading Protestant heresies. He was sensitive and well educated in the humanist tradition. And he had also travelled around the sheltered valleys of Piedmont and discussed the growing pressures of the new heresies with the authorities there.

However, the chief challenge to Catholic orthodoxy came, not from Luther, but from the teachings of the French divine, John Calvin. His little city state of Geneva had been governed with the help of fellow zealots from at least 1541, which is to say for most of Rizzio's youth, and during all that time the pastors there had laboured hard to export the pure milk of the reformed gospel to the rest of the known world.

At this stage Rizzio was only a choral singer, not a pleader for any particular branch of Christ's church. None the less, as his influence grew at court, he found it impossible to avoid being drawn into the religious controversies that beat down so heavily on Mary's kingdom. At first it seemed that the old faith there had collapsed without much of a fight. But the Roman Catholic Church was no insignificant structure. It regrouped, and reformed, although there was still much work to do by the time the mission from Savoy reached Edinburgh.

In many ways the religious changes demanded by the Reformation were more kindly handled in Scotland than in much of Europe. Despite the mean-minded attitude of some reformers, most of the clergy and bishops of the old faith were pensioned off with adequate support. The ministers of the new Kirk, or church, were then free to establish their own form of independent church government. And the Kirk, freed from control by prelate or prince, soon took a firm grip on the hearts and minds of its people.

Many merchants, farmers and traders, with their wives and families, took to the new Protestant teachings. It is no surprise the Protestant strongholds were to be found in parts of the country close to English influence, such as Ayrshire, Fife and the Borders. England, of course, had undergone its own reformation a generation earlier, in the time of King Henry VIII, and his son, Edward VI.

A people who believed themselves to be in direct covenant with God were often impervious to worldly reason and argument. Such a covenanted people could be taught that it was their duty to resist wicked rulers, put down tyranny and punish princely idolaters. These were the lessons that the increasingly literate Scots learnt from Knox and his friends, and from his 'Geneva Bible'. This was an edition of the testaments written in English and published only a year before Rizzio reached Scotland, where it was made popular by Knox and his fellow ministers.[2] The book was soon as effective in moulding public opinion to the Reformers' arguments as the other major works of Protestant propaganda, such as Foxe's *Book of Martyrs*, or Knox's own *History of the Reformation in Scotland*.

The reformed church in Scotland was Calvinist in theology. It adopted the teachings of John Calvin that the Word of God, as set out in the best available edition of the Scripture translated into a language the people understood, contained all that was necessary for man to know as to his faith. Such a doctrine appealed to the people, and encouraged clear thinking.

Less godly motives were also at work. Many of the Protestant leaders, like Lord James Stewart (later the Earl of Moray) and Mark Kerr, had managed to enrich themselves during the reformation process from the lands of the abbeys and churches of the old Roman Catholic faith, and this gave them an obvious incentive to maintain the new ecclesiastical arrangements.

The Protestant victory owed much to its musical appeal, which proved a powerful weapon in the Reformer's arsenal. There were the psalms, of course, with their clear message of salvation when sung in a language men and women could understand; but there were other radical ditties, which circulated just as widely and helped swing opinion against the old faith. It is an old lament that the devil has the best tunes, and the Scottish peasantry, like many others, were never averse to good bawdy song. The evidence here is *The Gude and Godlie Ballatis*, composed about then by unknown hands and sung lustily by the Protestant faithful.

One of the most powerful of these ballads, which mocked the Pope, was known as 'The Pope, that pagan full of pride'.[3] It described the greed and lechery of the nuns and monks, and showed what the Queen and her advisers were up against as they struggled to regain popular support:

> The Pope, that pagan full of pride,
> he has us blinded long;
> for when the blind, and blind think good,
> no wonder both go wrong,
>
> like prince and king, he led the ring
> of all iniquity;
> He trix, times go trix,
> under the green wood tree.

Of Scotland well, the friars of Faill
the villainy long has lasted,
the monks of Melrose made good soup
on Fridays when they fasted,

the silly nuns cast up their bums,
and hoist their hips on high,
He trix, times goes trix,
under the green wood tree.

John Knox, like Lenin and Cromwell, was a man who grasped that the time was ripe for revolution, and drove the process through to ruthless conclusion. He had the energy and the overpowering character to impose his will on the people, just as he tried to do with the young monarch. His was the very voice of the Reformation, and Knox's legacy came to be treasured by the various branches of the reformed churches that flourished in the light of his doctrines, so that his intellectual ferocity also made him an awesome antagonist to those who aroused his hatred. It was Rizzio's, and Mary's, misfortune to be numbered high on his list of adversaries.

His surviving writings and sermons are his best memorial. But it is still worth peering a little more closely into his background to understand why his spiritual revolution was such a success, and to appreciate how that made all Rizzio's attempts at counter-revolution so ineffectual.

Knox was born about 1513 in the Lothian countryside near Haddington, a few miles south of Edinburgh, where his parents owed their feudal allegiance to the local magnate, the Earl of Bothwell. They sent him to university at St Andrew's, in Fife, where he sat at the feet of the philosopher John Major with a view to taking holy orders.

But, without much family influence, the young cleric found it difficult to obtain a benefice in the old unreformed Church, and so, at the age of 25, he took to the law instead. He qualified as a notary, and opened a law business near his family home, where he specialised in property work. The practice ran for about three years. One of the title deeds he attested for important local clients, the Kerr family, still survives. It bears a standard notarial certification sealed in the name of the Pope, Paul III.[4] It says much for the economy of this small Lothian town in the reign of James V that enough work was generated there to keep him busy. The occasional lack of clients only gave the young Knox more time to study the teachings of the Reformers, and ponder again the iniquities of the current clerical regime.

For by now he was an enthusiast for reform. Imbued by the teachings of Calvin, he found inspiration in the example of George Wishart, that 'blessed man of God', who was burnt at the stake in St Andrew's during March 1546 after conviction for heresy by the authorities.[5] The sentence outraged local opinion, and soon provoked an armed uprising by a gang of fanatic Protestants, who were mainly small landowners from Fife, and came to be known as 'the Castilians'. Among them was the young lawyer James Balfour, who, in a surprising change of heart, was later to become one of Rizzio's closest allies.

The Protestant zealots managed to seize the castle at St Andrew's by a ruse, and, in revenge for the judicial execution of Wishart, then proceeded to slaughter the resident Cardinal Beaton, with particular savagery. And their revenge was all the sweeter since it was this Beaton who had sat in judgment at the ecclesiastical court that had convicted Wishart of heresy.

The Queen Mother, who was Regent for her daughter, Mary Queen of Scots, was naturally horrified by the violence. She ordered the arrest of the killers, who in turn were besieged by the royal forces in St Andrew's Castle. There was no evidence Knox played any part in the preliminary plots for Beaton's murder, but he most certainly approved of the proceedings. When he heard of the rebellion, he gave up his law practice, abandoned his clients and rushed across the Firth to join the Cardinal's murderers within the shelter of the castle walls, where he appointed himself to officiate as their chaplain.

The Castilians had hoped to find support from King Henry VIII of England, but that aged monarch, still enjoying his papal title as

'Defender of the Faith', was strangely timid in the face of this assault on that faith. Henry would not risk military intervention. Perhaps he thought it unwise to assist the killing of a cardinal, although his conscience had not been so tender when St Thomas More and Bishop John Fisher had held out against his claims to ecclesiastical supremacy. Henry's timidity led to the Castilians' defeat. Helped by the skilful application of French sea power, the levies of the Queen Regent managed to recapture the castle.

The French admiral was actually another Italian, a Florentine called Leone Strozzi. He set sail with a fleet of twenty galleys from Rouen, and on 5 July 1547 exposed the weakness of the English defences when he surprised Tynemouth, in Northumberland, by sending in landing parties to take on water. His squadron made the Fife coast by 24 July, and soon forced the rebellious garrison, outgunned and bombarded from sea as well as from land, to capitulate.

The militants, who were now imprisoned, contained some very disciplined and highly qualified individuals who were later to occupy distinguished positions in their country's service. They included the soldier Grange of Kirkcaldy, the jurist James Balfour, as well as Knox himself. However, Strozzi, unlike his fellow countryman Niccolò Machiaevelli, was of merciful disposition. The murderers were clapped in irons instead of dispatched for instant execution, and then taken back to France for judgment. Most were duly convicted, and condemned to hard labour in the penal galleys. In his *History* Knox described his time as a galley slave with understandable resentment. And his hard times may go some way to explain his hatred of Mary, and her mother, Mary of Guise, and his antipathy to any Italian presence in his native land, whether a Strozzi or a Rizzio, which the latter's ascendancy at court was only to inflame.

Once released from the galleys, Knox travelled widely throughout northern Europe as a self-appointed agitator in the Protestant cause. He was to be found with Calvin at Geneva, and in Germany at Frankfurt, teaching, writing and preaching to the faithful. Then came various ministries with reformed congregations in England and

France, at frontier outposts such as Berwick and Dieppe. By now he was a preacher with considerable spiritual influence over those congregations where the Reformers were in the ascendant.

Knox was then invited to visit England when it was undergoing its own more radical reformation during the reign of Edward VI. There he became close to the ruling regime, and was offered, but declined, the rich bishopric of Rochester, in Kent. He was not a man to end his days as an Anglican bishop. The secretary of state, Sir William Cecil, saw in him a valuable recruit for his grand strategy, and persuaded the 42-year-old Knox to return home in 1555. The suggestion was made the more appealing since England itself became far less attractive to extremist preachers of his persuasion after the premature death of the young King Edward, and the Roman Catholic reaction that set in under the rule of his successor and half-sister, Queen Mary Tudor, 'that wicked Jezebel of England', in 1553.[6]

The death of Mary Tudor in her turn, and the peaceful accession of her half-sister, the Princess Elizabeth, to the English throne in 1558, seemed at first to end any risk of counter-reformation doctrines re-establishing themselves in England. Not so in Scotland, where the religious, and therefore the political, future was still unsettled.

Mary of Guise had ruled there as Regent for her daughter, the young Queen of Scots, but her reign was comparatively benign when contrasted with Mary Tudor's in England. Once Knox was home, all this changed. By the time the northern spring reached Edinburgh in April 1560, the 47-year-old John Knox was to be found in comfortable occupation of his pulpit at St Giles, where he worked away as the minister of the new kirk in Edinburgh, and enjoyed the substantial salary and the other emoluments provided by the Burgh Council. These included a house in the High Street that had once been occupied by the Roman Catholic Abbot of Dunfermiline.

The rebel Protestants had moved quickly to consolidate their military success after the French defeat in 1560. Their leaders realised that, once victory was in their grasp, the radical religious changes they had in mind required parliamentary confirmation. Cecil may have suggested the process, but it was Knox who inspired the enactments of the Reformation Parliament held in Edinburgh during the summer of that year. The resulting legislation was among the most significant ever to be enacted by a Scottish Parliament.

The importance of the revolutionary work ahead was obvious to everyone that August. There was a large attendance. William Maitland of Lethington was elected presiding officer, or speaker. Many of the members, like Lord James Stewart (the future Earl of Moray) and Mark Kerr, were anxious to obtain statutory titles to their newly acquired church lands. Indeed, Lord James already held the lucrative post of Commendator, or lay abbot, of the Priory of St Andrews, at Pittenweem in Fife.

Most of the principal boroughs sent commissaries or representatives. Men – for of course there was no female representation – came from many distant parts of the kingdom. Burghs such as Aberdeen, Dundee, Ayr, Irvine, Glasgow, Peebles, Jedburgh, Selkirk, Cupar, Kinghorn, Banff, Forfar, Inverness, Montrose, Kirkcudbright and Wigtown were represented. More than most sixteenth-century assemblies, this Parliament was a manifestation of the whole national community.

However, the gathering was in no sense a product of a parliamentary democracy as understood today. There was no wide franchise. The electoral process whereby the members were elected was mostly obscure. Women had no vote, and the laws of the country were still feudal. The identities of many of the burgh commissaries, which struggled at their own expense to attend, remain unknown. What is remarkable is they made the effort to be there; to journey to Edinburgh from places as far to the north as Inverness, and as far in the south-west as Wigtown. Even Aberdeen, so often distinctively idiosyncratic in its outlook, sent representatives. This was not just an assembly of an urban elite, drawn from the capital and its immediate hinterland.

Although the names of most of the burgh representatives have been lost, the identities of some of the lesser gentry, or lairds, who were present as members have survived. They included lairds such as Cunningham of Caprington, Blair of Balneok, Nisbet of that ilk and James Tweedie of Drummelzier. At least 110 barons of Scotland were in attendance, and took part in the votes during the various sessions. So anxious were men to attend, and so important was the business in hand, that many lesser landowners insisted on exercising an ancient right of summons, as conferred by an old statute of King James I in 1427, and long thought obsolete. The overwhelming parliamentary majority for the religious changes was clear enough proof that the Reformers' teachings had won the battle for public opinion.

The statute book was printed in due course. Entitled in Latin *Acta Parliamentorum Mariae apud Edinburgh*, it recorded the outcome of the debates in much fascinating detail, and enacted the formal expression of religious belief, ever since known as 'the Scots Confession of Faith'. The draftsmen included colleagues of Knox, such as John Row, Paul Methven and John Winram, the prior of Portmoak.

The preamble to the Confession opened with a proud boast to supreme spiritual and political ascendancy, stating: 'The Estates of Scotland, with the inhabitants of the same, professing Christ Jesus his holy Evangel to their natural countrymen, and to all other realms and nations professing the same Christ Jesus . . .'.[7]

The Confession defined the Protestant position in no uncertain terms. The proper teachings for the new kirk were set out regarding God ('We confess and acknowledge one only God'), Original Sin ('by which transgression commonly called Original Sin was the image of God utterly defaced in man'), and as to 'the Continuance, Increase, and Preservation of Man', which were all construed with great particularity.[8] The relationship between the legislature, 'the Prince', and the executive, 'the Civil Magistrate', was most carefully defined. The statute expressed an ideal political theory for a model civil state, which the reformers hoped to establish in Scotland, just as John Calvin had achieved at Geneva.

Throughout the proceedings and debates the Reformers exhibited such a potent combination of religious zeal, and canny political skill, that any opposition from religious conservatives was overwhelmed. The disparaging description in the preamble to the statute to 'the Rage of Satan', and the continuing references in the texts to the fact that 'now we have been tossed a whole Serpent', show this well; for the serpent was an iconic image of evil to all good Protestants. Here was a clear and unambiguous message to anyone still inclining to the old beliefs that theirs was no longer the dominant majority. In the final analysis, the Catholics and conservatives failed to understand how the spiritual temper of the Scots people had changed. Yet this process was far from sudden, and deep pools of personal loyalty remained to the person of the Stewart sovereign, from the humblest subject to the ever-faithful Lord Seton. It may be unfair to blame David Rizzio, educated as he was in the entourage of an Italian Roman Catholic archbishop, for failing to help the young Queen navigate these turbulent waters. He did his best, and was vilified by Knox as a result. It is nonetheless possible to shed a silent tear to the memory of the very different state that Mary and Rizzio may have hoped to bring into being.

Inspired by sermons drawing on Old Testament prophets such as Haggai, the preachers were willing to concede some essential power to the sovereign. In particular, the new parliamentary statute defined the position and status of the 'Civil Magistrate'. It stated he derived his high office by the direct intervention of God. The function of a ruler was to act 'for the singular profit and commodity of mankind', and, as such, ' He is to be honoured, feared, and held in reverent esteem'. This was no theocracy. The law conceded that 'to Kings, Princes, Rulers, and Magistrates chiefly, and principally, pertain the conservation and purgation of religion'. Thus the Crown, and its law officers, was charged with the duty of maintaining 'true religion' and of suppressing idolatry and superstition. The difficulty, of course, for the parliamentarians then, and since, was on the precise definition of 'true religion'.

The Confession ended with a powerful prayer. 'Arise, O Lord, and let thy enemies be confounded. Let them flee then thy presence that hate thy Godly name: Give thy Servants strength to speak thy word in Boldness, and let all nations cleave to thy Knowledge. Amen.'[9] In succeeding years, as the triumph of Knox was confirmed, this form of service became the usual mode of confession in the Scots kirk, and as such was adopted by other reformed churches.

The victory of the reformed kirk owed much to the timely help received from England, as well as the wish to modernise the old Catholic ritual and do away with perceived abuses like a belief in purgatory. The new kirk emphasised the importance of the spoken word. Its energetic ministers delivered exhortatory sermons to their flocks instead of acting out the old seemingly empty rites. But the dead still needed to be buried, and the living given in marriage, or admonished in ways of personal improvement. Even so, as the changes slowly began to take effect, thanks to the calibre of the new ministers, coupled with the sagacity of their congregations, the bulk of the Scots people became attached to their Presbyterian form of church government, and to the independent habits of thought that this encouraged. This taste for theological and doctrinal argument was to spread wherever the Scots settled overseas.

Knox's triumph was complete. Such was Knox – a man at the height of his powers when David Rizzio reached Scottish shores; but a man who made the young Queen weep tears of frustration when she was confronted by his obstinate disregard for her opinions.

His supreme object was to establish the rule of the 'Evangel' in Scotland. This was both a religious and a political imperative, though to him there was very little difference between the two. He was always anxious that Mary, urged on by Rizzio and her other Catholic advisers, might somehow prevent the achievement of this holy task. Her suggestion in a letter to the exiled Archbishop of Glasgow dated March 1566, in which she expressed the hope she might do something 'anent the old faith' – that is, restore the Catholic religion – is one of the very few pieces of evidence she may really have hoped to do so.[10]

Knox enjoyed writing to the English secretary, Cecil. In a letter written about four weeks before the arrival of the Italian embassy, he gave a vivid report of the state of public opinion. He complained how people were by no means as zealous for the new faith as he was, and that Mary had begun to work her magic: 'I would have judged his counsel most wholesome if God had not so often trapped the men of most singular experience in their own wisdom. Men delighting to swim between two waters have often complained of his severity.'[11]

He went on to comment on the character of the young Queen, then a girl only 18 years old. Unsurprisingly, he found her devious. He discerned an undesirable inheritance in her character, as a result of her education under the influence of her Guise uncle, the Cardinal de Lorraine. 'In very deed her whole proceedings do declare that the Cardinal's lessons are so deeply printed in her heart, that the substance and the quality are like to perish together. I would be glad to be deceived, but fear I shall not; in communication with her I espied such craft as I have not found in such age'. He would not attend her court again. 'Since then has the Court been dead to me, and I to it.'[12]

The Savoy mission had reached Edinburgh about the same time as the delegates to the new General Assembly of the Kirk began to convene there in December 1561. Quoting the Apostle Paul, and the splendid doctrine that 'the mouth of the labouring ox ought not to be muzzled', the Reformers pressed for the establishment of a proper Protestant ministry, which was to include provision for state payments to the ministers.[13] They also urged that any remaining surplus ecclesiastical revenues left over by the acquisitive laity be spent on charitable purposes, such as help for the poor, and the encouragement of education, since 'the workman is worthy of his reward'.[14]

Such a programme was too radical for the times. Both sovereign and the Protestant majority on the Privy Council much preferred to leave matters as they were. After all, most of its members had only recently helped themselves to the assets, lands and leases of the old church. And any arguments against taking further steps towards church reform were strengthened by renewed turmoil on the southern borders. Lord James was sent down to bring the malefactors to heel. On 28 November 1561 he issued a formal proclamation from his headquarters at Jedburgh, in which he announced that, as 'the dearest brother' of the Queen, he held full powers to maintain public order over the reivers.[15]

All this police and judicial activity must have impressed the newly arrived Italian visitors, de Morreto and his private secretary, David Rizzio. There was much to report back home too on the charms of the Scots Queen, and the benefits to both Spain and the Holy See, if only the government would stand firm against the spreading Protestant heresy. This was easier said than done, since that government was by now firmly in the hands of a regime with closer links to Savoy's particular enemies, the Calvinist republicans over the Alps beside Lake Geneva.

Knox, however, remained a man of his time, and that time was the sixteenth century. For instance, he believed in witchcraft and the significance of heavenly signs. He gave these manifestations as much credit as did Horatio when the ghost of Hamlet's murdered father hove into view on the battlements at Elsinore.

Mary was suprisingly well briefed about his strange theories. She once accused him to his face of being a wizard, or 'necromancer'. 'He was also the cause of great sedition, and great slaughter in England; and that it was said to her that all that he did was by necromancy.'[16] So, too, was another of her later enemies, the Protestant fanatic Ruthven, who had a well-deserved reputation as a wizard and practitioner of the black arts.

Whether or not the Reformers actually indulged in witchcraft and necromancy, there was clearly a deep fissure at the heart of the land. And, sadly, it was to prove impossible to bridge the chasm where court and country were split by such fundamental questions of belief. While the Protestant preachers exhorted their flocks to chant the psalms of Clément Marot and look for salvation to Zion and Geneva, the young Queen and David Rizzio, along with her other courtiers and retinue, in contrast enjoyed their sweet songs of love, hoping to find their worldly pleasures here on this earth and so enjoy a life of *jouissance* to the full. The differences were to be irreconcilable.

THREE

English Policy

To have these two kingdoms perfectly knit in amity.
(Sir William Cecil, 1559)

E ngland's policy towards its turbulent northern neighbour was usually one of open hostility tempered by the occasional aspiration that one day it might be able 'to have these two kingdoms perfectly knit in amity'.[1] By 1559 peace had at last returned to most of Europe, but sadly that peace took time to reach Scotland, which was still just another pawn in the long-running conflict between the Valois and Hapsburgs dynasties. The death of Queen Mary Tudor on 17 November 1558 had put her half-sister Elizabeth on the English throne and made Sir William Cecil, the future Lord Burleigh, at the age of 38, her chief minister.

Cecil was the strategic genius behind English ambitions in the north, and in due time was to be Rizzio's nemesis. It took Cecil a little while to work out what a threat the Italian posed to English interests, but, once he had done so, he was to be utterly ruthless in dealing with his challenge.

William Cecil was born in 1520. After a conventional Cambridge education, he read for the bar at Gray's Inn in London. Intelligent and gifted, by the age of 27 he was working as private secretary to the Protector, Edward, Duke of Somerset, during the minority of Edward VI. And, unusually for a Tudor government servant, he had crossed the Channel on diplomatic business, and even tasted something of the discomforts of military life.

He also knew more about the Scots than many of his contemporaries, though he never felt any great fondness for them. Moray and Maitland were the only Scots politicians he seems to have approved of. Like Edward I, he thought the Scots deserved nothing better than a good 'hammering', and put his principles into practice when he accompanied the English army that invaded Scotland under Protector Somerset in 1547. During the campaign he worked in the Tudor equivalent of the army legal department as a judge in the Marshalsea Court, and was on the battlefield at Pinkie, albeit in a non-combatant capacity, where he learnt what it was like to face the enemy's fire.

He was also a devout Protestant, and inclined towards what today might be described as a low-church position. From his Cambridge days on he moved in a circle of friends of similar faith. However, prudence was always his watchword. His business skills were such that that he survived the restoration of the Catholic religion under Mary Tudor. He took no great office in her service, but as a country gentleman lived quietly on his Lincolnshire estates, and maybe even practised a little law from his town house near London at Wimbledon.

When Elizabeth came to the throne, he quickly took control of the nation's foreign policy. His perennial nightmare was that the country might suddenly be invaded by any one or more of a whole host of enemies; he even feared such a coalition might include minor states like Emmanuel Philibert's duchy of Savoy.

If Cecil had a fault, it was a tendency to wordiness. He summed up the dangers of the Catholic powers combining against her in a note to the Queen:

> So it may be feared that to stay the progress of religion against the See of Rome, the Emperor, the King Catholic [that is Spain], the Pope and the potentates of Italy, the Duke of Savoy, will rather conspire with the French King than suffer these two monarchies to be joined in one manner of religion. It may be doubted that many, as well Scots as English, that can like very well to have these two kingdoms perfectly knit in amity will not allow them to be knit in a like religion.[2]

His concerns about the threat from Rizzio's homeland are well shown by this dispatch. Even though it was only a minor player, he feared Savoy might be able to influence events in Scotland. His anxieties only confirmed the good sense of the Duke of Savoy when he sent de Moretto there to see how the country might be stopped being 'knit', with England, 'in one manner of religion'. On his way home, de Moretto naturally discussed developments in Edinburgh with the resident Spanish ambassador in London, de la Quadra. The Spaniard recorded their conversation, particularly Mary's comment to the Italian minister that she 'was determined to marry very highly' and so defeat all Cecil's plans.[3]

Cecil's strategic aim was to exploit any sign of weakness among his enemies. He was determined to expel French influence from north of the border, and hoped to force a political and religious revolution there, which was one reason why he encouraged Knox to come back from his exile. And he was understandably pleased by the havoc the radical preacher caused when he did eventually reach home in February 1559.

His short-term tactics were to encourage whatever faction would follow English imperatives. Happily for Cecil, religious sympathy, combined with the traditional impecuniosity of the native nobility, meant this presented little difficulty. The leading Protestant chiefs, who called themselves the 'Lords of the Congregation', were by now in outright rebellion against the regime of the Queen Mother, Mary of Guise, and desperate for support. Cecil believed that counter-attack was the best defence. So, soon after Elizabeth's accession, he argued the good sense of supporting the insurgent Protestants in their guerrilla campaign. This alliance between the English Queen and the Protestant Lords worked because they shared common religious beliefs, which encouraged a climate in which 'the amity' between the two could flourish. He set down his thinking in a powerful letter of advice to the rebels. His language did not underrate the dangers they faced. 'You know your chief adversaries. I mean the Popish kirkmen. They may have been noted wise in their generation. They be rich also, whereby they make many friends, by their wits with false persuasion, and by their riches, with corruption.'[4]

One of the other reasons for Cecil's success in Scotland was the good intelligence sent to him by the English minister there, Thomas Randolph.

Since so much of our information about Rizzio's time comes from Randolph, it is worth assessing what he says carefully. It is wise to treat him as a hostile witness, but it also helps to know a little of his academic and personal background before he took up his post in Edinburgh. His career was extraordinarily varied, even for one of Elizabeth's civil servants.

Randolph was a very different type of diplomat from the aristocratic Piedmontese Robertino Solarto, the Marquis de Moretto. He was no noble. Rather he was a typical thrusting and ambitious servant of the Tudor state, an example of the 'rising gentry' so often to be found in Elizabethan England, and an individual with something of the thug about him. His prolific correspondence with

William Cecil remains one of the most important sources for Rizzio's life.

Cecil rewarded Randolph for his successful time at Mary's court by sending him to Moscow as the English minister there. He was to negotiate with the Russian Czar, Ivan the Terrible, about the opportunities for increasing trade with Russia. When patiently waiting the Czar's pleasure in the pillared halls of the Kremlin, he must have occasionally mused fondly on his happy days back in Edinburgh. It is unlikely the Russian girls were as fetching as the Queen's four Maries clad in their beautiful white and black dresses as worn at her pre-Lenten feasts. And it was probably easier to bully the young Queen of Scots too than to talk business with the Czar.

Thomas Randolph was born in 1523, and so was about ten years older than David Rizzio. A loyal subject of King Henry VIII, he found himself, as a devout adherent to the reformed faith, very much in the fast stream for promotion during the rule of Henry's son, the boy king Edward VI. His abilities soon propelled him to high academic office. By 1549 he was Master of Pembroke College, Oxford, at the early age of 26, when the Protestant cause was very much in the ascendant. The death of Edward, and the ascent to the English throne of the Catholic Queen Mary Tudor in 1553, meant a career reverse. Randolph, ever the realist, was no martyr. He took the prudent decision to abandon his Oxford college, and made his way to Paris, where he joined the other English *émigrés* there, who were sheltering from the Roman Catholic reaction at home. The death of Queen Mary I, and the accession of Elizabeth to the Crown of England, meant the return of these 'Marian' exiles. Now, once again, they came into their own, home to a land flowing with Anglican milk and honey. John Knox was back. Thomas Randolph was back, but sadly the ambitious young puritan was not again to enjoy the quiet delights of academic life by the Cherwell. The way to preferment in Tudor times, as today, was hard. Cecil, who thought highly of him, decided to send him back to France on a confidential mission to escort the unruly and unstable son of the head of the great house of Hamilton, James, Earl of Arran, home to Scotland. Arran was a possible claimant to Mary's throne himself, and was also being talked of as a potential husband for Elizabeth. Randolph was about 35 years of age when he crossed the Scots border for the first time in 1558, where he was the accredited agent, or minister to, the 'Lords of the Congregation'. He soon played the intelligence game with the best, sometimes disguising himself under the alias of 'Mr Barnaby' as he spread his web of intrigue over the rebel Lords.[5] Cecil also put him into Parliament as pocket MP for his borough of Grantham in 1559, though he was far too busy in the north to have much time to attend to parliamentary duties in Westminster.

Randolph's work was made easier by the fact that there was already a long-standing pro-English party in Scotland. Its members agreed with him in seeing the economic advantages of closer union or 'amity' between the two countries. These merchants and traders shared advanced religious sentiments, and their commercial interests often stood to benefit from any change in policy that would establish closer trading links with English ports or with English trading entrepots, such as the staple in Antwerp across the North Sea. Moreover, the Scots currency was weak, which made for more anxiety among the Edinburgh capitalists. Between 1560 and 1567 the Scots pound had depreciated against the English pound sterling from an exchange rate of 4:1 to 5.5:1.[6] Although the advantages of any political or monetary union between the two kingdoms still lay a long way in the future, it was even then possible for far-sighted and intelligent individuals, of whom there was never a shortage in Caledonia, to discern the economic advantages that would follow from access to English markets and open trading opportunities. Rizzio's period in power seemed to put all these fair prospects in jeopardy.

The Knox family certainly stood to benefit from closer economic ties between the two kingdoms. One person who had already done so was John Knox's brother, William Knox, a ship-owner and merchant of Leith. As long ago as 1552, that is fourteen years before the date of Rizzio's murder, William Knox was in business with English associates and had obtained a licence from the Privy Council permitting him to trade with any port in a vessel of up to 100 tons dead weight.

It was the application of this English sea power that led to victory for the Protestant rebels in their struggle against the regency of Mary of Guise. Rizzio was no seaman and never quite appreciated how the careful use of naval forces could influence events far beyond England's borders. On this occasion, the fleet, under Admiral Winter, blockaded and patrolled the waters of the Firth of Forth to such effect during the winter of 1560 that the French forces sent to help the Regent were destroyed as an effective fighting force. Their galleys were unable to operate and their troops starved of supplies.

The first steps to success were taken when, as Secretary of State, Cecil drafted orders to the Duke of Norfolk, the English commander in the North, which suggested:

> It would be a great advantage to put 500 arquebusiers out of Berwick aboard to aid the Protestants in Fife. He is to take counsel with Sir Ralph Sadler, and, if it appear advantageous, to give order for the same, making it appear to be for the arming of the navy against any chance. William Winter shall have the landing of them where need shall require, adding such of his number that he can spare.[7]

Admiral Winter acted promptly. By Sunday 14 January, Norfolk was able to report that the fleet of fourteen men of war, with seventeen other vessels laden with munitions, armour and artillery, were at anchor in Lowestoft Roads.[8] A day later saw them off Flamborough Head. Within five days, despite the dangerous January weather, they had reached the great frontier fortress of Berwick-upon-Tweed, with its expensive new defences, where more men could be embarked.

The 500 arquesbusiers were landed without much difficulty at one of the little fishing ports that decorate the Fife coast. There they were embodied into mixed companies formed from the local Protestant volunteers, and the sailors drawn from the English warships, like the *Swallowe*, the *Fawcon* and the *Gerfawcon*.

Captain Holstocke, the commander of the *Swallowe*, and his men then showed their military skills. They advanced boldly on the enemy and drove them from their bastions. There were no great battles, but the end came near when the weakened French forces withdrew behind the walls of their last redoubt at Leith. Surrender soon followed.

The price for all this aid was paid with the treaty of Berwick, which embodied the terms agreed earlier in February 1560 between the Protestant nobles and lairds who made up 'the Lords of the Congregation' and the English negotiators.

Most of the leading Scotsmen involved in the uprising had made their way south, north-east or just east to join the peace conference that was held in the old border town at the mouth of the river Tweed. Lord James Stewart (later to be the Earl of Moray); Archibald, the 5th Earl of Argyll; Patrick, Lord Ruthven; Sir John Maxwell; Maitland of Lethington; John Wishart of Pitarrow; and Henry Balnaves of Halhill, who represented the Duke of Chatelherault and the Hamilton interests – all were there. Chatelherault, and his wayward son and heir, Arran, held the best claim to inherit the Crown should Mary, who was then still in France, die childless.

The Scots were in no position to resist Cecil's demands, and his envoys extorted many significant concessions from them. They were forced to recognise English ascendancy. In particular, they agreed that the Queen of England had power to act 'for the just and due preservation of Both these Kingdoms, thus contained in the one Isle, and in a little world by itself'.[9]

The English were especially keen to get any help the Scots could give them in Ireland. As part of the rescue package, the Protestant leadership agreed that Lord Argyll would take a force of Campbell clansmen to fight in the Irish wars beside the Lord Lieutenant, the Earl of Sussex. Argyll, known as 'Brown Archibald', was a modern but reform-minded individual, an effective and independent chief in his ancestral lands on the western seaboard, where he encouraged the spread of the new kirk. Protestant though he might be, in the end he was to prove a loyal subject to Mary and the Crown.

This Sussex was the same Radcliffe who only a few years before, during Somerset's invasion at the time of the 'rough wooings', had sailed his battle fleet out of Dublin to ravage and pillage the glens and settlements along the western seaboard of Arran and Ayrshire – an enterprise in which Matthew, Earl of Lennox, played an ignoble part.

By 11 June 1560 the Queen Regent, Mary of Guise, was dead, worn out by her long struggles to defend her daughter's throne from the rebels and aggressive English encroachments. She had fought hard to save her child's heritage and persuade her brothers to send a mighty power from France to save them both. Now, exhausted by all the conflicts, she expired in Edinburgh Castle at the age of only 45 years. Some patriots, like James, Earl of Bothwell, mourned her loss, but most of the Reformers, such as Knox, openly rejoiced.

For the English, it was all a neat revenge for the loss of Calais, and of the *Mary Rose* fifteen years before in the Solent. Clear strategy, good leadership and popular support, allied with command of the sea, gave them the victory. The lessons learnt in these wars about the effective use of sea power were to be asserted again and again as Elizabeth's reign continued and her seamen grew in confidence.

The English government had some justification for its worries. The fall of the ancient stronghold at Calais on the northern French coast in 1558, coupled with the failure to hold on to Le Havre ('Newhaven'), meant that Elizabeth and her council were often apprehensive of similar setbacks. Mary herself was not unsympathetic to the English ambition to retake Calais and once told the English envoy so: 'I ken what you mean, but in good faith I would you had Calais again, and the French Le Havre'[10] – an observation, including her pretty Scots way of speaking, that was immediately reported back to London.

Cecil's perennial objective was to prevent the return of any French, or other foreign, influence in the north. Now aged 40, he decided it was imperative that he revisit Edinburgh and personally negotiate the terms for French withdrawal. They clearly agreed to go, and the discussions concluded with the Treaty of Edinburgh, which was signed on 6 July 1560 by the French plenipotentiaries, the Bishop of Valence and M. de Randan, and by Cecil and his fellow commissioner, Dr Wooton. During his stay he met most of the Protestant leaders; he particularly approved of William Maitland of Lethington, writing: 'he is of most credit here for his wit, and almost sustains the whole burden of foresight.'[11]

So the safe homecoming of the young Queen of Scots in summer 1561 was very much a setback for English aspirations. 'The Scottish Queen', as Cecil usually called her, was French and Catholic, and so by definition extremely dangerous. He was perennially worried that militant Catholic or Guise arms might somehow come back with the young Queen in her fetching mourning clothes. Her arrival might also encourage the Scots to stay loyal to their old Catholic faith and the traditional French alliance. So he had refused to authorise the issue of passports for her, and her numerous entourage, to travel home overland through England, with the result that she was forced to face all the perils of a North Sea passage.

Cecil took the view that the Queen of Scots was just another enemy alien, and must be treated as such, because she had refused to ratify the terms of the Edinburgh treaty and give up most of her claims to the English throne. And he advised Elizabeth accordingly. Mary Stewart, miserable at the loss of her mother, persistently declined to sign the obnoxious document, which had been agreed by the Protestant rebels in her name.

But more troubles for Cecil lay ahead.

FOUR

The Courtly Singer

A merry fellow, and a good musician.

(Sir James Melville, 1565)

Despite dangerous rumblings from the Protestants, life was not always high politics. Mary's young court enjoyed many happy hours together, with heady days full of jouissance and girlish excitement as the Queen, the exotic new favourite and her Maries made music. Evenings were for innocent flirtation, dancing and dressing up, or playing simple games like running at the ring. But Knox and his friends would not share the fun. They saw Satan at work, began to inveigh at the Frenchified and idle ways of the Queen, and grumbled about the all too frequent moments when 'the dancing began to grow hot'.[1]

The early days of her personal rule saw Moray effectively chief minister, while Maitland continued as the principal secretary in charge of foreign policy. Theirs was a regime with close links to London and Geneva. Both men encouraged their young and impressionable monarch to roam round her kingdom in the better summer weather and get to know her subjects. So she was to be found planting chestnut trees at Balmerino Abbey by the River Tay, sitting on the bench in courts of justice trying suspected thieves on the borders, or, as on Maundy Thursday 1562, washing the feet of nineteen virgins on her nineteenth birthday in the chapel at Falkland Palace to celebrate the nineteenth year of her reign. Next year, 1563, saw her away in the west, in the Campbell country, dressed in Highland costume, as she enjoyed the hospitality of the 25-year-old Archibald, Earl of Argyll, and her half-sister, his wife Janet, at Inveraray.

As one of the leading characters around the court, Rizzio would sometimes accompany the Queen on her royal progress as part of her suite. This was the how he came to know the great clan chiefs, and grow to love the hills, moors and peaty smells of his mistress's country. She revolved in a fairly regular summer circuit moving from royal palaces, as at Stirling, to small burghs like St Andrew's, and on to important noblemen's strongholds such as Lord Atholl's Castle at Balvenie, in what is now Banffshire. Rizzio enjoyed being part of Mary's cavalcade and so shared in the hospitality of the leading barons and lairds. His clan hosts would occasionally lend him a horse on which he could forage forward through the heather, for he was an accomplished rider, with a good eye for a mount. It was a good moment to be alive, a time of which it was said 'sundry of the nobles attended upon him, and conveyed him to and thro'.[2] As they made their way over the rough moors and rocky hills, they sometimes put game up ahead – a black cock or the native grouse. Here in this savage country he found himself, for the moment, just an immigrant Italian, ensconced among these wild tribesmen. But perhaps, if he saved his money, and served his Queen loyally, he too might acquire noble status, and have his own baronial castle, complete with pit, and gallows? It was not an impossible dream.

After all, many Saxon, Norman or Flemish adventurers had come before him and done just that.

The English ambassador, Randolph, occasionally went with the royal party on these journeyings. He too enjoyed wearing the Highland garb, but complained about the costs involved, which he had to meet himself: 'She is from place to place which is more chargeable and painful for her attendants. How it may be borne on my allowance Your Honour can well conceive.'[3]

Mary took her regal duties seriously. She has sometimes been criticised for a lack of assertiveness in these early years of her personal rule, for just quietly sitting in council at her needlework, while letting Moray set policy. Although there is some truth in the charge, in her defence it may be said she was still relatively immature, and not yet developed into such a dominant personality as her cousin Elizabeth. However, in and out of council chamber, she was naturally kind and always anxious to help her own people with their problems, be they poor tacksmen, great courtiers or mere domestics – characteristics she had showed when she tried to save Cecil's eldest son, Thomas, from his own adolescent scrapes in Paris just before she left for home.

Her kindness was well illustrated in April of the year 1563, when she asked the unlikely figure of John Knox to help her sister, Janet, Countess of Argyll, and advise about her marital troubles. The episode is to the credit of both Queen and preacher. Argyll, good Protestant and great chief though he was, was susceptible to the black eyes of other Highland beauties, and Janet suffered as a result. Knox did his best to reconcile the warring spouses, and Mary gave him a rare and valuable clock afterwards in gratitude for his help. He mentions the story in one of the few favourable comments he makes about Mary.

Usually he made her cry.

Mary's tears were compounded by Knox's views on the part women should play in public office. She knew very well that he was the famous author of *The Blast of the Trumpet*, which, with annoying provocation, addressed its arguments against the 'Monstrous Regiment', or rule (*regio* in Latin), of female sovereigns.

He was summoned to court to explain himself, and described their conversation in his own inimitable style: 'The Queen accused John Knox, that he had raised a part of her subjects against her mother, and against herself. That he had written a book against her just authority; by which she meant the treatise against "the Regiment of Women".'[4]

He did not hesitate to defend himself. Grudgingly he said he was prepared to accept her as his sovereign, but went on, rather tactlessly, to compare her rule with the tyranny of the Roman emperor, Nero:

> If the Realm finds no inconvenience from the regiment of a woman, that which they approve shall I not further disallow than within my own breast, but shall be also well content to live under Your Grace, as Paul was to live under Nero.
>
> My hope is that so long as ye defile not your hands with the blood of the Saints of God, neither I, nor that book, shall either hurt you or your authority.[5]

He went on to expostulate, rather lamely, that his writings were really aimed at the English Queen Mary Tudor: 'In very deed Madame, that book was written most especially against that wicked Jezebel of England.'[6]

Knox argued for a political theory of government that defined relations between sovereign and people. Although subsequent constitutional analysts have built on his theories, he deserves credit for trying to define the duties of a model sovereign. While his views on the functions of a head of state sound almost modern, his teachings on women's place in government are entirely in contradiction with opinion today. It is unhistorical to expect anything else.

He was by no means unique, however, in his opinions on female participation in government. And his gender prejudices were usually shared by most of the other leading Protestant Reformers. An example was John Aylmer, the one-time tutor to the unfortunate Lady Jane Grey, and later Bishop of London, who was even more critical of female political leadership than Knox.[7] Aylmer, though a Protestant too, wrote a powerful critique of the book, in which he attacked 'the Regiment of Women' in his own very individual tome entitled *An Harborowe for faithful and true subjects against the late blown blast concerning the Government of Women.*

Here he argued, in beautiful and eloquent Elizabethan English, that, by virtue of their sex, women were entirely unsuited to play any part in public life. Because of their gender they were all 'foolish, flibbergibs, tattlers, triflers, wavering, witless, without counsel, feeble, careless, rash, proud, talebearers, eavesdroppers, rumour-raisers, evil tongued, worse-minded and in every wise doltified with the dregs of the Devil's dunghill'.[8]

But back in Edinburgh the Reformers' cause was still very much in the ascendant. In the meantime the preachers continued to rant away at the games, *joie de vivre* and overall extravagance of the court. And they raged away about the Catholic services that were once again being held in the Chapel Royal at Holyrood, and were now open to people at large, and not just confined to members of the royal household. The Queen, however, had other problems.

Although she could usually cope with the occasional domestic crises, like Janet Argyll's, she was conscious of her high rank and slightly reticent in her private morals. She was by no means the predatory harridan depicted by her enemies.

Most of her household, like Rizzio, were, of course, foreigners. She could afford to maintain a large staff, of whom many were recruited from abroad, and at times had over 240 retainers and domestics in service. There were French, Italians and local Scots; even a few English. Some of the French had lingered behind after the defeat of the French armies in 1560, while others had come over with the Queen on her galleys in the summer of 1561.

The accounts of the Lord High Treasurer give us a financial snapshot of life behind the scenes at court. Although the country was impoverished, the Queen herself was a rich heiress with large estates, who could afford to spend her private money to maintain her state and support her royal dignity. The accountancy of the Treasury clerks means a little intimate detail is preserved about her day-to-day concerns.

She always loved her pets, especially dogs, so it is not so surprising to find an entry in the royal accounts for January 1562 that mentions the cost of running her pack of deer hounds. The payments made to their keeper, who bore the good Scots name of Geddes, are also recorded.

The next entry in the royal accounts is even more interesting. It has one of the earliest references in the state archives to the dashing Italian newcomer, with his fine resonant voice and electric personality, who had just joined the choir, and so caught the Queen's interest that she ordered he be given a present of £10 Scots in cash. Mary grew very fond of him, and was always fond of her dogs, so it is worth setting out the entries in detail. They read as follows:

> The Expenses disbursed by the Queen's Grace's precept and special command, in this instant month of January 1562
>
> Item, the 8th day of January, to Anthony Geddes, for keeping of Her Grace's dogs . . . £12.00
>
> Item, to David Rizzio, varlet in the Queen Grace's chamber, £10.00.[9]

This reference confirms the immediate impact he had made on Mary. Within only a few weeks of his reaching Scotland, and having heard him sing for the first time at a requiem mass on 6 December, she was arranging for him to leave the chapel choir to work as one of the team of varlets in her private service.

The duties of the royal varlets were not just to be in daily attendance on the monarch. They still had to join her devotions in chapel, and take their parts in the proper performance of all the kyries, glorias and sanctuses as demanded by the holy mass. There were at least four other French choral singers to be found in the choir with David. They were called Michellet, Balthasar, Servais de

Conde and Adrian, and all recognised the immigrant from Piedmont as the best of their group, happily accepting his pre-eminence and christening him 'David le chantre' (David the singer). He got on well with them, which shows his diplomatic skills, while they all appreciated his peculiar talent and breadth of experience.

Of course, he also had to work at his domestic duties with the rest of the household, the Comptroller, Bartholomew de Villemore, the Master of the Wardrobe, but most of all with her 'Maries'. These were the four legendary beauties – Livingstone, Beaton, Fleming and Seton – all called Marie like the Queen and all of noble birth, who went with her everywhere.

The Treasurer's accounts contain two other references to David from this early period, and mention a little about his finances, which, thanks to the Queen's favour, were now fast improving. After that first payment of £10 on 8 January 1562, when he had been in the country for only five weeks or so, there is a record of another £50 given to 'David Rizzio, virlat of the Queen's Grace chalmer' soon afterwards. And three months later a further entry showed £45 was paid to him as 'chalmer cheild' on 16 April 1562.[10] They confirm his growing responsibilities.

The reference to the post of 'chalmer cheild' (chamber child, or varlet to the Queen), hints at the inevitable intimacy that was developing between them. It is difficult to be precise about the duties of chamber child as compared with varlet, since so much depended on the personalities concerned. In modern terms, the post of *varlet de chambre* might perhaps be compared to that of a favoured butler, an influential equerry, or aide de camp, to a high-ranking personage.

Not every varlet was musical, and not every chamber child was just a page in the bedchamber. David could play his part in both capacities. His career shows how a clever and trusted confidant could climb the winding stairway to power and influence to become first a popular courtier, and then principal minister, to the sovereign.

His domestic arrangements certainly improved with his finances. Once he had acquired status as an established palace servant, his whole lifestyle became of public interest, and, as it happened, Mary soon arranged for him to be well looked after and better housed. 'David le chantre' was now an interesting figure around the court; someone who ate with the rest of its leading members, for all the varlets worked and dined together. They were an eclectic group. Besides David, there were some other musicians, both Scots and French, and a Scots usher. The names of some of them have come down to us. There was René the perfumer, Maguichon the tailor, and four others called Guilliame, Denis Bassecontre, Guilliame Goudret and Martin Mingnon. They dined in style, and shared lavish daily rations of beef, mutton, and chicken at their meals, which included an allowance of a gallon and two quarts of wine.[11]

All the pressures and excitement of this close-knit life meant there was often a steady stream of drama well spiced by sexual attraction running parallel to their day-to-day work. David managed to keep himself aloof from most of it as he busied himself with the papers in foreign languages on which he was now expected to express an opinion. Usually he was careful not to get too involved and be caught up by such intimacies. However, tragedy sometimes lurked beneath the veneer of 'joyusitie' and cast a darker shadow on all the courtly camaraderie; one sad tale of love requited affected even him. A French apothecary, who had sailed over in the royal suite, made love to one of the Queen's maidens, who became pregnant.[12] The doctor procured an abortion for the girl, but the affair was discovered. There was great distress in the Household, but the law was implacable. It was said: 'Her Grace is so much offended it is thought they shall die.' Sure enough, 'they were both hanged this Friday, causing much sorrow at Court'.[13]

Their fate compared unfavourably with the milder sentence imposed on the Lord Treasurer of Scotland for a similar offence. His penalty, 'for getting a woman with child', was only, 'on Sunday next to do open penance before the whole congregation, and for Mr Knox to make the sermon'. The contrast between the punishments seems a little inequitable. The French foreigners were convicted of infanticide and hanged. The Lord Treasurer,

Richardson, as a great officer of state, had just to suffer public humiliation, which included being made to stand in a white sheet outside St Giles and then sit through a Sabbath sermon from John Knox. But there is still an air of hypocrisy about the incident that rankles. It was stories like these that her enemies used later to justify the Presbyterian historian Calderwood's complaints about Mary's promiscuous education at the French court, where all was debauchery and lust – filthy habits that followed her home. There, it was alleged, 'vice was free from punishment, and virgins and men's wives were made as common to King Henri, and Charles the Cardinal, their court and pages, as harlots in brothels, to their companions'.[14]

Back in the cold light of day, and away from the pleasures and travails of the summer jaunts, the deep religious divisions remained a constant dilemma. Mary continued to do her best to broker a compromise with the Protestants, and persuade them at least to modify in part their bitter opposition to the private exercise of her Catholic faith, but her difficulties in doing so were formidable, since the Reformers were not easy men to be moved. They suspected the Italian's influence at Mary's ear and discerned in him just another example of the Catholic and foreign entourage that provided her with such 'sinister counsel'.

Despite the constant attacks by the fanatics on the old church, not all its spokesmen were entirely overwhelmed. A few bold Roman Catholic priests remained who were prepared to stand up for their faith and challenge in open debate the supremacy of Knox and his friends. Some had come over with the Queen from France, and so were pledged to support her; while conservative-minded magnates such as Huntly had sheltered the others.

One such Catholic loyalist was Ninian Winzet, originally a schoolmaster from Linlithgow. Winzet was one of the confessors to the Queen, and worked hard to confute Knox and his doctrines. In July 1562 he was brave enough to write and publish an impressive assault on the Protestant position in a splendidly provocative work named *The Last Blast of the Trumpet of God's Word against the usurped Authority of John Knox, and his Calvinist Brethren, Intruded Preachers*.[15]

Knox and his allies were outraged. So much for free speech. The Edinburgh burgh council ordered the book be suppressed. The unfortunate printer, a man called Scott, was sent to jail. Winzet was forced to flee the country and take refuge in Paris with James Beaton, the long-serving but absentee Archbishop of Glasgow, in exile there. From Paris, Winzet took up his pen again, to compose another powerful polemic in confutation of the heretics, *The Book of Four Score Questions Touching Doctrine Orders and Manners Proposed to the Preachers of the Protestants in Scotland*. This was dedicated to the Queen of Scots, and found a sympathetic publisher at Louvain in the Spanish Netherlands. In energetic prose Winzet attacked Knox for having become too anglophile. He alleged that Knox had lost his native Scots accent as a result of his long residence in England, and, what was worse, had picked up an English way of speaking. Mary, of course, had a soft and attractive Scots accent, and Rizzio a Franco/Italian one.[16] Rizzio's early upbringing on the edge of the French- and Italian-speaking worlds had taught him the essential languages for his work; and he was already fluent in Italian, Latin and French. With his quick intelligence he had no trouble in picking up the Scots Doric, or rather English, when he reached Edinburgh. He was undoubtedly literate and well educated.

Knox was such an argumentative and provocative writer it did no harm to see him repaid by a little vulgar abuse in kind. Winzet went on to complain of Knox's anglican prose style. Among his other insults, he offered to translate Knox's writings into Latin, since Knox had forgotten his native Scots: 'you have forgot our old plain Scots tongue, which your mother taught you', he proudly told Knox, going on to sneer, 'I am not acquainted with your Southron' – that is, English.[17]

Even so, the Protestant camp was not without its own divisions. While Mary and her entourage continued to dance and sing the nights away, June 1564 saw fierce arguments when the eighth General Assembly of the Kirk met again in the grey summer of Presbyterian Edinburgh. There Knox and the current Secretary of State, Maitland, settled down to a serious debate on the limits of resistance to 'ungodly rulers'. Knox quoted extensively from the Old Testament to argue his case that the 'people may execute judgment against their King, being an offender'; Maitland in reply defended sovereign authority. He used arguments taken from the best of the modern Reformers, 'the judgments of Luther, Melanchthon, the minds of Bucer, Musculus, and Calvin, as to how Christians should behave themselves in time of persecution' in support of the status quo.[18] The debate foreshadowed years of constitutional disagreements about the precise power of the Crown.

Knox set down his considered views on the point later. In *The History of the Reformation in Scotland* he described his part in the religious revolution. This left his readers in no doubt how much he detested all that Mary stood for. So, when she came to open the Scots Parliament in 1563 and gave a graceful speech from the throne, most people were charmed; but he remained highly critical. He attacked the ceremony in his usual ferocious prose, and claimed that the parliamentary proceedings showed 'such stinking pride of women, as was seen at that Parliament, and was never seen before in Scotland'.[19]

In March, Knox, by now a widower aged about 50, took a new young wife, Margaret Ochiltree, who was only 17 years old. The Queen disapproved of the age disparity. Knox himself had a vigorous sex drive, which led to further troubles. It was about now that he found it necessary to bring proceedings for slander against a charge by an Edinburgh housewife, one Effie Dundas, that he was in the habit of consorting with common whores on the town.

The great preacher was not cast down by the litigation and stayed in sardonic form. He continued to scorn all the masques, parties and other festivities the courtly singer was starting to arrange for Mary. When told how the Queen's ladies in waiting were ready to leave for yet another banquet, dressed in all their evening finery, his irritation knew no bounds. He fulminated at them from his pulpit in St Giles and warned of the doom that lay ahead:

O, fair ladies! how pleasing were this life of yours, if it should ever abide, and then in the end that we might pass to Heaven with all this gay gear! But fie upon that knave Death that will come whether we will or not! And when he hath laid on his arrest, the foul worms will be busy with this flesh, be it never so fair and so tender; and the Silly Soul, I fear, shall be so feeble that it can neither carry with it gold, or garnishing, targetting, pearl, nor precious stones.[20]

But, however much Knox might thunder to his congregation, it was the Italian singer David Rizzio who had the ear of the Queen. His immediate appeal to Mary was based on his music. It was that deep, masculine, bass voice resounding in the regular discipline of the mass that had first caught her interest. His appeal was not promiscuously broadcast over the media like modern stars today. Instead, it was individual, directed with all the charm of his Latin allure on the single and susceptible person of the young lady sovereign herself.

As a consequence, he had by now become an important personage around the court. And at last he could also put to use his good classical education and that early clerical training with the seminarians back in Piedmont. He shared with the young Queen a love of cards, music and the masque. Away from all the paper work, he advised on court ceremonial. He reminded her of France, and knew all the latest fashions from Italy, and how modern monarchs should best order their courts. He composed happy songs of love and organised spectacular pageants in the best Italian style. His growing importance came from his ability to keep secrets, give impartial advice that was free from local factions, and control access to the royal person. Knox complained later of how 'a little before the troubles, which Satan raised in the body of the Kirk, began Davie to grow great in Court. The Queen used him for Secretary, in things that appertained to her secret affairs in France or elsewhere. Great men made court to him that their suits were the better heard.'[21] He may have begun life in Scotland as just a choral singer, but, as Mary's feelings for this very 'special servant' developed, their relationship inevitably was to change.

Now he could look out to wider horizons and hope to have some say on the country's place within Europe. Once installed as her private secretary, he could whisper his views into her ear, take charge of her incoming letters and advise as one of her leading functionaries with the authority of an older man, and of a classical scholar.

The Queen's more established advisers watched the Italian's rise with interest, and sometimes with no little misgiving. Some have left a record of their impressions. One of the best descriptions of his impact on Edinburgh comes from the quill of Sir James Melville. Sir James gave years of distinguished service to the Scots Crown, and, like many retired diplomats then and today, wrote up his memoirs in old age. In them he described how there arrived from Italy, 'with the Ambassador of Savoy, one David Riccio, who was a merry fellow, and a good musician'.[22] The Queen wanted a singer to make up her small choir since 'Her Majesty had three varlets of her chamber who sung three parts, and there wanted a bass to sing the fourth part. Therefore they told Her Majesty of this man, as one fit to make the fourth in concert, and thus he was drawn in to sing sometimes with the rest.'[23]

Another summary account of 'David le Chantre' came from Mary's loyal supporter, John, Lord Herries. Herries died in 1583, and in his *Historical Memoirs*, published long afterwards, he outlined his career in Scotland succinctly. There was 'one David Rizzio, an Italian who had served the Queen for many years, and who from a musician became her Secretary of State, an active politic man, whose counsel the Queen made use of in her greatest affairs'.[24]

So he was energetic: an active, politic person, with an attractive personality, and a fine bass voice, whose advice was worth having. Yet his were dangerous gifts. Melville says he was a 'merry fellow', and his Latin charm and wit clearly amused Mary and her ladies. The difficulty was that the royal court was an insecure power base –

a Catholic cosmopolitan establishment, in which a girlish sovereign encouraged a spirit of 'joyusitie', but where favour could be fickle.

The sentiments at the court contrasted with the new Calvinist culture of severity, which discouraged pleasures of the flesh. Edinburgh was still but a small city, though its citizens, as ever, held a high opinion of their own worth. Throughout the land, vendettas and feuds were rife, as cattle, grazing rights, title and disputes over women made for long-standing hatreds between men of rival clans and kin. Life for the Reformers was a serious business. They had little liking for the Italian's quips and jokes.

FIVE

The New Secretary

An Italian occupieth now his place . . .
(Randolph to Cecil, 15 December 1564)

The turn of the year 1564 started with ferocious cold weather. January saw 'the rain falling and freezing that the ground was like a sheet of ice. The fowls of the air died and might not flee, and the sea stood still neither ebbing nor flowing for twenty-four hours.'[1] By way of contrast, and to cheer everyone up for the approaching austerities of Lent, Mary gave orders for yet another great feast. She enjoyed parties, and this time her hospitality was to be very special, complete with all the latest *divertissements* her Italian favourite could suggest. Some of the nobles were beginning to find her constant round of entertainments too much. Indeed,

Argyll grumbled that he could never do any business in Holyrood, because everyone was either just recovering from the last festivity or preparing for the next one. The cream of Edinburgh, including many of the judges and other important 'men of law', were asked to this particular extravaganza, which was again held in the great hall at the palace. Randolph, the English resident, was one of the 300 or so guests present.

Mary made a great fuss of him during the meal, and he clearly enjoyed himself. Her four Maries – Livingston, Beaton, Fleming and Seton – were all dutifully in attendance that evening and served the more important guests with their dishes. For Randolph there was an extra special *frisson* in their company. He found Marie Beaton particularly attractive and was doing his best to capture her affections. The next day he wrote up a description of the festivities, which, dour Puritan though he was, he had clearly enjoyed, even though he complained about the strange order in which the various courses reached him from the kitchen. Sadly we do not know the full details of the menu.

> The Queen dined privately with the chief Lords and Ladies, willing me to be so placed at the Lords' table that she might speak with me, as she did much of the dinner time. The four Maries served Her Grace, the lords were attended by the rest of her own gentlewomen, maidens apparelled as herself, and the other four all in white and black.
>
> The solemnities of the supper are too long to describe, but I remember three divers courses brought in, the strange order I let pass, but the last was served by gentlemen apparelled all in white and black, and divers amongst them sang the verses, which herewith I send your honour.[2]

The entertainments during the dinner were the fruit of an interesting partnership between Rizzio and George Buchanan, the Queen's new poet laureate and a celebrated Latin scholar, and were put on with all the splendour and elegance of a competitive Renaissance court at its zenith. At intervals between the different courses a group of children dressed as Cupid, Charity and Time darted out among the guests, singing graceful odes in Latin to wish peace and harmony to the two British Queens. Then, amid the feasting, drinking and general merriment, just before the end of the meal, another troop of dancers, this time all dressed in black and white, burst suddenly into the great hall, where they chanted an Italian love song that Rizzio had composed. The English ambassador was sufficiently impressed by the verses to copy them to Queen Elizabeth.

Mary was in her element at a grand state occasion such as this; she enjoyed playing the leading part in the revels, took them very seriously and made sure all the players were dressed appropriately. It seems that the black and white garments worn by the masquers and her Maries were meant to symbolise her regal authority, while the contrasting colours were believed to have magical qualities too.[3] Here indeed was a Renaissance court at full high water.

With such a welcome it is little wonder the English envoy looked back on the evening fondly and appreciated being made so much of by all 'the chief lords and ladies' in attendance. There were formal courtesies and much good drinking. Many a loyal toast was downed to the health of the Queen of Scots, and also to that of the English Queen. Randolph claimed that he stayed sober enough to reply to them as best he could.

My Sovereign was drunk unto openly, not one of 300 persons or more but heard the words spoken and saw the cups pass between. I gave Her Majesty thanks in my Sovereign's name in as good words as I could.

She answered me, it was more in heart than outer show, as these verses shall testify, which she gave me in my hand, the self same that were sung, and willed me to do with them as I liked.

I trust that your Honour will present them to the Queen's Majesty, with my humble suit that I write not, trusting to your report.[4]

Then Rizzio took up his lute. He plucked away and then began his song about the amorous blindness of Cupid. He was not called 'David le Chantre' for nothing. As the years went by, many compositions were afterwards ascribed to him. Most of the attributions are false, but this particular lyric, which he did write and sang to the guests that night, has come down to us.

Here is the melancholy ballad of love. It is the only genuine fragment of his work to have been preserved:

> Quest' e colui che'l mondo chiamo amore
> Amaro come vedi et vedrai meglio
> Quando fia tuo, com'e nostro signore
> Mansueto fanciulo et fiero veglio
> ben sa ch'il prova, et fiati cosa piana,
> anzi mill' anni e infin adhor ti sueglio.
> El nacque d'otio et di lascivia humana,
> nutrito dipensier dolci et soavi,
> fatto signor et dio da gente vana
> quale e morto da lui, qual co' piu gravi
> leggi, mena sua vita aspra et accerba,
> sotto mille cathena et mille chiavi.[5]

> (What is the power that the world calls love?
> Bitter if known, worse when he is thine own
> when you are in his power, he will prove,
> child or tyrant, you before him prone,
> is not this felt by those his talents rue,
> I tell you, and my words are true,
> if you should live a thousand years or so,
> Love's born of leisure, and desire,
> feeds on sweet thoughts, and fair words won,
> is made a god, by those who feed his fires,
> some die for him, others he keeps in
> shackled locks and chains.)

The singer, however, was by now more than just another *troubadour* or aide-de-camp to the sovereign. He formed part of the Queen's inner circle, and was by way of becoming quite an important figure among the secretariat. His opinions counted, and he did not hesitate to express them to her in private, especially on the question of her choice of husband. Her marriage was a matter of prime importance for all her advisers, and one on which he spoke with some authority. He had worked with de Moretto, knew the latest techniques of Italian and Spanish diplomacy, and was familiar with the type of man King Philip II, and his own Duke back in Savoy, hoped to see as her consort. So it is hard not to believe the new private secretary was behind a letter she wrote to her uncle in Lyons on 9 September 1564 when away on another of her summer circuits through the Highlands. This year the royal progress had taken her from Perth up north to Inverness, and then south-east over the hills to Aberdeen. Now she wrote to Duke Emmanuel Philibert from her quarters near Dundee. It was just a brief and formal little letter, which confirmed how attached she was to her Savoy uncle and aunt, and wished them good health and a long life.[6] The Duke doubtless appreciated the message from far-off Scotland, and was as yet ignorant of a recent diplomatic slight on Elizabeth's part. His arms and insignia as a Knight of the Garter had just been taken down from the wall over his stall in St George's Chapel, Windsor, and replaced by the achievements of the French king. This heraldic slur may have indicated the growing English disquiet at Savoy's status as a Spanish satellite, and one that was duly reported back to King Philip by his new envoy in London, Don Guzman de Silva.[7]

Other evidence of Rizzio's growing influence around the court now begins to come into the open. Most of our information about his ascendancy comes from the dispatches of Thomas Randolph, who watched his increasing prominence with a certain fastidious distaste. It was not long before Randolph sent a dispatch with all the latest gossip from Edinburgh in which he mentioned recent changes to Mary's advisers; and in it gave the news that 'an Italian "Piedmontese", that came in with Monsieur Moretto, is her new Secretary for French affairs'.[8] The Italian 'Piedmontese', of course, was David Rizzio, whose increasing grip over the Queen was to dominate the political scene in future.

Soon further references to the influential Italian, who was already an important personage in Mary's household, begin to appear in his files. As usual Randolph was on constant alert to discover every scrap of news from her circle. Rizzio apparently had 'crept in on suspicion gathered against Raulet, whose case and what befell him, your Honor has heard'. Some questions arise here. Who was Raulet, and how had Rizzio 'crept in' to his post, which was that of the secretary in charge of the Queen's French correspondence?

The answer seems to be that Raulet, another of her French entourage, who had returned with Mary in summer 1561, had made a mistake in the long-winded diplomatic negotiations about her marriage. Raulet, though French, was arguing for a Spanish match, and had steered her towards the Hapsburg candidate, the Infante Don Carlos of Spain. As secretary for 'French Affairs', he pressed her case with the Spaniards, and drafted the necessary correspondence with the Hapsburg authorities in Madrid and Brussels.[9]

By December the ever-vigilant Randolph could write that 'Raulet, her old Secretary, is clean out of favour – some think for being familiar with me, which indeed is not so', and, more interestingly, that 'Riccio, an Italian, occupieth now his place'.[10] Raulet, whose arguments for marriage with Don Carlos ended in such failure, was also suspected of taking bribes from the English. This may well be why he was dismissed, but, none the less, he did not depart in disgrace, his wife stayed on at court, and he received a generous annual pension of 200 *livres*, which was charged on the revenues of Mary's French estates.

Randolph, of course, denied Raulet was ever 'familiar' with him. His denial is not very convincing, since he always tried to extract intelligence and buy up such officials, courtiers and peers as his limited resources allowed. His other persona, 'Mr Barnaby', was usually engaged to the same end too.

In contrast to the attitude of Raulet, Rizzio's loyalty to the Scots Crown does him credit. His enemies were often to accuse him of corruption, and the evidence of his steadily mounting wealth does support the charge, but in his defence it must be remembered that standards in public life in the sixteenth century were very different from today. Sir William Cecil himself profited mightily from the many great offices of state he held, such as the keepership of the court of wards. It has never been suggested that Rizzio himself took English money to betray Scotland's secrets. He never did so, for his fidelity to Mary remained absolute.

In pursuit of Don Carlos, Mary had little difficulty in rejecting other inferior suitors.

So, when an ambassador arrived from the Swedish king, Eric XIV, in the summer of 1562 to seek Mary's hand for his master, Raulet advised against him. Public opinion supported the decision. In his own inimitable language even Knox cautioned rejection of this Nordic suitor: 'Such a man was too base for her estate. Had she not been a great Queen of France? Fie of Sweden. What is it?'[11] Eric was persistent and refused to be rebuffed. He wrote to her a year later, saying that he 'marvels at the Queen's constancy in remaining so long unmarried on his account, and still hopes that she will marry him'.[12]

Despite her diplomatic pleasantries to the emissaries from England, Sweden or elsewhere, Mary's attitude to marriage was in many ways 'fie' upon the lot of them. Especially 'fie' on Elizabeth's former lover, Robert Dudley, the newly minted Earl of Leicester, who was now commended by cousin Elizabeth as the best candidate for her hand. Mary had no hesitation in rejecting Elizabeth's patronising offer to play the part of a generous elder sister and subsidise her lifestyle if she took Leicester and lived with him 'in household', even though the English Queen promised to cover the costs of their 'family', 'as shall be meet for one sister to do for another'.[13]

Nevertheless, Raulet had made a poor choice in backing the Spanish prince. Unfortunately for him, Don Carlos was a repellent lunatic, like so many of Mary's other suitors who emanated from the rather inbred royal houses of Europe. King Philip of Spain, ever the realist where women were concerned, soon realised his son was an impossible consort for the Scottish Queen, and called a halt to the business. Raulet fell as a casualty to the failed negotiations. However, his loss of place made room for David Rizzio to put his first footsteps on the serpentine staircase to power and influence.

Mary's choice of husband was critical for the future direction of the state. Another French prince as king consort would renew France's grip on the country, and especially that of the Guise family, would confuse and confound the heretics, and so would consolidate the old Catholic faith. The best opinion in the Vatican, and therefore in the universal Church, inclined to a Spanish match, despite all Philip's reservations. England itself presented a good example of such an arrangement. It was not easy to remember that it was only six years since Philip himself had reigned there as king, consort and husband to Mary Tudor.

Mary Stewart's beauty and femininity were never in doubt. It is sometimes hard to pierce through to her real emotions, since so much of the evidence, buried in the cold calendars of the state papers, is essentially formal in its nature. (Later on she was not ashamed to defend her liaison with Bothwell with some passion. And so, in May 1567 she wrote to her representative in France asking him to justify her third marriage to her supporters there, for which she gave the following rather feeble explanation. 'Bothwell had us in his puissance,' the Queen explained. She continued her justification by saying that, since Bothwell was not willing to postpone consummation of the marriage, 'He must be considered our husband, who we will both love and honour, so that all that profess themselves to be our friends must profess the like friendship towards him, who is inseparably joined with us.14) The records, moreover, confirm her sex appeal. She was attractive, a reigning queen and in every respect eligible for marriage and motherhood.

In this, as in so much else, Mary was unlike her 'Right mighty Princess, and good sister', Elizabeth of England. Elizabeth, despite her occasional protestations to the contrary, was strangely disinclined to exchange the state of virginity for matrimony. Philip himself had wooed her shortly after her succession in 1558, and suggested she marry immediately, since 'it would be better for herself and her kingdom, if she would take a consort who might relieve her of those labours which are only fit for men'.[15] The English Queen had little difficulty in ignoring Philip's wise advice. She was perfectly capable of performing 'those labours which are only fit for men' herself. Mary, however, was different. She had been taught by her family, and her Church, to believe that in this world the work of a woman privileged such as her, called by God to rule, could be performed only with the help of a man.

Not every piece of state diplomatic business was about her marriage, however. Commercial opportunities were not neglected. So, for example, in June 1564 William Douglas of Whittinghame was sent to negotiate better terms for trade in the Baltic with the King of Denmark. The return home of Matthew, Earl of Lennox, at first seemed another exception to the rule. Later that summer Lennox had crossed over the border from England, where he had been living in exile for many years. He was then about 48 years old, and arrived with a blighted reputation. Most good Scots disliked his treasonable conduct during Henry VIII's invasions, when, unlike Rizzio, he happily took English gold and commanded a division in their armies. He was condemned as a traitor, and his estates were then made forfeit.

Leicester too was now playing his own, rather difficult, hand in this complicated game of royal matrimonial chess. He was unwilling to fall in with Cecil's plans and be exiled to Scotland as Mary's consort. As a counter-ploy, he seems to have encouraged Lennox to ask permission from Elizabeth to return north with the ostensible object of launching a legal process to recover his forfeited estates. His request was granted, and he was given a temporary passport, which allowed him to leave England. Elizabeth stayed suspicious of the Lennoxes, who had been far too close to her half-sister, Queen Mary Tudor, for comfort, and refused to let his wife, Margaret, Countess of Lennox, accompany her husband. Lady Lennox was to be kept under restraint as a hostage for his obedience. But Mary Stewart and her government fell in with Elizabeth's wishes and welcomed the visitor to her court.

The Scottish Parliament was now on the point of meeting, and the young Queen had begun to rehearse the speech she would deliver from the Throne. This was drafted by the principal Secretary of State, Maitland of Lethington, and as yet showed little sign of input by Rizzio. His hour had not yet come, and what influence he had on domestic policy was well behind the *arras*.

The previous year's parliament in 1563 had been the first one to be held since the great Reformation sessions of 1560. Much of the business this time was routine, with statutes enacted against perceived threats to good order, such as the prevalence of witchcraft, which was described as 'the highest abominable superstition used by divers lieges of the realm in witchcraft sorcery, or necromancy'; and against poaching. Punishing poachers was always a cause dear to the hearts of country gentlemen, who may have found it a relief to have something familiar to grumble about as a change from the long theological debates of recent years. The previous year's sporting had been poor, and poachers were blamed. The threat they offered was defined as 'shooting with half hag, culverin, or pistol at deer and other wild beasts . . . and against wild fowls, wherefore the noblemen of the realm can get no pastime of hawking or hunting, like has been in times past'.[16] But this year, 1564, the parliamentary programme was much more interesting.

Moray was still in power and governed in coalition with Maitland, so the parliamentary business stayed Protestant and reformist. Higher taxation loomed, with a land tax proposed that was to claw back some of the excess profits from the sale of the old church lands, and with a general tightening of the penal laws against Catholics. The general Protestant and reformist bias of the legislation was confirmed by the increased penalties enacted against sexual offences, especially fornication and adultery. (The new statute provided, doubtless more in hope than in expectation, that offenders charged with fornication were to be fined £10 on first conviction. On a second conviction the punishment was to stand at the market cross, with head and face shaven; and after a third conviction the guilty parties were to be permanently banished from their homes. The legislation against the practice of the Catholic religion was equally penal. It was to be a capital offence to hear the mass, saving an express exemption for the Queen to follow her faith privately, 'Herself and those of her House excepted'. The lands and goods of all so convicted were to be forfeit.)

However, one interesting private and particular piece of legislation in hand was the motion that the Earl of Lennox have his hereditary lands and honours returned to him. In an optimistic speech to the members of parliament present, the secretary, William Maitland, emphasised that Lennox had returned with Elizabeth's permission. Speaking in the absence of the Lord Chancellor, Morton, in a debate held on 23 September 1564, he said that the government's reservations about allowing Lennox back were overcome only because Mary had 'tenderly looked on the request from her good sister, the Queen of England'.[17] The fragments of Maitland's speech that survive read well. It was a successful piece of oratory, which appeared to confirm the happy state of the realm under Mary's benign rule, so that the Three Estates (nobles, clergy and burgesses) duly enacted the required measures, even though Lennox's restoration required some readjustment of clan allegiances in the West Country. The Hamiltons, and Campbells, lost out, and former Lennox clients, like the Buchanans, who had given bonds of man rent, or promises of allegiance to the Campbell Earl of Argyll, were now forced to return to their old loyalties.

During his speech Maitland spoke with a typical politician's optimism: 'It may be affirmed Scotland in no many age that presently lives was in greater tranquillity. It is the duty of all Her loving subjects to acknowledge the same, and the most high benefits proceeding from the good Government of Her Majesty.' Mary was actually sitting on her throne under her elegant cloth of state during the proceedings, and may have been relieved when her minister ended his remarks, saying, as he sat down, that, if he continued, 'he fears he might offend Her Highness, whose presence and modest nature abhors long speaking, and adulation' – which was true enough, even though she had been cheered to the rafters by the fickle crowd as she made her way up the Royal Mile to the Parliament House.[18] The mob even shouted how like she was to the Goddess Diana.

Knox was not alone in his concern at these developments. By the end of January 1565 the French ambassador down in London, de Foix, had joined the critics. He had learnt through the diplomatic grapevine of a rumour that Lennox's young son Darnley would soon be allowed to leave for the north. In the meantime, rather tongue in cheek, he reported to Catherine de' Medici that he was worried by the 'dissipated' behaviour of the Scots court, where all was hunting and hawking in the morning, and dancing and masquing at night.[19] On one occasion the Queen of Scots was even said to have taken the middle-aged Lennox as her partner in the dance. Maitland, however, had no cause to worry, although he may have tempted the fates when he praised the efforts of her government to keep the peace, since her final choice of husband, Lennox's son, Henry Lord Darnley, was to start a civil war and lead on to catastrophe. When winter did eventually return, conditions were even worse than before; indeed, there was something of a mini ice age, which gripped Europe in the mid-sixteenth century. It was so cold for the four days just before Christmas from 20 to 24 December 1564 that the Queen was confined to her rooms at Holyrood. And, if Seigneur Davie may have pined occasionally to be back near the warmer Mediterranean shores at Nice, in the meantime he could take some comfort from his growing precedence in the royal household.

SIX

The Arrival of Lord Darnley

I intend to be a wife indeed.
  (Mary quoted in a letter from Randolph to Cecil, 1 March 1565)

Meanwhile, early in February 1565, when Elizabeth allowed Henry, Lord Darnley, to journey north to join his father Lennox, the 'tranquillity' of which Maitland had boasted so eloquently was soon found to be just a sham after all. Mary, though, did not mind. She was intrigued at the thought of meeting the visitor.

Harry Darnley was 19 years old. His ambitious parents had brought him up as a Catholic, and at first blush he seemed well qualified for Mary's hand, in default of the 'strong Catholic Prince' that the Papal nuncio Father de Gouda hoped might be found for her. Since Lennox himself was Protestant, it could be argued that a match between them would appeal to moderate opinion on both sides of the confessional divide. His weak character was still well hidden, although Mary's worldly-wise uncle, the Cardinal de Lorraine, knew enough about him to warn of his inadequacy. The Holy Father was less well briefed, while, far away in Madrid, King Philip approved the match.

Lennox produced good reasons to persuade Cecil to let his son join him. He had obtained counsel's opinion that it was necessary for them both to be enfeoffed together so as better to secure the family entail over their estates.[1] Furthermore they must actually be physically present within Scotland when the legal formalities took place. Lennox explained the problem in a letter sent on 10 March 1565, in which he asked permission to stay on for another three months beyond the time marked on his passport, since 'I cannot proceed so soon as I thought in the assurance of my lands to my son, the laws here requiring three or four months at the least'.[2]

Lennox himself was well received at the Scots court, where he soon became a figure of importance. He was made much of, and great efforts were made to see that he was kept comfortable. Expensive presents came his way, which included a 'house well hanged, two chambers very well furnished, and a special rich and fair bed, where his Lordship lieth himself'.[3] Beds were rare and costly pieces of furniture in Marian Scotland.

Randolph was not impressed at his arrival. He noticed his pride and his poverty. 'Thus your honour sees how things are. Such pride, excess in vanities, proud looks and deceitful words, and so poor a purse as I had never heard of.'[4]

He had not yet appreciated quite what efforts Lennox and his wife were putting into the marriage project, and that Rizzio was involved in it too. Lennox was playing for high stakes in order to gain a kingdom for his boy and had mortgaged himself to the hilt to do so. He distributed lavish presents to potential allies around the household like Rizzio, though there was nothing for Moray, and soon got into financial difficulties, despite the return of his hereditary estates. 'Lennox is now quite without money. He borrowed 500 crowns of Lethington and has scarcely what will pay for his horsemeat. His men are now bolder and saucier with the Queen's self and many noble men.'[5] Lennox and his entourage seem to have behaved rather like King Lear and his train of knights, of whose conduct his evil daughters Goneril and Regan complained so much. Shakespeare knew very well how Elizabethan magnates were expected to maintain their troops of followers, who were likely to be bold and saucy as they swaggered around the court. And, far worse for Randolph, the Catholics were resurgent. 'Divers resort to mass and glory in their doing so.'[6]

Darnley duly met Mary on Saturday 17 February 1565, in Wemyss Castle, about four miles east of the small port of Kirkcaldy on the north shore of the Firth of Forth. She had ridden there from St Andrews, where she had been living simply, pretending to be just a little bourgeois housewife, in a small town house well away from the cares of court. Randolph saw her during her stay there, and found her in high spirits, as she argued vigorously for female empowerment: 'may not some notable things be wrought by us women, as have been done by our predecessors?'[7] There is no record Rizzio was around at Wemyss on this momentous occasion, but he has always been credited with encouraging Darnley to aim high, pressed his case on Mary, and must have done his best to make him welcome. At first Darnley appeared to respect the older man, and a friendship sprang up between them.

David Rizzio, with his influential position close to the Queen and the ability to whisper his opinions into her ear, was someone Darnley, and his father, soon realised it made sense to cultivate. This may have been why Lennox got special permission for 'Harry', as he called his son fondly, to have 'a licence' to bring 'three or four geldings' with him up to Scotland.[8] Good English horses were rare and valuable commodities abroad, and their export was strictly controlled. Lennox knew they would make attractive gifts for influential courtiers, like Rizzio.

Meanwhile, as the spring blossoms came into bloom, the attraction between Mary and Darnley grew. Before long an annoying, but not life-threatening, illness – perhaps measles or chicken pox – struck the visitor down. This gave Mary the opportunity to play the nurse, and she began to visit Darnley in his sick chamber at Stirling Castle carrying comforts and sweetmeats.

Mary's independent attitude to her marriage had made for difficulties not only with the English government, but also with the French one as well, for there the influence of her Guise connections was now on the wane. France was more than ever under the spell of her formidable mother-in-law, Catherine de' Medici, who suspected pro-Spanish elements were at work in Edinburgh, and took appropriate counter-action.

Her doctor, Leseure, like her apothecary and most of her household, was, of course, French. There was a certain amount of skulduggery abroad that December, which it not easy to interpret, and this time the doctor was implicated. Leseure was about to leave for home. The English emissary suspected he was working as a spy for Catherine, while the Scots thought he was in the pay of the English. Randolph, always alert for French intrigues in Scotland, recommended, in his rather sinister way, that Leseure 'were well used when passing through England'. Dr Leseure was to leave in two weeks. Once he departed there would be no 'other Frenchmen of credit, wisdom, or honesty' in the Queen's household. However, Scottish counter-intelligence scored a local triumph, and managed to intercept the French doctor's papers before he left the stage of history.[9]

But Mary's matrimonial future was still unsettled. As her trusted confidant, Rizzio thought she should accept Darnley but still keep negotiations open with other suitors. It was too early to make it obvious, at least in public, that she had lost interest in them. In the meantime he was instructed to bankroll Darnley's expenses: 'as he had no proper establishment, the Queen directed the French Secretary Rizzio to attend him, and to receive and pay money for him.'[10] This was the moment when Elizabeth, always something of a tease, now resurrected the suggestion that her own lover, Robert Dudley, the new Earl of Leicester, might be a fit consort for the Scottish Queen. Randolph was instructed to urge his case and, once again, did his best to do so at one of the many masques, banquets and entertainments she delighted in giving.

Randolph was ever watchful to catch the latest court secrets. It was at another such party that Moray took him aside and whispered a plea to him for English help to 'bring us from Papistry'.[11]

The Scots Lords were proud of their Queen's sex appeal. Although the politicians refused to stop discussing her wedding plans, she in turn enjoyed keeping up the pretence there were no commitments to any of her suitors. So, when Moray and his wife Agnes, Lady Moray, hosted yet another reception in March, the English Ambassador and other local grandees were all invited.

Mary was the principal guest. She had now been widowed for nearly five years, and many couriers had travelled the weary way between Brussels, Edinburgh, London, Paris and Rome on the business of her marriage. The Protestants still hoped her choice would fall on a prince with full English approval – the understanding being that Elizabeth would confirm such approval by nominating, so far as she was able, the younger woman as her heir and successor. Both Maitland and Moray were proponents of this arrangement, and continued to urge Mary to choose a candidate both who was Protestant in faith, and whom the English Parliament would welcome as a fit consort for her.

During this dinner, Randolph again pressed the case for Leicester as the most eligible spouse for her. Some of the Scots Lords, by now pretty well gone in their drink, belittled the idea. One of them, Wishart of Pitarrow, who acted as Moray's 'controller' or chamberlain, argued she could do much better than Leicester.

He went on to underline her charms in rather vulgar detail, all of which was faithfully reported back to Cecil. Pointing at his young monarch's fetching person, Wishart said admiringly, in a rather drunken way: 'You see the lustiness of her body . . . you know what these things require . . .'.[12]

Perhaps Wishart was right. Mary's first boy husband, Francis, may have been too immature to cope with 'what these things require' and so may have failed to appreciate the delightful 'lustiness' of her body to the full. Nearly six feet tall, red haired in reflection of her Celtic ancestry, and with her soft appealing Scots accent, Mary was an attractive beauty, with much of her father's Stewart good looks.[13]

But there was to be still more extravagant eating and drinking at court that March. Rizzio was kept busy organising the festivities, and had his work cut out to make sure everything stayed seemly and in order.

Again we are indebted to Thomas Randolph for setting the scene. He records a conversation he had with Mary at yet another grand banquet on Sunday 4 March 1565. They discussed her plans. He usually enjoyed a good gossip with his hostess, not to mention her attendant Maries, and most especially attempting to seduce Marie Beaton. He again pressed her to accept Leicester, who was still Elizabeth's nominee. He described their talk together: 'We then fell on her marriage. She said to that she was minded. I prayed God that her choice might be good.'[14]

For once his sources failed him. He had not calculated what an impact Lennox's son would have on Mary, and that the Italian Secretary was already putting the case for this particular candidate. It is little wonder Mary sounded somewhat indecisive as she tried to voice her feelings. Still, she replied to the diplomat's rather impertinent questions as honestly as she could. She said her choice of husband was in the hands of the Almighty. 'He must be such a one as God will give me.' To which the Englishman replied: 'I said that God had made a fair offer in him, for whom I had been so often times in hand with Her Grace,' by which he meant Leicester. 'Of this matter', saith she, 'I have said enough, except that I saw greater likelihood, nor I may not apply, and set my mind.'[15]

She went on to say that, of course, she hoped to marry: 'I intend to be a wife indeed. And in good faith no creature living shall make me break more of my will, than the Queen [that is Elizabeth], my good sister, if she will use me as a sister. If not, I must do as I may, and yet not fail unto her in any thing that is my part.'[16] That is as much as Randolph tells of their conversation, but it is enough to confirm her understandable doubts, and hesitations. The kernel of his analysis was that he felt the Scots Queen told the truth when she said that she wished to be on good terms with Elizabeth, but that the tough-minded female continued to be unimpressed by these expressions of sisterly devotion.

For now, as the first green shoots of the spring began to put their heads above the ground in the new warmth, she had at last made up her mind. Her eventual choice of husband was to be not Leicester, nor Arran, nor a prince of Spain or Austria, nor yet another Frenchman, nor even a Swede. She agreed with David Rizzio: Darnley must be her man.

Cecil was greatly irritated when he heard the news. He decided England's objections to the match must be reinforced, and dispatched the veteran diplomat Sir Nicholas Throgmorton post haste to the Scots court at Stirling, to protest in the name of Queen Elizabeth at this proposal, which was made 'not only without our knowledge, but also contrary to the speeches of his friends here, wherewith we take ourselves very far abused'.[17] Elizabeth herself was equally furious. The French ambassador found her in a 'très grand mescontentement' about it, finding it strange that a reigning queen could deign to marry one of her vassals.[18] And in her annoyance, when she learnt what was planned, she packed Darnley's meddlesome mother, Margaret, Countess of Lennox, back off to the Tower of London.

Randolph realised that he had been outwitted. He grew tired of watching the growing romance played out at Stirling, and decided to take a little leave and slip away south towards Carlisle to look at the border defences there from the Scots side. Rumour had it they were being strengthened despite the supposed 'amity' that existed between the two countries. The Master of Maxwell on his lands near Annan had just built a great peel tower with an emergency fire beacon. This was capable of holding a strong fighting force, and was well worth a look. 'In Annan town he has built a fair tower able to receive about one hundred persons at ease, and forty or fifty horses, with a beacon and watch tower of great height.'[19]

The next two months were among the most eventful of all Rizzio's time in Scotland. Much of the political and romantic interest of the kingdom was now confined behind the walls of the beautiful new Renaissance palace and privy gardens of Stirling Castle, where Mary mulled over her decision. She was beginning to trust his judgement, and, the more she put her confidence in him, the more his status increased. She agreed with his analysis that, if she married Darnley, she would please the King of Spain, and perhaps also rid herself of the tutelage of her increasingly obnoxious older brother, Moray. Sir James Melville described how this was a time when Rizzio was Darnley's 'great friend at the Queen's hand, so that she took ever the longer, the better liking of him [Darnley] and at length determined to marry him'.[20] And even Knox confirmed his present ascendancy: 'her Council at this time was only the Earl of Lennox, and Atholl, the Lord Ruthven, but chiefly David Rizzio the Italian ruled all.'[21]

Hitherto, cloaked by Mary's name and crown, Moray had been the effective ruler of Scotland. But the installation of a king or prince consort beside the Queen would inevitably alter the balance of power within the structure of politics. And it might also open ways for a new faction to take control, perhaps one more likely to play the patriot card and return to the country's traditional anti-English policies. Baser motives were also at work. Rizzio's enemies were later to claim that he had encouraged Darnley's proposal to protect himself from his rivals like Moray, 'who signified by his very countenance that he disdained him'. They went on to allege that 'to strengthen himself against those who hated him he insinuated himself into the favours of Lord Darnley, so far that they would lie sometimes in one bed together. He assured him that by his procurement the Queen had fastened her eyes on him.'[22]

Whatever the truth of the allegations, he still had to keep up his other responsibilities as these momentous events unfolded.

He continued to do his best to encourage the already sound musical standards of the court and organised a particularly jubilant Catholic Easter Day service in the chapel at Stirling Castle. There the congregation enjoyed a veritable feast of music during the High Mass, which included contributions from the bagpipes, drums and trumpets: 'organs were wont to be the common music. She wanted now neither trumpet, drum, nor fife, bagpipe or tabor.'[23]

If Mary's interest in Darnley was first aroused when he fell sick, there was still state business to be dealt with, despite the demands of the invalid. She might be in love, but Rizzio, by now one of her principal private secretaries, insisted that she must not neglect her paperwork.

So, on 3 May 1565, she sent a short letter in French to the English secretary, Sir William Cecil. This accompanied a packet of confidential instructions for her special envoy, William Maitland of Lethington, who was down in London on yet another mission to press once again her case to be accepted as the heir to the English throne.[24]

This letter is of great interest. It is drafted for signature in a firm and educated italic hand, which must be that of David Rizzio. By now he was her most prominent courtier and in charge of much of the day-to-day secretarial business in the household. The back side of the paper is addressed to 'Monsieur Cecille' and has on it a wafer embossed with the royal seal of Scotland, the Lyon Rampant. The reverse carries an endorsement in dark black ink by Cecil's own hand, as a reminder to himself before filing of what it contained, 'the Scottishe Queen to W C'.

The precise contents themselves are not so very remarkable. Cecil is asked to pass the accompanying papers on to Maitland. Mary says she will be just as ready to oblige him in his turn. She closes the note with the pious hope that he will continue to enjoy good health and a long and happy life. She signed it, in her own large, firm, and easily recognisable hand, with diplomatic nicety as 'Votre bien bonne amye, Marie. R.' (Your very good friend, Mary. R.).

The survival of this document in Cecil's records is itself something of a triumph of archival care – a remarkable physical microcosm, which records the actual link between Rizzio and Sir William. It is strange to think that they must both have actually handled this small scrap of paper, which was, of course, the closest they ever came to meeting.

The bad news from Scotland, and Rizzio's growing prominence there, continued to vex Elizabeth's first minister. He had always harboured a particular antipathy for Italy, and Italians. This attitude seems to have affected his views about the Italian secretary once he realised the hold he had obtained on the levers of power at the court of 'the Scottish Queen', and the antipathy long lingered. When he came to advise his own, second son, Robert, on how to bring up his family, he particularly warned him to 'marry thy daughters in time, less they marry themselves. And suffer not your sons to pass the Alps, for they shall learn nothing there but pride, blasphemy, and atheism.'[25]

On the very same day, 3 May, that Mary wrote her letter to Cecil, Thomas Randolph sent another of his regular dispatches to the English council. In it he described his border tour, and gave more intriguing intelligence about Rizzio's growing popularity with the Queen. He bemoaned the usual border feuds, and the weak state of the economy, as well as the collapse of law and order. 'The country is broken. Daily slaughter between Scotts and Elliots. Stealing on all hands – justice nowhere.'[26] However, there was something to tell that was even more important than reports of the usual border turmoils.

Lennox had an agent, his principal man of business, called Fowler, who was just back in the north. He had arrived with a long message in cipher from Maitland, who was still in London: 'Fowler came in as I wrote on Saturday night late, communed long that night with the Queen and the Lords.'

The mysterious Mr T. Fowler was an individual who had made many secret missions to Scotland on behalf of the family. This time: 'He brought Her Grace a letter of five or six sheets of paper in cipher from Lethington. Fowler has said the Queen's Majesty openly said she had no liking of it . . . and all good Protestants driven out of the country, which she would not suffer.'

It is worth noting this last comment. It is further evidence of Mary's tolerant approach to her country's religious divisions. She had no wish for 'all good Protestants' to be 'driven out of the country'. She was no persecutor of Protestant heretics, unlike her cousin and namesake Mary Tudor of England, though she did her best to protect Catholics when she could.

Randolph went on to analyse the divisions among Mary's leading advisers. 'Lethington [that is, Maitland] is suspected to favour Darnley more than he would seem, and yet I assure you he is scarcely trusted amongst them.' Then he mentions the new leadership. 'The chief dealers in these matters are David Rizzio, the Italian, Mingo, valet de chambre, Atholl and Ruthven, whom I should have named first.'[27]

This was his first recognition of Rizzio's increasing importance. He had at last realised that she was on the point of coming to a final decision about her choice of husband. She was being urged to take Darnley by an unlikely coalition of radical Protestants, such as Patrick, 3rd Lord Ruthven, the Lennox Stewart family interests, and foreign courtiers and favourites in the Royal Household, like Rizzio and Mingo.

Now though it was time to celebrate the approaching nuptials. The first step was to organise a grand investiture ceremony in an attempt to consolidate support for the marriage among the nobility. This was held on 15 May 1565. And so there, in the Great Hall at Stirling Castle, Darnley proceeded to dub fourteen of his Stewart kinsmen as knights, complete with all the ancient honours of Scottish chivalry, in an effort to embolden his kinsmen's belief in the benefits of the alliance. The new knights were mainly Lennox Stewart cousins or clan allies, so it is little surprise that most of the newly beknighted gentlemen had historic Scots surnames such as Douglas, Maxwell, Ruthven, Hume or Drummond.

During the proceedings Lord Darnley himself took a solemn oath that he would always be true and loyal to his Princess and Sovereign Dame, the Queen of Scots: 'Je suis loyal et veritable à ma Princesse et Souverine Dame, la Royne d'Ecosse' – an obligation that he was to test to the limit. He went on to swear, by the Holy Evangel, and by God himself, that he would fortify, maintain and defend each and every member of the Noble Order of Knighthood, in their hour of need.[28]

By 3 June 1565 it was quite clear that Lord Leicester was no longer a serious candidate for Mary's hand despite Elizabeth's strong recommendations, and that the match with the Lennox boy was almost impossible to stop. The English government had miscalculated when it let him go north. 'Great tokens of love daily pass between them' was how their ambassador noted the affection between Mary and Darnley with growing chagrin.[29]

Randolph may have been a little slow in finding out that Mary's choice had lighted on Darnley, but he was still suspicious of French intrigues. His dispatches now become ever more partisan, if not just a little spiced by sour grapes, as when he commented how she had lost much of her looks once her new love became public.

He could write to Leicester more frankly than to Cecil. He told him how Mary's new love changed her appearance, 'which in her has wrought so strange an effect that shame is laid aside'. Her 'princely honour' was lost in the process. Worse for him was the fact that her pro-English advisers were about to lose power and that 'Her counsellors now are those she liked worst': 'The nearest of her kin are now the farthest from her heart.'[30] In the result, Moray fell from favour, and no longer had his sister's ear. Even Maitland lost influence, and so had time to concentrate on his own affairs of the heart.

Then he came to the central problem. His shrewd analysis had revealed that the Italian favourite was now the principal adviser. 'David is he that now works all. Chief Secretary to the Queen, and only guv'nor to her good man.'[31] 'Governor', or 'Guv' today, is just a slightly jocular form of address, used by taxi drivers to their fares, but his meaning is clear. Rizzio controlled Darnley.

Jealousy of his success with the Queen was inevitably on the increase. Here Randolph echoed Moray's own bitter comments: 'There is hatred of Darnley. His pride is intolerable, and his words not to be borne. This Queen is determined to make a divorce with England, yet you shall not lack fine words till she can make a better party.'[32] He then proceeded, in a rather unkind way, to tell Leicester that he thought Mary was bewitched, and that much of her beauty was gone, despite her being so much in love. She was now 'a woman more to be pitied than any other that I ever saw. The saying is that surely she is bewitched.'[33] Mary and Rizzio though were happily ignorant of his comments. Later that June a large and well-horsed party left the court at Stirling Castle on a little summer jaunt to visit Darnley's kinsman, Ruthven, near Perth. There they remained beneath the battlements of his castle at Huntingtower, a mile or so outside the town, while they enjoyed his hospitality and discussed the plans for the wedding. 'They remained there that night, and the whole day until after supper, when she took her horse,' accompanied by an escort, which included Lennox himself, Darnley of course, 'David Rizzio the Italian', the ubiquitous Mr Fowler, Lady Erskine, Lady Seton and Madame Roulet.[34] Lord Ruthven's territorial wealth was based on extensive family lands and estates around Perthshire, where he held 'the land and barony of Ruthven, with the tower, fortalice, manor, mills, multures, mill-lands, salmon and other fisheries, etc.', and where he was also the hereditary sheriff of Perth.[35] From Ruthven's Castle the happy pair proceeded on to Dunkeld, where they stayed for another four days with Lord Atholl, and than back home through Perth.

In the meantime, down in London, the French ambassador was well aware of the approaching trouble in Scotland. He told Catherine de' Medici that Moray and Maitland were on the point of losing power, and that the real leader of Mary's council, to whom she listened, was a musician called David, who had been in the country only for the last four years or so.

De Foix went to discuss the business at a private audience with Elizabeth. She, shrewd as ever, enjoyed the joust; she looked down at her chessboard, and complained bitterly of Lennox's disloyalty, saying his son Darnley, of course, was only a pawn. When de Foix suggested his own king, Charles IX, might be a better and worthier spouse for her, she heaved a melancholy sigh, and replied: 'Alas, I am not worthy of one so good.'[36] Yet another bravura performance.

Randolph was instructed to make one last-ditch effort to bring Lennox and his wayward son back to their allegiance. And so he went to see them both a week before the day fixed for the wedding. In the face of his expostulations Lennox prevaricated, and claimed that it was much too dangerous for him to return to England while his wife was imprisoned in the Tower. But Darnley gave a more arrogant answer, saying:

> I do now acknowledge no other duty nor obedience but to the Queen here, whom I serve and honour; and seeing that the other, your Mistress, is so envious of my good fortune, I doubt not but she may have need of me, as you shall know within a few days. Wherefore to return I intend not. I find myself very well where I am, and so purpose to keep me; and this shall be your answer.[37]

Spoilt, as always, he would make the most of his good fortune.

SEVEN

The Fall of Moray

Married . . . with great magnificence.
> (*A Diurnal of Remarkable Occurents*, 1565)

The Darnley marriage was a great setback for English diplomacy. With hindsight, it proved to be a disaster for Mary, but at the time it was a triumph for David Rizzio. It was also a triumph for everyone who hoped to see the country free from English influence, and true to its old Catholic faith. And it was a particular victory for the Lennox family and thus a bitter blow to Mary's brother Moray.

Loyal and faithful subjects argued that marriage to this young cousin might strengthen Mary's claims to the English throne, please her friends abroad and release her from her brother's influence. Mary agreed. She delighted in her suitor's presence and heaped high honours on him. Darnley was quickly accelerated within the Scots peerage: he had already been made Lord of Ardmanach, Earl of Ross and Duke of Rothesay; now he was advanced to yet another dukedom, that of Albany, only days before the wedding ceremony. Parliament was summoned to give the necessary consents, and this was achieved, despite complaints from disgruntled Protestants and a few lawyers, who queried the right of the Queen to name a king consort without parliamentary approval.[1]

Moray was dismayed by his sister's choice and quickly realised that the marriage would mean the loss of his influence and power. He also feared any children that might result from it, 'thinking to keep her fruitless in her body and without issue or heir to the crown', to which he still had his own aspirations.[2] Her uncle, the Cardinal de Lorraine, agreed with Moray but for different reasons. He advised against marriage with this young man who was just a figure of fun, a mere coxcomb ('un houtendeau'[3]). But far away in Rome, the Pope, Pius IV, gave the necessary dispensation for the match between the cousins and spoke out in favour of it at a special consistory. The Protestant extremists soon began to say that Rizzio had himself in fact secretly married the affianced pair in his private chambers at Stirling Castle before the formal dispensation arrived from the Vatican, so that they could slake their passions before the actual ceremony. This seems a little unlikely, not least because the Italian secretary held no valid priestly office to conduct a nuptial mass.

For much of the summer he was with the Queen, her ladies, Darnley and the court at Stirling, where they hunted, hawked and made merry while they enjoyed the bracing air and distant views from the castle ramparts over the old battlefield of Bannockburn. Moray was intelligent enough to realise that power would soon slip from his grasp, and, feeling estranged and unwanted, retired from court with the excuse that he wished to visit his mother at her castle by Loch Leven. He then arranged to meet his brother-in-law, Argyll, about 15 July, to discuss how they might make one last effort together to stop the marriage, which he realised would strengthen the Lennox Stewart family, irritate Elizabeth and endanger the

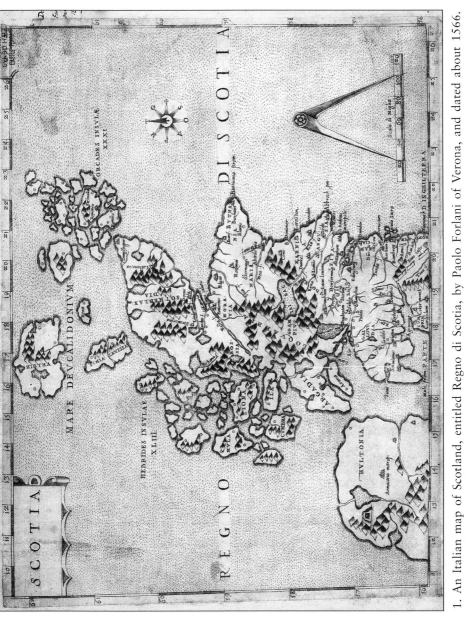

1. An Italian map of Scotland, entitled Regno di Scotia, by Paolo Forlani of Verona, and dated about 1566. (*National Library of Scotland*)

2. David Rizzio, or Rizio (1534–66). Tradition says this is 'from an original picture painted in 1564', but the attribution is dubious. *(Heinz archive, National Portrait Gallery, London)*

3. Queen Marie Stuart, Mary Queen of Scots, aged about 16, drawn on the occasion of her marriage to the Dauphin François, by François Clouet, 1558 *(Bibliothèque Nationale de France, Paris)*

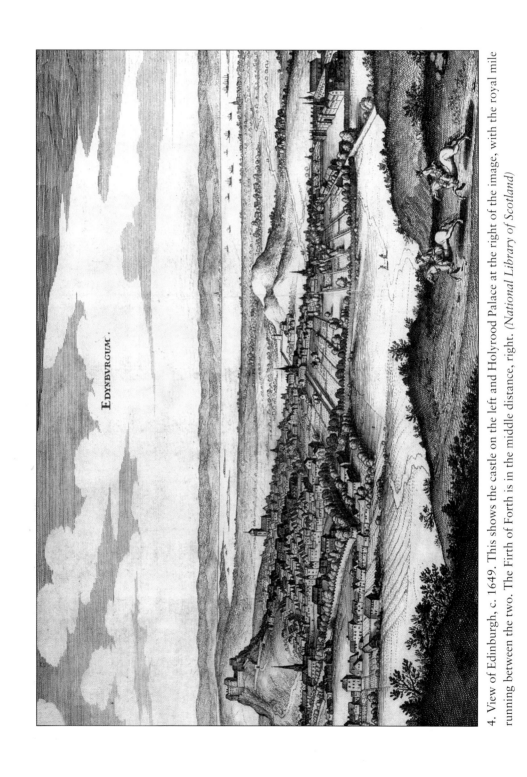

EDINBVRGVM.

4. View of Edinburgh, c. 1649. This shows the castle on the left and Holyrood Palace at the right of the image, with the royal mile running between the two. The Firth of Forth is in the middle distance, right. *(National Library of Scotland)*

5. Sir William Cecil (1520–98) painted about 1565, by Hans Eworth. He is wearing a black bejewelled suit with a closely fitting ruff. His right hand holds a small red book, and rests on an open wooden case, which contains four hour glasses. *(Reproduction by courtesy of the Most Hon. the Marquess of Salisbury)*

6. Emmanuel Philibert, the Duke of Savoy (1533–80). An energetic and intelligent prince nicknamed by the French 'Iron Head' (tête de fer). *(Heinz archive, National Portrait Gallery, London)*

7. Lord James Stuart, later Earl of Moray (1531–70), artist unknown, but said to be of the school of Antonio Mor. *(Author's collection of Scottish prints)*

8. James Hamilton, Duke of Chatelherault (1516–75) painted about 1573, by Arnold Bronckhorst. *(Author's collection of Scottish prints)*

9. Henry Stewart, Lord Darnley (1545–67), at about the age of 10, by Hans Eworth, 1555. *(Scottish National Portrait Gallery)*

11. James Hepburn, Earl of Bothwell (1537–78), by an unknown artist. He married his first wife, Lady Jean Gordon, on 24 February 1566, and the miniature may have been painted in celebration. *(Scottish National Portrait Gallery)*

10. *Above:* Silver coin, ryal, 1565, and inscribed in Latin 'Mary and Henry, by the grace of God, Queen and King of Scots', with an image of a tortoise climbing up a palm tree on the obverse. *(The Trustees of the National Museums of Scotland)*

12. James Douglas, Earl of Morton (1515–81) painted about 1580, attributed to Arnold Bronckhorst. *(Author's collection of Scottish prints)*

13. Queen Mary's Closet, Holyrood. A nineteenth-century engraving entitled *Scene of the Murder of Rizzio. (Author's collection of Scottish prints)*

'amity' with the English. The two brothers-in-law agreed they must fight to keep their supremacy. And so Argyll gave orders to send the fiery cross round his glens, and raised the standard of rebellion.

Rumours of the rising soon circulated. As the date for the wedding drew near, the talk in Edinburgh was that Argyll, with a body of Campbell clansmen, his 'redshanks', planned to kidnap the bridal couple on their way down from Perth.[4]

As dawn broke over Arthur's Seat around six o'clock early in the summer morning of Sunday 29 July 1565, the magnificent music of a full nuptial mass could be heard rising from the palace chapel at Holyrood. The wedding service itself was taken with 'great magnificence' by the Dean of Restalrig, John Sinclair, who officiated with full Catholic rites and every pomp that Rizzio and the church could suggest. 'The whole nobility of the realm' was there.[5] Rizzio's imposing figure stood out among the guests. There he was in a place of honour by the altar, wearing a splendid cloak of black velvet brocaded with gold. At last he was free from the anxieties of the previous weeks, and so happy was he to see the business over at last that he could not be stopped from shouting out in his attractive resonant voice, as the final anthem came to its triumphant conclusion: 'Praise be to God, now the marriage cannot be broken!'[6]

Rizzio made sure the entertainments that followed were the best that could be had. Edinburgh was to see nothing like them for a long time. A clever choreographer and stage director, he arranged for three celebratory masques. In the first spectacle, happy figures dressed up as pagan gods and goddesses scampered in a golden pantomime through the royal presence chamber of Holyroodhouse, while all the while the Goddess Diana recited melancholy Latin verses, in which she complained how miserable was her lot now that her bright handmaiden Mary was to be taken from her side by the jealous power of Love. On the second night, male dancers disguised as black African slaves and ever faithful knights serenaded the bridal pair to lyrics of his composition. And then, on the third, the four maiden Maries, all clad in virginal white like nymphs, joined the play as they prettily chanted praises to the great God of Health.[7]

The English ambassador stayed firmly unimpressed. He noted sardonically how Mary seemed a little reluctant to leave the festivities and change out of her wedding dress to join her husband upstairs to consummate the marriage and thought this delay deliberate. All she had to do was act out her bridal duty, 'to show that it was not lust that moved her to marry, but the necessity of her country, not to leave it without a male heir'. Well informed as always, he claimed there had been no premarital intercourse before the legal ceremony, and sent this interesting information down to Cecil. 'Suspicious men, or such as are given of all things to make the worst, would that it should be believed that they knew each other before they came there. I would not that your Lordship should believe it, the likelihood is so great to the contrary.'[8]

Soon afterwards the Lyon King of Arms marched up the Canongate to the Mercat Cross with his heralds, where they proclaimed King Henry to be Scotland's rightful sovereign.

But Rizzio saw with no little foreboding that Moray's estrangement would inevitably lead to war, and suggested they mobilise their defences. It was now a race as to who would strike the first blow. In the event, Rizzio and the Queen won. Great effort was made to gather in as much support as possible, and special steps were made to garner assistance from the nobility. Some powerful but uncommitted feudal magnates, such as John, 5th Lord Erskine, were promoted in the peerage better to cement their allegiance. This was how Erskine, who controlled the key fortress of Edinburgh Castle, came to be granted 'the earldom of Mar, and the lordship and regality of Gairoch, with all the usual privileges incident and belonging thereto, together with the lands of Strathdon, Braemar, Cromar, and Strathdee'.[9]

Another pointer to the changed security situation was seen on 3 August, when George, Lord Gordon, was let free from his cell in Dunbar Castle, and his lands and honours as the lawful Earl of Huntly were returned to him. The Gordons had suffered much under Moray's ascendancy and had good cause for feud. Their chief,

Huntly, had been charged with treason after his defeat at Corrichie by the royal army in 1562, and his extensive estates had fallen into Moray's hands. Happily Gordon bore no grudges against the Queen for his treatment and was welcomed back to his father's old place on the Council.

The heralds were kept busy that August. No sooner had they to proclaim Huntly's restoration than they had to pronounce on Moray's fate.[10] Rizzio suggested he be dealt with harshly. So on 6 August he was 'put to the horn' – that is, outlawed – by Peter Thomson and the same heralds who only seven days before had announced the royal marriage at the Mercat Cross. Moray was now the accused, summoned to justice.

His fall was not quite as tragic as Lucifer's but was pitiful enough. Ousted from government, with the Lennox faction dominant at court, and with Rizzio jousting with Maitland for control of foreign policy, he was where Gordon's father had found himself three years before: an over-mighty subject facing a charge of treason. He had played for high stakes in the game of royal and matrimonial politics, and lost.

Moray was canny though. He knew there were other clans such as the Hamiltons who were dissatisfied with developments and would be only too willing to challenge the new Lennox supremacy.

James Hamilton, the elderly and rather indecisive Duke of Chatelherault, was still the nominal head of his formidable Hamilton family combination. Chatelherault himself had served as regent during Mary's minority many years before. Nimble footwork then saw him rewarded with the French dukedom of Chatelherault when he agreed to retire as regent in favour of the Queen Mother, Mary of Guise. Moray now persuaded the duke that his reversionary prospects as the heir presumptive to the throne would be diminished by the Darnley marriage. And, since Chatelherault had his own long-standing feuds and quarrels with Lennox, he agreed to join the insurrection and send his fighting men to serve with Moray. The Campbells too were happy to support anyone when so commanded by their chief, Archibald, 5th Earl of Argyll, the *Mac Cailein Mor*, an individual who united in his person the different worlds of Gaelic and Lowland Scots. Rather unoriginally, the allies styled themselves 'the Protestant Lords'.

They did at least share Moray's Protestant fervour and his jealousy of 'new men' such as Rizzio and Balfour. Scotland had a long history of disgruntled barons attempting to kidnap their lawful sovereign, and Moray seems to have calculated that a quick coup might just work if he could but seize the Queen and her husband, dispose of Darnley and hold Mary somewhere under close arrest. With them both out of the way, he would be back in his rightful place as first minister.

Events now moved fast. On Saturday 25 August 1565, Rizzio and the council learnt that Moray was about to strike, and soon good intelligence arrived of how his forces planned to threaten the capital. As the omens grew worse and disorder broke out, security was tightened throughout the town, and the municipal administration was quickly reorganised, with the loyalist Simon Preston of Craigmillar put in as provost in place of Archibald Douglas: 'The provost . . . put out of office and Cragmillour in his place. The controller, Pitarrow, removed and the laird of Tillibarne in his place, who within the last four days had four villages spoiled, and eleven men slain by the Highlandmen. Stealing and killing on every part.'[11] The secret council now included Atholl, Huntly, Lennox and James Balfour.

Rizzio had even persuaded the new king, a somewhat lukewarm Catholic, to attend a reformed service in St Giles on the previous Sabbath, where together they sat through a long sermon by John Knox about the duties of kingship. We know exactly what Knox said that morning since he published it soon afterwards. The text fills over forty pages of his *Collected Works*.[12] They got little immediate benefit from the preacher's words. But the significance is that Rizzio, who was never a religious bigot, thought it was worth their while to be there. A formal proclamation of religious toleration was also issued in which Mary sensibly offered such a benefit to all her subjects. She announced that: 'She cannot leave the religion wherein she had been nourished and brought up, against her own conscience, but leaves them to worship God as they please, leaving her to do the same. That religion cannot be established by her consent alone, but by the Three Estates in Parliament, which done she will confirm it.'[13] Nevertheless Darnley was unhappy at being held up to Knox's congregation as a fine example of an impenitent sinner and resented the secretary for having made him take part in this public humiliation.

By now William Maitland of Lethington had ceased to act as one of the Crown's advisers and lay low; it was not for nothing that contemporaries called him the Scottish Machiavelli. But even now his political skills were such that he managed to keep his hands clean from active involvement in this attempted coup. And in his absence David Rizzio was effectively the secretary of state in his place, though he never seems to have received formal confirmation in the office.

Rizzio's hand may also be discerned in the arrangements to muster the royal forces in the face of the insurgency. Yet another example of his administrative skills was seen on 23 August when the King and Queen issued a royal proclamation asking every loyal vassal for help.[14] Writs were sent out that commanded all feudal lieges to attend them at a place of rendezvous in a camp outside Edinburgh and bring with them sufficient victuals for fifteen days' campaign in the field. Very soon large numbers of Douglases and Gordons appeared in obedience to the mobilisation summons, anxious to revenge old quarrels with Moray. And most came with alacrity and excitement. The Crown forces amounted to about 4,000–5,000 men and outnumbered the rebels by a ratio of roughly five to one. They wore leather jacks or tunics and brought with them the usual swords, daggers and traditional long spears of the Scots infantry. Overall they were generally better equipped than their adversaries with heavier firepower, which included a few pieces of field artillery and several companies of trained arquebusiers. Randolph described their departure from Edinburgh: 'This Sunday, 26 August, they departed out of town at about 4 o'clock, after dinner to Linlithgow, from thence to Stirling or Glasgow. What their power will be is uncertain. Six hundred arquesbusiers, with two hundred spears, follow tomorrow, with six field pieces of artillery.'[15]

With the castle garrison secure on its rock, the Queen's forces saw little point in making great efforts to defend the capital. They decided on a strategic retreat towards the west in the general direction of Glasgow with the object of intimidating Argyll's Campbells and keeping him under restraint within his own country.

The newly wed pair, and their new advisers, were glad that the rebel storm had at last broken. Now there was to be no more waiting on rumours. It was time for action. Unlike Elizabeth, Mary had some military experience. Three years earlier she had accompanied Moray when together they had invaded the Gordons in their Grampian fastness; and she had seen the brutal fruits of victory on the battlefield at Corrichie, there outside Aberdeen. Then the Gordon, Earl of Huntly, was the enemy; but now everything was different. Her emotions were in confusion. She felt betrayed by this trusted elder brother, who had plotted to kill her new husband and steal her Crown. She was outraged by his treason and treachery, and now insisted on riding out with her army against him, like a modern Joan of Arc, in armour especially tailored to her elegant figure, with a steel bonnet on her head and a brace of pistols at her belt. Her blood was up. Even Knox commended her courage: 'albeit the most part waxed weary, yet the Queen's courage increased manlike so much, that she was ever with the foremost.'[16] And, as her forces mobilised for battle, Darnley's father, with all the strength of the Lennox Stewarts, joined her. He was put in command of the advance guard.

James, 4th Earl of Morton, the Lord Chancellor, even for the times an unusually devious figure and the effective head of the great Douglas confederation, headed the main army, 'the middle battle', while Mary and Darnley rode with the rearguard. Lord Ruthven was there too, a sick and reluctant individual torn between his strong Protestant beliefs and his feudal obligations and strong kinship links with Lennox.

The enemy, in the persons of Moray and the Protestant Lords, had by now mustered their levies from clans Hamilton and Campbell. They might be outnumbered, but they had the benefit of having on their side one of the best generals of the day, Sir William Kirkcaldy of Grange. Grange advised their only chance lay in a lightning attack on the capital. So the rebel army, whose leaders also included the Lords Rothes, Glencairn and Boyd, trotted towards Edinburgh over the moorland hills as fast as their scraggy ponies would allow. On 30 August they entered the city gates with some 600–1,200 light horse. They expected to find support from the townsfolk, but most of the leading citizens and burgesses saw that the court was good for business, and kept true to the government.[17] The new Earl of Mar with the castle garrison, whose heavy guns commanded the city below, stayed loyal too. The rebels did, however, have one key supporter in John Knox, who later complained how the 'terrible roaring' of the big guns in the castle artillery disturbed him as he worked away in his manse in the High Street below on his sermon for the next sabbath.[18]

August can be wet in Scotland, and this year was no exception, as heavy rains carried by Atlantic depressions swept in to slow progress. The swollen rivers in the Galloway hill country were particularly difficult and delayed the royal forces so much that, when they heard of Moray's daring raid on Edinburgh, they turned back to bring him to battle or at the very least prevent him linking up with his confederates.

This was Rizzio's first experience of real war. And it was not particularly comfortable for him, or for any of those involved. It made a strange honeymoon for Mary and Darnley too, their passions heightened by the added spice of danger. Their men camped for the night in the field or among the heather, sheltered from the midges and the wet only by their plaids, while the leaders slept on straw mattresses in simple bivouacs or *palyeonis*. There was little hand-to-hand fighting and few casualties during the short campaign. But even so there was the inevitable brutality of any civil war. The Campbells, in particular, took every opportunity to rape, pillage and burn the Lennox country around them, while in the south wilder tribes, the Armstrongs and Elliotts, seized the chance given by the collapse of order to break out from their bleak border country of Liddesdale and ravish and steal to within eight miles of the walls of the capital. But, since there was no major battle, the campaign itself was overall more an affair of feints and skirmishes; of fast-moving manœuvres in the summer's light; of hard riding and hurried exchanges of oaths and insults as men cursed each other viciously when they met as foes.

EIGHT

Bothwell to the Rescue

False and Untrue as a Devil . . .

(Randolph to Cecil, 22 January 1563)

Cecil was irritated by all this trouble in the north. He soon realised the omens were not propitious, and that Scotland's foreign relations were now being directed against the interests of his Queen. Signs of Rizzio's hands on the diplomatic tiller did not take long to appear. Rizzio knew that the Queen of Scots must find counterbalancing support abroad, and that their best hope was from Spain. Now he had the opportunity to put into practice some of the lessons of great power diplomacy he had learnt from de Moretto. And so, on 10 September, he drafted a letter from their camp in the hills above Glasgow for Mary to send to Madrid.[1] This correspondence confirms that the Scots civil war was already of international concern, and points to some of the changes he hoped to achieve if he was able to free the country of English influence. He seems to have believed, bravely, even rashly, that Scotland was capable of challenging the English hegemony within the British Isles, and that a powerful combination to this end might be formed with Spain at the head. After all, his native land of Savoy had won freedom from French occupation when it put its trust in the Hapsburg alliance. It was only six years since the Spanish King had helped Duke Emmanuel Philibert recover his duchy's independence at the treaty of Cateau-Cambrensis. Perhaps he could repeat the trick for Mary.

In her letter she asked Philip 'to support our Catholic religion'.[2] She said she was sending him a special envoy, 'a faithful Catholic English gentleman', to ask his help in defending 'the liberty of the Church'.[3] The faithful Catholic English gentleman was a retired English Member of Parliament, originally from Suffolk, called Francis Yaxley. Well briefed by Rizzio, he duly set sail for the Spanish coast from Dumbarton.

Randolph's sources of information were, as usual, excellent. He soon knew something was afoot, and wrote with the worrying news of Yaxley's departure. 'His journey is to Spain, to seek support, and put the Queen and country under King Philip's protection.'[4] Mary's letter reached Philip about 20 October. Yaxley arrived soon afterwards, managing to avoid the English navy's attempts to catch him on the dangerous voyage across the Irish Sea and the Bay of Biscay. He was well received by Philip in the Escurial and sent on to Brussels, where the Spanish authorities were given orders to do what was necessary to support the noble cause of the Queen of Scots. Rizzio and Yaxley then set up a correspondence in a specially devised secret code, which Randolph and his agents for a time were unable to crack, so that for the moment it looked as if Rizzio's plans might succeed.[5]

By long tradition Scotland was the special daughter of the Holy See, and now in its need turned once again to the Holy Father. William Chisholm, the Bishop of Dunblane, was sent on the long journey to Rome with another 'dispiteful letter' from the Queen of Scots to seek what support the aged Pope Pius IV could make available. The Pontiff was encouraging, and promised the considerable sum of 300,000 ducats by way of subsidy, so the embassy was by no means in vain.

Rizzio then infuriated Cecil by persuading the Queen of Scots to stir up trouble in Ireland, where the usual intermittent warfare between the Gael and Saxon continued as the native Irish tried their best to resist the persistent English aggression. Two Gaelic-speaking Highlanders were sent over the water to track down the great Irish chieftain Shane O'Neill in his Ulster refuge. Their orders were to persuade him to launch another onslaught on the English settlements and their local allies in the names of Queen Mary and King Henry of Scotland. O'Neill needed little urging to attack the enemy. He was understandably delighted by the Scots approach, and assured the messengers that he would be only too pleased to join Mary Stewart's cause, and longed for the day when he would see her crowned as the great High Queen of Ireland. This news soon reached London, where it intrigued the French ambassador, de Foix. He wrote to Catherine de' Medici:

> about fifteen days ago news reached us that the Great O'Neill had captured two major fortresses of the Queen of England in Ireland, and that O'Neill wished to serve the Queen of Scots, and name her Queen of Ireland. I know, because someone brought me word, that the Queen of Scots had sent two gentlemen from the savage part of Scotland to negotiate since they speak the same language.[6]

Mary's advisers now included 'new men' like David Rizzio; another Italian, Francisco de Busso; a Frenchman, Sebastian Danclourt, as well as great feudal magnates such as Atholl and Huntly. Rizzio's was the most influential voice among them, in a formidable alliance with James Balfour of Mountquhanie, an ambitious and gifted lawyer who had switched to her side. Balfour, who went on to become a close colleague of Rizzio's, had served as an extraordinary Lord of Session from 1561, and also sat as a part-time judge in the church courts. He joined the Privy Council in 1565 and soon became one of the Crown's principal advisers about domestic and legal business. As such he was closely associated with the ruling regime and was perhaps among the most able of the new team of ministers. Darnley himself took little part in setting government policy, although he shared the general mistrust of Moray, and was once heard to observe rather petulantly that his estates were already far too large. The council was keen to consolidate royal authority in the face of rebellion, and moved quickly to suppress any signs of dissent. The records show Mary was in St Andrews on 12 September, Dundee on the 13th, and back in Holyrood by the 17th. Under the Italian's guidance the King and Queen now made another attempt to widen their appeal. They issued a formal proclamation of religious tolerance on 15 September in a further effort to attract moderate opinion: 'Their Majesties, on the advice of their Council, wish it to be known that they have no intention of making any person act outside their conscience.'[7] The efficiency of Rizzio, Balfour and the rest of Mary's counsellors is well shown by the way they kept the machinery of government working despite the constant travel required by the emergency.

The rebel Lords decided there was little point in trying to make a stand in Edinburgh. Moray was naturally cautious, and realised that, since Protestant opinion was split and he was heavily outnumbered, it was better to abandon any plans to fight a defensive battle in the streets of the town. He decided to retreat south-westwards, through Peebles, over the high moorland hills of the Southern Uplands towards Dumfries and the English frontier, where his men rested as he sent increasingly desperate pleas to Cecil for help.

Somehow he also found time to compose a wordy proclamation to justify the rising, which was published on 19 September.[8] Like many political manifestos the document is a little verbose. It began by saying that it was issued by 'The Nobility and Congregation professing the right religion of Jesus Christ within this realm of

Scotland, presently pursued for their lives by the Queen, their Sovereign', and proceeded to set out their religious credentials, and list their grievances. Moray and his colleagues very much objected to the 'ungodly and wicked religion wherein Her Grace had been brought up'.[9] They feared Popery was on the point of being re-established, and blamed this decision for the constant disorder, which included 'taking some ancient and aged barons out of their houses and beds, and that under silence of night, without any order of law'.[10]

Moray and his friends had other grievances. They were now deprived of their hereditary rights, as noblemen and counsellors, to play their proper part in the government of the realm. And they resented the fact that their places were filled by persons of 'base degree', who looked only to their self-interest and private profit. This charge was clearly aimed at David Rizzio and his colleagues such as de Busso, Danclourt and Fowler, whom they called 'strangers, as have neither judgement or experience of the ancient laws and government of this realm'.

The 'sinister counsel' of the Italian Rizzio made them particularly unhappy, especially on 'the most weighty matter of Her Majesty's marriage'. That business had been mishandled. Offence had been given to the English government, and worse, because Elizabeth's candidate for Mary's hand had been so decisively rebuffed, and, as Mary had been persuaded to 'proclaim a King over us', the ancient laws and liberties of the realm had been broken.[11] Furthermore the same 'fountain of sinister counsel' was wasting the Crown revenues, and increasing taxes, all of which fell especially hard on the nobility and barons.

This document is a formidable, if one-sided, production. It was intended for English eyes, and in particular for Queen Elizabeth and Cecil. The Scots ignored it completely. For the moment both public opinion and the stronger army were with Mary and her secretary. And on 17 September a powerful reinforcement arrived at their side. As the contemporary author of the *Diurnal of Remarkable Occurents* dryly noted, this was the moment when 'James, Earl Bothwell arrived in Scotland, out of France, and on 20 September the said James Earl Bothwell got presence of our Sovereigns in Holyroodhouse, and was thankfully received of them'.[12]

James Hepburn, 4th Earl of Bothwell, was a remarkable and charismatic figure, now about 30 years old, a man whose life stands comparison with other famous Cavalier heroes like Montrose or Dundee. For many months he had been eking out a parsimonious existence in exile on the Continent after an audacious escape from dubiously legal imprisonment three years before. Now hearing from one of Rizzio's couriers of the emergency, and realising that his hour was at hand, he risked returning to face justice. But he also hoped to turn Moray's troubles to advantage. The English had had a healthy respect for his energy and abilities ever since he had caught their emissaries sent with money for the rebel Lords in the Queen Dowager's time, when he had confiscated their saddlebags full of gold coin for the Scots Crown. Cecil's men put out much black propaganda about him, and considered him 'as mortal an enemy to our whole nation as any man alive, despiteful out of measure, false and untrue as a devil . . .'.[13]

This time the rumour was that he planned to come back by way of Ireland. In London the French ambassador picked up talk that he planned to sail for Ulster from Flanders to reinforce O'Neill with at least two ships full of Spanish professional soldiers. This was not exactly true, but, as so often with Bothwell, his actions were daring enough. The enemy had warships watching the Scots coast for him. They even hired a Swedish pirate vessel to catch him, which was owned by a suspiciously Anglo-Saxon-sounding individual named Wilson. However, Bothwell's courage and seamanship saw him through. Not for nothing was he the hereditary 'Admiral of Scotland', and he certainly knew the ways of the sea. He managed to out-sail the Swede, and land safely with eight men and some arms in the harbour of the little fishing village of Eymouth just up the coast from Berwick. There was no question of being sent back to jail. He was warmly welcomed at court, most of his lands and feudal honours were restored to him, and he was made Lieutenant General of the East, Middle and West Marches, despite the fact that Darnley wanted the post for his father. He then rode south-west with two companies of infantry to take command of the loyalist forces based outside Dumfries, where it was hoped his presence would encourage more of the moss troopers to rally to Mary's standard. Randolph grumbled sardonically when he heard the news that 'Bothwell takes great things on him, and promises much. A fit captain for so loose a company as now hang upon him.'[14]

Rizzio and Bothwell were very different personalities, the one a cosmopolitan artefact of Renaissance civilisation, the other a bold, bad, fighting man, but they shared a common loyalty to Mary that she returned. There was never any rivalry between them.

Now once again Bothwell had the chance to show his fierce Scots patriotism. After all, these borderlands were his own country. His Hepburn strongholds controlled most of the key points along the southern marches from the lowering walls of Hermitage Castle, squatting brutally among the bleak Liddlesdale hills, to his fortress at Dunbar on the rocky eastern seaboard. The Hepburn family motto was 'keep traist [trust], keep faith', and in the coming crisis he did not deviate from that injunction.

For a few days Moray hung on in Dumfries, from where he sent ever more desperate appeals for English help, but he remained cut off from Argyll and any hope of reinforcement by the Campbells. Meanwhile Randolph continued to send encouraging messages from Edinburgh, saying how much he sympathised with his plight, and was pressing his pleas for money on Cecil. They were, however, too late, even though de Foix, the French ambassador in London, learnt Elizabeth was minded to authorise the secret release of a further £6,000 in gold pieces to support the insurrection. By 22 September Randolph was able to write to Cecil and assert that the Italian's influential position at Mary's side was the real reason why she had taken such energetic measures to punish her half-brother, 'The hatred conceived against Moray was because he would not allow or authorise Davy in his abuses.'[15]

Moray himself then wrote despondently that the reason why he and his friends were being hunted down like wolves was that 'a stranger subject to another realm had intruded himself into the name and authority of a King'. It was because of Rizzio that 'as honest men they were hunted for a prey. Crafty and rude strangers, chiefly two Italians Davy and Francisco, together with Master Fowler, Englishmen and other unworthy persons occupy the place of native councillors, and manage all weighty affairs.'[16]

At length, with the royal army approaching, which included numerous Gordons only too eager to avenge their earlier wrongs, with the Maxwells about to switch sides, and with Bothwell and his Hepburns massing on their eastern flank, Moray and 'the Protestant Lords' accepted the inevitable. They were well aware that 'a great force comes from the North with my Lord Gordon, who imputeth the overthrow of his father to Moray'.[17] By 6 October they had crossed the frontier into England. Their revolt had failed.

On 23 September another interesting visitor reached the capital. Catherine de' Medici, the French Queen Mother, shared all Cecil's alarm at the disturbances in Scotland. She had no wish to see the country fall back under English influence, or even worse into the hands of Spain, so now sent her own special agent to assess the situation. The envoy, Castlenau de Mauvissière, was instructed to do his best to reconcile the competing factions.

Mary was pleased to see him. She always enjoyed news from France, but still waxed indignant at her brother's treachery. The envoy reported there were tears in her eyes when she told him she was entirely confident of French support; but that, if France failed her, she feared nothing could now stop her country from turning into a Calvinist republic. De Mauvissière made sympathetic noises, but warned her that sadly France was also distracted by its own civil wars of religion and was in no position to send another expeditionary force to Scotland. One of Cecil's numerous spies, a Captain Cockburn, described the tense atmosphere in Edinburgh. The Queen seemed very nervous and 'wept wondrous sore'. She had taken to her room two days after the Frenchman's arrival, and wept again when she heard what he had to say. Maitland was quite out of power and 'has leisure to speak with his friends at this present, but so has not Dave [that is, Rizzio] or Mr James Balfour'.[18] On the next day the ambassador and the Queen saw each other again in the gardens at Holyrood, where de Mauvissière found Mary walking in the autumn sunshine with her husband and James Balfour. He thought that a night's reflection had slightly cooled her indignation at her brother and that she now seemed a little more inclined to consider his mediation proposals.[19]

De Mauvissière does not mention meeting Rizzio. It is hard, however, to avoid the conclusion he knew Rizzio was arguing the benefits of a Spanish alliance and so kept away from what would have been a difficult confrontation.

Once safe over the English border, Moray hurried down to London to plead for asylum. Elizabeth allowed him to attend court, where she subjected him to a lecture of breathtaking hypocrisy as she reproved him for the treason showed to his lawful sovereign by his rebellion. Nonetheless he was graciously permitted to make a discreet retirement to the north country with his followers, where they lurked in rather straitened circumstances in the environs of Newcastle for the rest of the winter. Only old Chatelherault was allowed to cross the Channel and retire gracefully to enjoy life on the revenues of his ducal estates in France.

Meanwhile Rizzio and Balfour remained anxious for the security of Edinburgh. This time the castle garrison had stayed loyal, but there was little money in the treasury for a permanent defence force. The government coffers needed to be refilled to cover the costs of all those arquebusiers, gunners and the other military paraphernalia that had been so essential to put down the rising. An obvious solution was to tax the merchants and dealers suspected of supporting or sympathising with the rebels. Some seventeen of them were invited to attend before the council at Holyrood on 27 September, where they were subjected to a pretty little speech by

Mary, in which she asked them each to lend a thousand marks to her treasury. Understandably the assembled burgesses found this suggestion not entirely welcome. Those who demurred were then admonished in a bullying harangue by James Balfour and threatened with imprisonment or even the gallows if it could be proved they had helped 'the Protestant Lords'. Six of the more obstinate were incarcerated in the castle until they paid up. They were taken there under close arrest, 'sent in the night to the castle of Edinburgh, conveyed with musketeers round about them, as if they had been murderers, or the most vile persons'.[20] Other funds were then raised at a lower rate of interest once the customs revenues from the port of Leith had been pledged as security. Despite all the disorders, the lawyers had prospered during the early years of Mary's personal rule. And now their well-honed plea-bargaining skills secured them exemption from making compulsory contributions to the new loan issue.[21]

During the autumn of 1565, with the rising defeated and with the hope of help arriving from Spain and the Vatican, Rizzio might have thought that his new administration would now settle down. With Bothwell back from France, Huntly freed from prison, Moray crushed and Elizabeth checked, perhaps life might once again be prosperous and tranquil, and long so continue in sweet paths of tolerance. One hostile observer described his ascendancy then:

The Queen was governed by the Earls of Lennox and Atholl; but in matters most weighty and of greatest importance, by David Rizzio, the Italian afore mentioned, who went under the name of the French Secretary; by whose means all grave matters, of what weight soever must pass; provided always that his hands were anointed.[22]

And so his great adventure had worked. Now he would enjoy the fruits of his triumph.

NINE

Rizzio Resplendent

A gentleman of such pleasing appearance . . .
    (Pietro Bizari, *Historia de la guerra in Hungaria*, 1568)

Now it was time for Rizzio to enjoy his reward for encouraging the Queen to follow her heart, and take the tall, petulant, but good-looking Lord Darnley for a husband.

Mary was a rich young woman with much money at her command. And formal 'Inventories' survive that list her personal assets and possessions in some detail. They show how soon he was recompensed for having so successfully outwitted Cecil and engineered the marriage. These records, known as the *Inventaires de la Royne Descosse*, hold a great deal of informative detail about her private finances, and tell how she spent much of her income –

mainly derived from the lands and estates in France that had been settled on her by way of dowry when she married the Dauphin. These endowments gave her the wherewithal to be lavish when she wanted. Furthermore, her annual receipts as a Queen Dowager of France were high, possibly as much as £12,000 sterling, often more than the Crown revenues of Scotland itself; and, though the money was sometimes a little erratic in reaching her, she could usually draw down funds on account when she wanted, and be as open handed as she wished.

David Rizzio was one of her beneficiaries. In July 1565 the Queen gave him an expensive roll of 'black velvet, brocaded with gold', which must have been the one made up into the fine clothes he sported on her wedding day.[1] Later that December he got another present, 'plus au Secretary David, four yards of black velvet'; and finally in January 1566 there is another entry, 'given to Secretary David four yards of Cloth of Gold'. The secretary's fashionable and elegant clothes, cut from these rich fabrics in the best French style, ensured that he was always dressed quite *à la mode*. A rich jewel usually hung from his neck on an elegant gold chain, so that he must have been a wonderful sight as he tripped along the draughty corridors of Holyrood palace in the autumn days of 1565, with his arms full of papers requiring Her Grace's urgent attention. And this royal favour meant that other rewards soon came his way. With his ready access to the Queen, he controlled petitioners to the royal fount of honour and power. The petitioners, of course, had to pay for the privilege of introduction, and riches resulted. Now he could live in magnificent splendour in his chambers at Holyrood rather like a Medici prince, where a steady press of suitors anxious to find favour thronged his morning levées. One morning the visitors even included emissaries from his old enemy, Moray. It was a particularly pleasing occasion when Moray's brother, Douglas of Lochleven, arrived early to solicit his good will with Her Grace. His aim was to bribe him to persuade her to allow Moray back from his exile. According to Douglas, Rizzio bargained shrewdly, setting a price of £20,000 for his help. Douglas offered £1,000. They settled for a sum somewhere in between. Moray himself was sensible enough to know this was the moment to be humble. He accompanied the money with a grovelling letter in which he asked for the Queen's mercy, and sent a gift of a finely cut diamond as another little token of his friendship.

In the months that followed the consummation of the marriage, Rizzio might reasonably have thought he had got everything that might be hoped for. Moray and the militant Protestants were ousted from the seats of power. English aggression was in temporary check. But all was not well. The darkest of the lowering clouds that loomed above the horizon was the rather juvenile behaviour of the new king, Henry. And his father, Lennox, continued to fret, while his spoilt and immature son showed little appetite for the day-to-day grind of state business. He might condescend to attend the occasional church service according to Catholic rites, but it was obvious that the minutiae of government work was not for him. He was not over-bright, and preferred to spend the short winter days hunting, hawking, drinking and wenching, rather than dealing with paperwork, while his behaviour became increasingly irrational.

We now get the occasional brief glimpse of the exotic figure of Seigneur Davie in his days of glory. Most important visitors to the capital did their best to meet him during their stay. And their testimony sometimes contrasts sharply with later libels from his ill-wishers. But this is not the case for all those who mention him in their writing: Adam Blackwood, Pietro Bizari and Louis Guryan were certainly not just Marian hagiographers, although Blackwood might be thought more than a little partisan.

Blackwood was a Catholic priest who went to France to escape the Protestant Reformation. Devoted to Mary's cause, he rose there to minor government office, and became the *Conseillor du Roi, au Siege Presidial de Poictiers*. He wrote about Rizzio twenty-one years after his death in kindly terms, when he praised him for the 'fidelity, wisdom, prudence, virtue, and his other good qualities of mind, with which he was richly adorned', as exhibited during his time in power. He described him as 'a man of great and long experience, who understood best the affairs of the state, well respected by his mistress for his singular wit'.[2]

There was also Pietro Bizari. His evidence is more credible than Blackwood's, since it was almost contemporaneous. Bizari, like Rizzio, was an Italian, but came from Umbria, and was also a Protestant.[3] He reached Edinburgh in the autumn of 1564, at the time of Rizzio's growing ascendancy, as a sort of literary tourist, armed with letters of introduction to the Scots court from Lord Bedford, the English Governor at Berwick, and with an interesting present for the Queen. This was a beautifully bound presentation copy of a treatise he had written in Latin, called 'de Bello ac Pace', which he had dedicated to Mary. Mary kept a fine library at Holyrood that included a recent history of Savoy, and undoubtedly appreciated the gift.[4] She gave Bizari a valuable gold collar in return, and invested him with it herself. Rizzio took care to see his fellow countryman was made much of, and enjoyed the opportunity to talk his native language, and discuss current literary and political business together. It was a delight to introduce the distinguished Protestant scholar to the Queen, and the visitor certainly appreciated his reception. He was a prolific author, and wrote up the visit in a small tract published in France five years later, where he said that Rizzio was well educated, good looking and much loved by everyone at Mary's court.

His precise comments about Rizzio were that he was a 'Gentleman who, besides his knowledge of belles lettres, was of such pleasing appearance, and such courteous manners, that he made himself beloved by everyone, as I indeed knew very well when I was at that court, and had familiar converse with him'.[5]

This is a favourable impression of the secretary at work from an impartial source with no particular axe to grind. Further corroboration of Bizari's assessment that he was indeed a pleasing artefact of Renaissance civilisation comes from Louis Guryon, another French official (*Conseiller de Finances*) who also came to Scotland on business, and saw him at work. Guryon wrote: 'I was well acquainted with David Rizzio from whom I received many civilities in that Court. He was in years of dark hue, and very ill favoured, but of a rare prudence, and very skilful in business.'[6]

Despite the clear conflict of evidence as to his good looks, or otherwise, his intelligence is also shown by the way he encouraged people to be tolerant towards their religion. It was on his advice earlier, as we have seen, that Mary had tried to widen her popular appeal during the battles with Moray, when her proclamation of tolerance was issued from her camp at Dundee on 15 September 1565: 'Their Majesties, on the advice of their Council, wish it to be known that they have no intention of making any person act outside their conscience.'[7]

His participation in a Presbyterian communion service was another sign of his wish to conciliate every form of Christian belief, and one in which he was clearly well ahead of his time. Late in the autumn he took communion in the old kirk of the Canongate according to the rites of the Reformed church.[8] The church records for the year have the names of those who communicated then: 'The persons that new communicated, the time of their decease, the day and year, beginning anno 1565.' Among the names included were 'Monsieur Signior David, who was slain in Holyrood house the 9 March 1566', and fourteen others, of whom one was Darnley. The records also show the names of the principal harlots in the parish. There were at least fifty-three of these poor women, who included 'Isabel Lyell, common harlot, and Janet Witt, harlot to John Hunter', and fifty-one other ladies, who must have found the proximity of the court good for business.[9]

His enemies were not convinced by these concessions, and continued to spit out propaganda then, and afterwards, that he was essentially corrupt. They alleged that he was offered rich inducements to make the regime adopt a pro-Catholic position. George Buchanan wrote during the 1570s in his great, but biased, work, *Rerum Scoticarum Historia*, how, 'if Mary adhered to the Council of Trent, Rizzio was promised honours, ecclesiastical dignities, heaps of money, and unrivalled power to himself'.[10]

He certainly did his best to support the old faith when he could. Among the many adventurers and rather serpentine characters attracted north by the interesting opportunities at the Queen of Scots' court was an Englishman named Fowler, who now turned up in Scotland again as an agent, or follower, of Lord Lennox. Fowler had been one of Darnley's tutors when he was a boy and now crossed the border to advise Lennox and his son. Lady Margaret Lennox was, of course, still locked up in the Tower of London as punishment for Darnley's breach of faith in marrying without the Queen of England's consent. Fowler succeeded in ingratiating himself at the Scots' court and was soon high in Lennox's counsels. He professed to be devoted to the interests of the Lennox family, although there is a suggestion that he had already been turned by Randolph and his master, Cecil, and was in fact all the time working as a double agent. Fowler was no mean poet, and could pen an ode in the finest Elizabethan style with the best of them.[11] Now he wrote to Lady Lennox to profess that his 'simple carcass whilst it had life, would always work to serve her, and hers', and went on to say that Darnley was in good health, and that she should be 'assured of the good heart, and affectionate disposition of the King, her son'.

The English government had ordered that Fowler be arrested should he slip back to London with any messages for Lady Lennox. But, after a difficult journey, he was able to find his way back in a fishing boat, which picked him up from the little fishing village of Pittenweem on the Fife coast loaded with a cargo of herrings for the London market. Though he avoided immediate capture, his correspondence was intercepted by Cecil's men, and ended up in the Salisbury muniments at Hatfield House. It included a rather touching epistle from Lennox to his wife, Lady Margaret, still in her prison in the Tower, in which he wrote with great affection from his home by Glasgow. He called her 'my sweet Mage', and told her that their son, the King, 'continues in good health', and that 'the Queen was great with child'.[12] The news confirmed all Cecil's worst suspicions about life north of the border.

David Rizzio did not leave us many clues as to his thinking for the short time of his ascendancy during the autumn and winter of 1565 and 1566, and it is important not to stretch what scraps of information that do survive too far. Since his policies failed, and history is usually written by the victors, it is not so easy to see how the state of the country might have changed had he continued at the centre of affairs.

What is clear, nonetheless, is that his regime proudly set out to embrace an assertive anti-English policy. Scotland was weak and impoverished, barely recovered from civil war, but under his guidance had little hesitation in challenging the English supremacy within the British Isles.

Some of his actions have already been considered; for example, the unusual diplomatic activity abroad in the crisis of Moray's rebellion. This included Yaxley's embassy to King Philip of Spain, and his return with the Spanish money, shipwreck and death, on the bleak northern coastline of Northumbria. The failure to recover this lost gold rankled, and was made worse by the fact that the local magnate, Lord Northumberland, kept the cash, despite the fact that he was a devoted adherent of the old faith.

Then again there was the mission of the Bishop of Dunblane to the Vatican. The purpose here was to encourage the Pope to support the Queen of Scots in her change of tack. The Bishop was made much of in Rome, where the Jesuit Fathers seem to have felt that her kingdom really might be on the point of returning to the true faith. The new Pope, Pius V, though hard pressed financially by the Ottoman threat and the needs of the Knights of Malta, said that he himself would send 20,000 scudi to Scotland 'to assist the Queen to restore the ancient religion in her country' and pledged more if necessary.[13] And the Scots Jesuit priest Father Hay was able to rejoice that those who supported 'the Bastard', that is Moray, were now either in exile or in prison and that better men were back in power, by which he meant Bothwell, Huntly and Rizzio.

While relations with Rome blossomed, they were now icy with England. Most Scots had no particular liking for the 'auld enemy', despite all the efforts of Knox and the kirk ministers to reconcile the two peoples. In the face of a deteriorating situation, the Edinburgh government did what it could to strengthen its border defences. In early October 400 men were sent to garrison the town of Kelso, while at the same time 50 arquebusiers occupied Hume Castle, to deter any incursion from the south. The growing antipathy between the two realms was well illustrated by the reception given to one of Elizabeth's warships, *The Aid*, with a crew of 200 men aboard, when she sailed uninvited into Scots territorial waters the same month.

The Scots coastal artillery on Inchkeith island in the Firth of Forth immediately put a salvo across her bows, which made her captain, Antony Jenkinson, complain, when the battery eventually ceased fire, that this certainly showed 'the Scots were not our friends'.[14] The Scots then dispatched a trumpeter aboard a small boat to challenge the intruder. He blew his instrument lustily while summoning the captain to explain himself. Jenkinson said that he was hunting for Nordic pirates in the North Sea, but that autumn gales had forced him to seek shelter in the nearest haven. He was politely disbelieved – the real reason for his encroachment into Scots waters being that he hoped to catch either Bothwell or Seton on their way home. Sentiments then slightly thawed to the extent that Jenkinson, and the Leith port authorities, exchanged modest gifts. The Scots gave Jenkinson a gold chain and double gilt silver cup, and received in return a pot of jam, or maybe marmalade, with a set of bow and arrows – not really equivalent, but a good low-key reaction to this early example of gunboat diplomacy.

By October Randolph, the English Ambassador, was also finding his life in the capital rather uncomfortable. Guards were placed outside his front door, and his movements were restricted. He complained about Rizzio's and Balfour's growing influence, and grumbled how they ran the government in partnership together: 'Mr James Balfour, that once that did row in a galley, and now except David, no man so great with her, the whole Governor of this Estate.'[15] He was depressed by the recent turn of events, and complained to Leicester about Seigneur Davie's ascendancy, saying most Scots disliked the fact that 'a stranger, a varlet, should have the whole guiding of the Queen, and her country'. He went on to observe, with typical male arrogance, how sorry he was that Leicester 'was not here to have enjoyed both the Queen, and her country'.[16]

The Scottish coinage has interesting evidence of the changes Rizzio may have hoped to see. In late 1565 a silver coin, known as a 'ryal', was minted with a value of thirty shillings. It was issued in the names of the King and Queen and carried an intriguing and novel design. The obverse depicted a crowned palm tree with a tortoise shown climbing up it. Across the top was a scroll with a quotation from the Latin poet, Ovid, 'Dat gloria vires' (Glory gives strength). Palm trees, and even tortoises, do not flourish in Scotland save in the few fortunate places along the western seaboard warmed by the Gulf Stream. Certainly palms do not grow as they do in North Africa, so the symbolism behind the coin is a little mysterious. For a long time the silver ryal was thought to show a yew tree that grew in the garden of a house at Crookston, near Glasgow, where Mary and Darnley had lingered during their fighting honeymoon along Clydesdale; and that it was struck to celebrate the wedding. It now appears much more likely that the iconic image originated from the Mediterranean, and that it was minted at Rizzio's suggestion, to celebrate the great sea battles fought that year in the waters around Malta, where after a long siege the Ottoman fleet had been driven from the walls of Valetta.[17] This glorious victory was a significant triumph for the Knights of St John, and for Catholic arms. Rizzio, who had spent some of his youth at the Duke of Savoy's court in Nice, at a time when it was under constant threat from Barbary pirates, must have appreciated the value of this victory over the infidel.[18] He took a close interest in currency matters, and seems to have persuaded the Queen to approve the new issue in triumphant exultation of the strength of Roman Catholic arms. He may very well have actually authorised the coinage himself, since he was about to be appointed master of the mint, a position rich with lucrative possibilities.

In the meantime the Bishop of Dunblane was still working away for the Queen of Scots in Rome. There the Jesuits remained supportive and pondered how they might best help her. Father Polanco SJ was able to write cheerfully in November: 'as to the return of the Scots to the bosom of the church, we thank God for having opened wide the door, and we daily hope for better things. When the state of affairs shall call for it, the Society will not refuse such little help as she can give to that Kingdom.'[19]

The 'tortoise jewel' that Rizzio gave Mary about now as a token of his love and in appreciation for her support supports the numismatic testimony. She described this later as 'une autre enseigne garnye de dix rubiz en tortue avec une perle pendante au bout'.[20] This was an age where the elite delighted to give each other expensive and mysterious presents, which often hid messages and secret symbols. Mary grew extremely fond of the piece. Rizzio had a soft spot for tortoises, whether as pets or depicted on coins or jewels, so the tortoise image, redolent of wisdom and the warm south, doubtless had a powerful symbolic meaning for them both that is too cryptic for us to unravel today.

This was a violent society, yet also an increasingly litigious one. The lawyers as usual were doing well, and the Writers to the Signet were already established as a distinct cadre among them. And their pleadings and deeds often had to be sealed with the Crown seal or signet before they could be used in the law courts. However, there were occasional state papers of importance, and numerous urgent legal documents that required the actual signatures of both the sovereigns. These papers piled up when Darnley was away at his pleasures. Rizzio now had the bright idea of arranging for a metal stamp to be made up that carried the king's signature, and that was then impressed on the relevant writings in his absence and so avoided any hold-up to Crown business.[21] It sounds a tidy piece of secretarial practice, and is yet another small example to illustrate his administrative abilities and secretarial skills, albeit in a minor key.

King James V had reformed the administration of justice when he established the College of Justice in 1532. The judges were described as Senators of the College of Justice or Lords of Session, and by now consisted of the Lord Chancellor, the Lord President, fourteen ordinary Lords or Senators, with additional supernumerary judges who were known as the Extraordinary Lords. A Senator received an annual salary of £1,600 Scots. The rather repulsive figure of Morton had been appointed Lord Chancellor in January 1563 after the previous post-holder, Huntly, had died of a stroke on the battlefield at Corrichie. Rizzio's close ally James Balfour, a jurist of eminence and the author of a leading legal casebook, Balfour's *Pratiques*, became an ordinary Senator the same year.

All the judicial appointments during Rizzio's period in power seem perfectly proper, with little hint of corruption in the choice. Working with Balfour and Bothwell, he seems to have tried to put the best men on the bench without regard for sectarian obligations, as witnessed by the appointments for the three months between November 1565 and January 1566. This was the moment when his influence was at its peak. Promotions to the bench then included the distinguished Roman lawyer, Dr Edward Henryson, previously a law professor at Calvin's old university at Bourges, in France, and Bothwell's former comrade in arms, David Chambers, who took over the seat of Henry Sinclair, the late Bishop of Ross.[22]

During these winter months, with the challenge from Moray apparently over, he could at last enjoy some of the benefits of his position. Although little documentary evidence survives, such that does confirms his growing wealth and status. For example, in the bad Latin of the day, there is a note recording that for the year 1566 a pension of £80 was paid to the Queen's servant David Rizzio.[23] The entry is sandwiched between two others that show the larger sum of £133.6.8 paid to John Spens of Condie, the Queen's Advocate, and the lesser sum of £40 due to the royal herald, the Lord Lyon. The emoluments confirm his status as an important figure in the royal household, someone paid less than the Crown Counsel, but more than the court herald. He was undoubtedly a powerful individual in court circles, since he controlled access to the monarch and could influence her decisions. His other sources of income fluctuated, but presents from petitioners certainly contributed to his store of value, since his support was now worth having. Notions of corruption have changed since his time. But in the sixteenth century it was not unusual for litigants and petitioners to give substantial inducements to buy the goodwill of a powerful patron, and this must have been the basis for much of his wealth.

As yet another mark of royal favour he now received the lucrative monopoly of the mint. The mint, or *cunzehouse*, was to be found in the Canongate, close to the palace at Holyrood, and the proprietor effectively had a licence to coin money. On 28 February 1566 he was credited with £2,000 as the first instalment of the profits due to him under the contract, which was expressly stated to be paid by the Queen's Graces' special precept.[24] He was probably taking a commission from the debasement of the coinage as well, though the records here are unclear, and the reports are too slight to be unduly dogmatic about it. What is clear is that there was a great hoard of gold specie secreted away in his rooms, where it aroused the interested cupidity of the English ambassador, and the suspicion must be that this represented secret profits creamed off from the mint.

He was now at his zenith: effectively he was the chief minister, who fronted the government in alliance with the jurist James Balfour. His political support came from powerful clans like the Hepburns (Bothwell), the Gordons (Huntly), the Athol Stewarts (Atholl) and still, but only just, the Lennox Stewarts, Darnley's own family. The reality was that the royal favour was his only real power base.

Life at court among these quarrelsome, opinionated and heretical Scotsmen was never easy, despite the royal patronage and despite the opportunities to garner wealth given by his status so close to the throne. His problem was that he had no party, or body of support, behind him to help him outwit the many enemies who were gathering fast. Many of his so-called friends and former comrades in arms who had fought beside him against Moray and the rebels, such as Morton and Ruthven, proved false, while the other foreigners in government service, like de Busso and Danclourt, were just over-promoted lightweights. Treachery was everywhere. Even Fowler, Lennox's apparently faithful man of business, in the end turned out to be a double agent in the pay of Walsingham and Cecil.

In contrast, Rizzio was wholly devoted to his mistress, but this was to stand him in little stead. He may never have taken English bribes, but it was of little avail when he had no trustworthy friends beside him who could share his hopes and help him carry forward the patriotic dream of saving a proud and independent nation from the perennial southern challenge. No one else seemed to share his conception of all that was needed to make a nominally Catholic Scotland fit happily within the Christian comity of nations.

The English ambassador, always poking around for tittle-tattle about his country's enemies, did his best to find out everything he could about the favourite.[25] He reported it all to Cecil, including all that he discovered about Rizzio's tastes in decor. Randolph confirmed that Rizzio had spent lavishly when he decorated his rooms in the palace at Holyroodhouse, where 'his Chamber was well furnished'.[26] His standards of interior design do seem suprisingly martial for someone whose influence originally came from his skill in drafting documents and singing lyrics. Maybe he felt his position required him to adopt this early example of the 'Scots Baronial' style when he furnished his accommodation. He took the chance to display on the walls of his rooms some of the weaponry captured during the previous summer's civil war. He may have felt that the familiar warlike decor might make the jealous Scottish nobility think a little more kindly of him. His chambers were festooned with daggers, guns and pieces of armour, which included 'daggs, pistoletts, harquebusses, and twenty-two swords, and that of all this nothing is spoiled or lacking, saving two or three daggs'.[27] The furnishings make his tastes seem closer to Balmoral in the heyday of Queen Victoria and the Prince Consort than to a royal palace in Renaissance Britain. Only the carpets and curtains in loud clan tartans seem to be wanting.

So he was civilised and cultured, a good sportsman, and athletic – someone who enjoyed all the aristocratic pastimes of the age and shared the young King's passion for hawking and hunting. When exercise was not possible, and as relaxation from pressing state business, he talked to the young Queen, read in her fine library and concentrated on his growing collection of local *objets d'art*. Rizzio was well educated in the humanist tradition and always confident in his eye. He liked to collect the medals and coins of his northern Italian Renaissance homeland, and, of course, if other pastimes failed, there was always his music.[28]

What else is known about Seigneur Davie? There is controversy about his appearance. Even his friend Louis Guryon said he was 'very ill favoured', while his enemies said that his features were 'verrie black', and no compliment was intended, for he was alleged to be dark, ugly, indeed swarthy, and thus unlike the conventional idea of male beauty in Tudor times. Others said that he was physically handicapped, 'a dwarfish and deformed person', like Shakespeare's King Richard III, though this is a little difficult to reconcile with the records of his sporting prowess. His bitter opponent, the great Calvinist historian George Buchanan, said that all the fine clothes cut by the best Edinburgh tailors could not hide his deformities. However, the independent testimony of Pietro Bizari, who said that he was of 'pleasing appearance', must be accepted as the closest contemporary statement of the truth in the absence of alternative evidence to the contrary. Even so it is hard to form a true judgement, since no genuine, contemporary, print or portrait of him survives.[29] The picture of him playing on his lute, which now hangs at the modern palace of Holyroodhouse, dates from much later.[30]

His interests were by no means limited to making money, playing music and exploring the latest tricks of interior decoration. He was fond of riding, and other field sports, despite all the alleged physical handicaps. He liked good horses and built up a fine stable. It was said afterwards that his furniture, clothes and horses were better than Darnley's, which only made the latter the more jealous of the sophisticated Italian: 'he excelled the King in household stuff, apparel, and number of good horse.'[31] He also liked his tennis, that is real tennis, which he played with Darnley, especially on the open court at Falkland Palace; indeed, they played so much that he was once accused of 'haunting' the court.[32] There are no records that he took up golf, unlike the Queen, who enjoyed her game. But he enjoyed playing cards at night, and was typically Italian in his love of clothes. This was a society where colourful, expensive and elaborate dress was as acceptable for men as for women. And display was so important. Well-cut and luxurious clothes and rich jewels confirmed the status of the wearer. An inventory of his wardrobe showed he owned at least eighteen pairs of velvet hose, and that even for a light and informal supper with the Queen he dressed in a stylish nightgown of furred damask, with a satin doublet, and wore hose of russet velvet.[33]

His early upbringing on the edge of the French- and Italian-speaking worlds had taught him the essential elements of the various languages required for his day-to-day work, although Sir James Melville claimed long afterwards that he was never very impressed by the Secretary's linguistic abilities. But he was already fluent in Italian, Latin and French when he arrived in Scotland. With his quick intelligence he had no trouble in picking up the Scots Doric, or rather English, when he reached Edinburgh, which he spoke, as we have seen, with a rather excitable and voluble Franco/Italian accent, so unlike the Queen, with her pretty Scots one.

Here was a Renaissance court at its peak with a particularly fine ornament of Italian sophistication at the epicentre. In contrast to the native nobility, David Rizzio was altogether an interesting and civilised individual for the Queen to have around her. No wonder she preferred his company to theirs.

TEN

The Fatal Conspiracy

The Seigneur, his credit increased daily.
(Calderwood, *History of the Kirk in Scotland*, 1566)

David Rizzio was now at the very pinnacle of achievement. Scotland had been good to him. He had the ear and affection of the Queen, and both she and the council enthusiastically agreed with him that they must do all that they could to avoid the English embrace. People now addressed him as the 'Seigneur', my Lord, as he walked along the High Street, perhaps deferentially to his face, like the sessions clerk in the parish church at Canongate, or maybe behind his back, with no little sarcasm in their voice.

As he bustled around the court, in his elegant clothes, with his jewelled chain of office hanging from his neck, he was able to give some thought to his investments. Inevitably our information is a little sparse, and only a few hints survive about his banking arrangements and private finances. What is known is that he placed his business in the hands of another Italian, Timothy Cagnoli, who was a Lombard. Lombards were well known for their acumen, having invented the wonders of double-entry book keeping, so his assets were well managed.

He kept most of his money in gold specie, locked in a strong box at his chambers in Holyrood. This hoard was additional to his credit entries in Signor Cagnoli's ledgers, and included some of the gold ducats that had been struck by the Edinburgh mint to celebrate Mary's marriage with her first husband, François, the Dauphin of France.[1] It was said later: 'of the great substance he had there is much spoken. Some say in gold to the value of £2000 sterling.'[2]

He was now at the very centre of power, though his influence was behind the scenes, informal, yet all pervasive. He was the *éminence grise* near the throne, but as yet without any formal office, so it is not surprising his name hardly appears in the formal records of the *Register of the Privy Council*, which lists the men who sat as the 'Lords of the Secret Council', with a summary note of their decisions.[3]

A typical entry, for 3 November 1565, showed the councillors then present included Huntly, his kinsman Alexander Gordon, the Bishop of Galloway (*Candida Casa*), who also boasted the rather exotic ecclesiastical title of Titular Archbishop of Athens, and Sir John Maxwell of Terregles, with the versatile Sir James Balfour as secretary, so giving a substantial Gordon preponderance. The business that day was yet again on the subject of further disturbances in the western country. This time Argyll and his clansmen were condemned for having 'done great hurt to the town of Glasgow'. The proclamation was ordered to be read out from every market cross in the land, the usual method of communicating with common people in an illiterate age.[4]

Just occasionally, Darnley would condescend to put in an appearance at council. He did so just before Christmas. The question of whom to appoint as one of the commissioners to arbitrate on outstanding border issues vexed them. This was important business, and even the King saw fit to air his views. The debate illustrates policy towards England during the period of Rizzio's supremacy: 'much was said why she needed to send any commissioners, for offence she had none. She desired but to live in peace' with Elizabeth. On learning about it, Randolph, the English minister, grumbled how the new men on the council were entirely inadequate: 'the old courtiers she likes not, and the new so unfit for it as for their places.'[5]

Bothwell was eventually chosen to represent the Scots side, confirming again his alliance with the Italian, but the English refused to have anything to do with him, and the Scots, in turn, declined to accept the English nominee, Bedford. So the stand-off between the two realms continued.

Christmas 1565 was a time for glorious celebration for everyone at court, as on the surface all seemed calm and peaceful. Darnley, not very interested in matters of faith, nonetheless condescended to attend church with Mary on Christmas Day itself. There the King and Queen heard the usual three masses celebrated in full canonical form: 'On Christmas Day last was the first day the King went openly to Mass since he came into his realm, on which day he went in despite of, who would say nay, to all the service, and heard three Masses one after another.'[6] Darnley seems to have been making a positive attempt to accommodate himself to Mary's Catholicism, and his attendance at this mass, however much it irritated the Protestants, was a visible manifestation of the policy of toleration that Rizzio was urging on them both. He was glad to see that they both made the service, since they had been up all night playing cards together: 'She herself the most part of the night sat up at cards, and went to bed when it was almost day.'[7]

Six weeks later saw the feast of Candlemas, the traditional Christian festival kept to celebrate the purification of the Blessed Virgin Mary. A splendid ceremony was held according to the usual

Catholic rites in the chapel at Holyrood, when the Queen and King, with his father, Lennox, and Lords Atholl, Cassillis, Caithness and Seton, processed into church, all holding up great lighted candles of beeswax, while Rizzio conducted the chapel choir in a glorious setting of the 'Nunc dimittis'.

Randolph was there too and continued to complain about the Seigneur's position so close to the seats of power: 'David yet retaineth still his place . . .'.[8]

However, the Protestants were still very fretful. The General Assembly of the kirk had met again in the Upper Tolbooth on Christmas Day, which to 'the Godly' was just another day for business. They were unhappy at all this Romeish resurgence, and at the growing numbers of people attending mass and remained fearful of a Catholic revival. The Assembly decided the Protestant faithful must observe a solemn fast the next Lent to show their concern at the Queen's failure to repent from her papistry.

There were other incidents that pointed to more troubles ahead. An assault on the person of Friar John Black was especially disturbing. A well-known Dominican priest, Black was no good advertisement for the old Catholic clergy, being notorious for loose living and corrupting the affections of his female parishioners. After being dismissed from his post in Edinburgh for adultery, he took refuge across the border in Newcastle, where he occupied himself in begetting yet another bastard child on a poor servant girl. These tales of sexual misconduct by priests, of course, lost nothing in their telling by their opponents, and played into the hands of the militant reformers, whose fanatical hatred for the whole Catholic Church burnt more fiercely as a result.

Excited by the news of Catholic renaissance, Father Black was now back in Edinburgh and in high favour at court. There he was pressing for more Catholic churches to be built, so that the growing numbers of faithful might worship according to the old rites once again. The Catholic population of Edinburgh was then thought to be about 9,000 souls.

In late January Black got his come-uppance. Late one evening, as he walked down the High Street, he was ambushed and badly hurt by a gang of Liddesdale border reivers, most of them ne'er-do-wells from the notorious Armstrong clan. The incident was described thus: 'About two months past he was met late at night suspiciously, and got two or three blows with cudgel, and one with a dagger, like to have cost him his life. Much trouble ensued, and many were imprisoned thereon.'[9] The municipal authorities, who suspected the Armstrongs were in the pay of militants, were much irritated by this breach of the peace and prosecuted some of the leading merchants suspected of colluding with them.

The international situation stayed tense. Protestant paranoia was not helped by the news of the recent conference at Bayonne between the Catholic powers of France and Spain, which the Reformers imagined was to lead to a combination, 'in devilish devices', to extinguish Protestantism entirely.[10] These were nightmare times for Knox, as for Cecil. Cecil had the additional worry that Bothwell, Lennox, Huntly and Rizzio might try to invade England next summer at the head of a Scottish army. Only the previous year Mary's troops had conclusively crushed Moray and his dissident friends. Now the English minister feared she might be emboldened to lead her forces south to raise the Catholics in the northern shires and try to seat herself on the throne of St Edward.

It was just as well Knox did not know that the Bishop of Mondovi, the newly appointed papal nuncio to Scotland, planned to stop over in Turin on his way there. He was to discuss with Rizzio's old master, Emmanuel Philibert, the Duke of Savoy, how best to extinguish the Protestant stronghold on Lake Geneva; as he put it, to talk 'about overwhelming Calvinism at the fountainhead, by the reconquest of Geneva'.[11]

Over in France, Catherine de' Medici had graciously recognised Darnley to be King of Scotland, and it followed that he was entitled to all the usual honours routinely exchanged between Christian sovereigns. So, early in February 1566, yet another French diplomat, Jacques d'Augennes, Seigneur de Rambouillet, made his way to Edinburgh. He brought with him the insignia of the prestigious order of St Michael, or the golden cockleshell, which he was to confer on King Henry by command of the French King.

The investiture ceremony was another splendid occasion, which included a solemn mass and provided another excuse to display all the cultural extravaganza of Mary's court. Rizzio took time off from the cares of state to devise a special entertainment for the event, which the Queen, her four Maries and three other ladies in waiting acted out. Mary had always liked cross-dressing, and insisted that this time they all perform the masque in men's clothing. Afterwards she gave Rambouillet and his attendants the rather unfeminine and warlike offerings of some daggers, beautifully ornamented in black velvet sheaths.[12]

The French envoy travelled home through London, where he saw the Spanish ambassador Guzman de Silva; they discussed the news from Scotland. He reported that 'the King and Queen are well and the kingdom quiet. They are treating matters connected with the Catholic religion with great solicitude, they themselves offering a good example to the people.'[13] Rambouillet's analytical skills seem to have let him down with this rather complacent analysis, since he showed little inkling of the storm that was about to break.

The nights might have been dark outside in the winter frosts, but the court stayed snug and cheerful within the palace of Holyroodhouse. Even Darnley appeared to be a little happier within himself, though his general frustration was on the increase. However, he was pleased by this international recognition of his royal status, and duly wrote back to the young French king, Henri III, in his best hand with his thanks, as one monarch to another.

There was another happy occasion on 24 February: the marriage of Bothwell with Huntly's 21-year-old sister, Lady Jane Gordon, which was held according to the rites of the Reformed Church. We do not know if Rizzio suggested this alliance between the two great noble houses, which were among Mary's most consistent supporters, but he would have been delighted by the match, which consolidated the governing coalition's grasp on power in a very traditional way.

But the Lord Chancellor, James Douglas, the Earl of Morton, had now become a bitter enemy to the Italian favourite, though for the moment his hostility was well masked. By now their service together in the previous year's campaign against Moray's rebellion was well in the past. Morton was the effective head of the great Douglas family confederation, a brutal and rather distasteful figure. Catholic writers, like Blackwood, saw in him evil personified, and gleefully wrote up stories of how even his own father found him repulsive. They circulated a tale of how Morton, when a small boy, once found a toad in his garden, which he insisted on eating live.[14] As a result, 'from his very youth he had been renowned for his treachery, and of whom his father had no good opinion'.[15]

Rumours were also abroad that Mary was on the point of raising Rizzio to the peerage and giving him an earldom, so that he could act as Crown spokesman in the Parliament, which was summoned to meet in March. He was to be naturalized as a subject, and Mary would 'give him some style of an Earl in Scotland'.[16] This shows how his debating skills were thought good enough to speak for the government, and that his command of the Scots tongue was sufficient to appeal to the assembly directly as their first minister. His opponent Buchanan, writing about ten years afterwards, told the story of how 'the Queen tried to elevate him to the rank of a Lord of Parliament, by loading him with wealth and honours. Her chief reason was that by procuring him the right of voting in Parliament, he could manage that assembly according to the Queen's wishes.' In anticipation of the honour, 'David went around them individually to plumb their minds, and discover what each would do if he were elected President by the rest of the Assembly'.[17]

Meanwhile he was working hard to whip up support for the legislation required to sequester the property of Moray and his confederates. But little did he know that the parliamentary process to forfeit the estates of the defeated Protestant rebels meant that there was a critical deadline before which any *coup d'état* to change the government must be launched, so triggering the timing for the final attack on the regime.

For the moment, he chose to ignore the danger signs, and kept himself busy with his private and public cares. Nevertheless, he now had enough money to contemplate an investment in an estate a few miles from Edinburgh and was encouraged in his ambitions by the Queen, who set her heart on making him a laird. He opened negotiations to buy a hunting lodge at Melville Castle, on the River Esk in Midlothian, and she said she would help with the cost, since she was keen for her favourite to have a baronial status like her other vassals. On more than one occasion they rode out to look at the property together. Local legend has it they even planted some young sapling oaks or chestnuts to celebrate the purchase, which are still to be seen growing in the policies there.[18]

Land prices have moved since the mid-sixteenth century. Even so, a cash pile of gold coin, when exchanged into the depreciated Scots pounds of the day, would have funded the price of a very substantial property, and allowed the suave and elegant figure of Seigneur Davie to loom large over the impecunious native nobility. And the purchase of Melville would have allowed him to live, and entertain, as a nobleman of Scotland ought, and given him a suitable home in which to show off his treasures – the fine furnishings, continental tapestries and other beautiful *objets d'art* from his collection.

However, the landowner, a cousin of Morton's and therefore a Douglas, refused to sell. The English ambassador, Randolph, confirmed the story: 'Displeasure is grown towards my lord of Morton. The seal is taken from him and, as some say, shall be given to keep to David. The ground of displeasure is that Morton will not give over a piece of ground, that thus David may come by a piece of lande with a fair house called Melvin within iij miles of Edenburg.'[19] The secretary's ambitions to acquire his kinsman's property only served to invigorate Morton's dislike for the favourite.

The elderly diplomat Sir James Melville, writing about thirty years afterwards and so with the benefit of hindsight, described his rise rather well. He knew all about court jangles and jealousies, and explained how the Italian interloper had failed to finesse his position with the great magnates, who hated his proximity to the Queen. 'And as he thereby entered in greater credit, so he had not the prudence to manage the same rightly; for frequently in presence of the Nobility, he would be publicly speaking to Her, even when there was the greatest conventions of the Estates.' Sir James also thought Rizzio aroused their jealousy because he controlled the flow of papers presented to the monarch, 'which made him to be much envied, and hated, especially when he became so great that he presented all signatures to be subscribed by Her Majesty . . .'.[20]

One hitherto underappreciated factor in the drama was his courage in the face of the looming danger. He knew that he had numerous enemies and that they were mustering. And he knew too that the Scots barons were a ruthless lot and that a conspiracy to overthrow him was almost certainly afoot. It was about now that a French Catholic priest, Father Jean Damiot, one of the Queen's confessors, warned him 'to beware of the Bastard', by which he meant Moray. Rizzio replied, 'I will take good care he never sets foot in Scotland again', and appeared to take the advice on board, even though he had just accepted Moray's gift of a diamond in return for permission to allow him home.[21] But in fact the priest meant another illegitimate sprig of the nobility, Darnley's uncle, George Douglas the Postulate, who was usually known as 'the Bastard of Angus'. Buchanan confirms the story: 'John Damiot had frequently warned Rizzio to take himself off now that he had made his fortune, that he might escape the hatred of the nobles, whom he could not hope to equal.'[22]

Seigneur Davie, however, stayed sanguine. He told Father Damiot, 'paroles, paroles, nothing but words, the Scots will boast, but rarely perform their brags'.[23] He was not frightened by the risks and went on to say that his enemies were 'but ducks; strike one of them and the rest would lie in'.[24] The priest replied that, to the contrary, they were geese. 'You will find them geese, if you handle one of them the rest will fly upon you and pluck you so that they will not leave a feather of down upon you.'[25] But Rizzio stayed confident and rejected Damiot's advice to leave with all his money and retire back to Savoy, 'to order his business, and get from hence'.[26] Sir James Melville too warned him about the dangers ahead of him. Unlike Randolph, Sir James claimed to be his friend. He wrote later that then 'I entered with Signor David in the same manner, for then he and I were under great friendship. But he distained all danger, and despised counsel, so that I was compelled to say I feared over late repentance.'[27]

Rizzio's concern was not for himself (he had no family in the country – his brother Joseph had not yet arrived) but for the Queen to whom he had pledged his loyalty. He had made Scotland his home, and there he would stay. This may have been the time he suggested she recruit a personal bodyguard, and, despite his bold words to Father Damiot, he certainly began to think how to improve security around the court. His enemies were to say later that, having defeated Moray's rebellion, he now planned to purge the country of other dissidents and institute a reign of terror. In pursuance of such policies he would not hesitate 'to cut off some of the nobility for a terror to the others'.[28]

This led to another rumour that 200 German, or Italian, mercenaries were to be secretly imported into the country. Rizzio himself was to be given a guard of fifty halbadiers. Since no Scots could be found for the work, he was also said to have advised that foreign professionals be recruited, mainly from 'Italians, who were void of all sense of religion, brought up under tyranny, and accustomed to mischief'. The suggestion was that the men were to be brought over to Edinburgh from Flanders, 'one by one, less their purpose should be discovered, and that there was greater danger to offend one of them than to offend the Queen herself'.[29] Rizzio himself would be in personal command.

There is no evidence any such mercenary force ever arrived in Scotland. For one thing there was no money to pay them. The Medici princes might be able to afford to keep up a private army of Swiss lancers, but Edinburgh was not Florence. A company of

Hepburn borderers, or Gordon highlanders, might have kept guard over the Queen and her secretary, but clansmen could not be away from their glens for long-term service like this.

For the moment Rizzio and Darnley were still allies, but any earlier liking was rapidly corroding under the pressures of life together. And their attentions were on other matters – Rizzio on his work and Darnley on his fun. The latter was already rather too fond of the local whisky and was also increasingly envious of the secretary's status and lifestyle – not to mention his close links with his wife. He was also prone to sudden mood swings, which may perhaps have signified the onset of depression, and was particularly irritated by the way the Italian cut a better figure and kept a better stable than he did.

Gold and silver ryals had been minted to honour the marriage with Darnley in 1565. They were handsome pieces worth thirty shillings, with portraits of the King and Queen, who looked at each other, face to face. On the obverse were depicted two crowned thistle heads joined together, with a prayer above inscribed in Latin, 'Quos deus coniunxit homo non separet' (Whom God hath joined together let no man put asunder) – an injunction that proved sadly ineffective, as Rizzio's camaraderie with Darnley started to falter, and the whispers spread about his growing intimacy with the Queen.

Many of the difficulties in the royal marriage came down to Darnley's own tensions, much increased by his sexual frustration, since Mary now declined to let him near her in bed. Her advancing pregnancy may be sufficient explanation, but his jealous imaginings that his wife was in an adulterous relationship with another only made for yet more misery. His mood swings grew yet more volatile. And the disgruntled nobles, especially Ruthven and Morton, encouraged them for their own reasons. Their next suggestion was to engineer an argument about the score at one of the games of tennis they still enjoyed playing together on the palace court, and then stab the Italian. But this was too much, even for Darnley.

The English minister, Randolph, was in a difficult position. He was still suspected of being behind the rebellion the previous year. In October, anonymous gunmen fired at his lodgings. 'Two arquebusiers shot into my lodgings one night at the door where Mr Colwith lodged. They were worst meant than any harm done.'[30] Now in the middle of February 1566 he was suddenly summoned to appear before the Queen and council, where he was accused of having supported Moray and his co-conspirators in the insurgency and of 'lending her rebels 3000 crowns to levy men against her'.[31] He was then declared *persona non grata* and packed off in disgrace across the English frontier to Berwick. Relations with England became colder than ever.

There was little sign of early spring that year, and in the continued frost Rizzio's numerous enemies continued to muster. They were motivated by fervent religious zeal and well fired up by the rich brew of sexual and personal jealousies now simmering away at the very heart of court. The disturbed imaginings of Darnley that he was being cuckolded only added yet another bitter herb to the cocktail of hatreds that were brewing.

The list of enemies now included Moray's supporters and allies, 'the Protestant Lords', as well as the ministers of the kirk, who mourned because these godly men were in exile for conscience's sake, and urged the brethren to brace themselves for a coming sacrifice. Moray and his associates still smarted from their defeat the previous year, and were keen to return for another round, to turn off the 'fountain of sinister counsel' that had swept them away from their proper position in government. High on the list, too, was the cryptic figure of Maitland, the former secretary, jealous of Rizzio's preferment in his place. Maitland now threw his own devious proposal into the pot by suggesting that the Italian take over the great state office of Lord Chancellor, since the present incumbent, Morton, was so 'unlettered and unskilful'.[32] Randolph, of course, soon knew all about it. And so did Knox, who confirms this was to be so: 'at the Parliament which was to be, he was ordained to be Chancellor, which made the Lords conspire against him.'[33]

The friends of the 'Amity' with England, mainly Protestants, of course, also hoped for regime change, and to be rid of the interloper. Randolph and his agents were by now deeply involved with the plotters, and were well aware of Maitland's dissatisfaction. Before his expulsion, in early December 1565, he told Cecil that both Maitland and Morton were out of favour with the ruling clique and that 'Maitland has leave to play his own solicitor with the Queen, and David, but I hear of no other credit except to entertain his mistress, whether he has more leisure than many a wise man would take to so idle an office'.[34]

Maitland now put forward an argument that Rizzio's present position as the informal, but highly influential, royal favourite, and effective chief minister, had no legal standing under proper constitutional practice, but that his elegant mind had hit on a solution. He suggested a deal be struck whereby Morton resign his position as Lord Chancellor in favour of Rizzio. Morton was to be compensated by being granted the revenues of the vacant earldom of Angus, which included custody of the key fortress at Tantallon, with its castle perched above the East Lothian coast. Rizzio, in turn, as we have seen, would be naturalised as a Scot, and Mary would 'give him some style as Earl of Scotland'.[35]

This offer, if true, and we have little means of checking, is interesting. It sounds just the sort of negotiating talk common among politicians today. The proposal confirms that at least his key contemporaries thought Seigneur Davie sufficiently well educated, and more up to the job, than the current Chancellor, Morton. Rizzio was no lawyer, but had doubtless picked up the basic principles of Roman jurisprudence as part of his humanist education when at university in Italy, and, anyway, the chancellorship was not then essentially a judicial office. As 'the Earl of Melville', any of his judgments could have been written up with the help of his close ally, James Balfour of Mountquhannie, who had one of the most powerful legal brains of the era.

Morton soon learnt of the proposal to evict him from office, and was further enraged by an adverse court judgment against his own good claims to the Angus estates. And so he was more than glad to join the incipient conspiracy to get rid of the Italian intruder; and he then brought all his many Douglas kinsmen with him to the vendetta.

On 9 February 1566 Maitland broke cover. He wrote to Cecil from Edinburgh to recommend firm measures, though his advice was, even more than usual, wrapped up in the customary Tudor circumlocution. 'I see no certain way, unless we chop at the very root. You know where it lieth, and so far as my judgement can reach, the sooner all things be packed up the less danger there is of any inconvenience.'[36] It was very worldly counsel, but the message was quite clear. Murder was planned.

The members of the Privy Council had met that same day, 9 February, quite unaware of what was afoot. They discussed routine business, in particular whether to vary the customs duties on imported French wine. The magnates present included Lennox, Bothwell and Caithness, again with James Balfour as secretary. There is no record that Seigneur Davie joined in their deliberations, as, on the surface of government, everything seemed at ease.

However, two days earlier, Randolph had presciently reported: 'David yet retaineth still his place, not without grief to many that see their Sovereign guided by such a fellow.'[37]

From his new vantage point over the border in Berwick, Randolph was in a good position to observe the various conspiracies now in hand against the Seigneur. He was pleased when he learnt the news of Darnley's dissatisfaction, and noted how 'the suspicion of this King towards David is so great that it must shortly grow to a scabbe among them'.[38] Queen Elizabeth meanwhile complained to Mary about the 'strange and uncourteous usage of Randolph in ordering him to quit her kingdom without proof of his offence', and threatened to treat the Scots envoy in London in similar fashion.[39] And then, three days later, 6 March, the news arrived that the formal bonds were at last ready from the lawyers, and that 'a matter of no small consequence was intended in Scotland'.[40] This was the slaughter of the favourite.

Bonds of 'man rent' were traditional legal devices long in use by the barons and lairds. Their purpose was to record the precise obligations and personal service owed to feudal superiors by lesser persons in return for their protection. Times were suspicious. A written paper in a formal contract drawn up by a notary would remain as evidence of agreement and endure longer than a mere word or handshake. But on this occasion the legal documents were prepared, not as contractual agreements about property or feudal service, but for political assassination. On 1 March 1566 Darnley signed such a bond with the leading malcontents, who included Ruthven, Morton and others of his Douglas kinsmen. Having rejected the idea that Darnley run through his rival after one of their games of tennis, the conspirators calculated that the killing might better be justified if he could be seen to have been caught *in flagrante delicto* with the Queen. So it could then be dressed up as a *crime passionel*. The purpose of the contract as finally drafted defined its principal object to be to rid the country of 'a stranger Italian called Davie'.[41]

Twenty-four hours later, Moray and his friends down in Newcastle put their hands to confirmatory contracts in which they promised to support Darnley in his quest for the 'Crown Matrimonial'. The agreements survive and bear an endorsement in a sixteenth-century hand: 'Ane band maid by my lord of Murray and certain other noblemen with him before the slauchtir of Davie.'[42]

Further and better particulars are in the documents themselves. The first one is headed:

Certain Articles to be fulfilled by Archibald, Earl of Argyll, James, Earl of Moray, Alexander, Earl of Glencairn, Andrew, Earl of Rothes, Robert, Lord Boyd, Andrew, Lord Ochiltree, and their accomplices; to Our Noble and Mighty Prince Henry, King of

Scotland, husband to Our Sovereign Lady, which articles the said persons offer with most humility, lowliness, and service to the said Noble Prince, for whom to God they pray with long life, and good succession to his body.

1. They bind themselves as true subjects to support him in all his lawful and just actions, to be friends to his friends, and enemies to his enemies, etc., etc.[43]

The second was a counterpart duly signed by Darnley, whereby he promised to stop their forfeiture, and restore their estates, support them in the exercise of the reformed religion, and maintain them, as a good master should. He subscribed it 'Henry, R.'.

Cecil dated the copy on his file, 1 March 1565.

So Randolph, Bedford and Cecil knew all about the plans for assassination. They knew that they, the exiled 'Protestant Lords' – that is, Moray himself, Argyll, Glencairn, Ochiltree and Boyd – and Darnley himself were all deeply implicated. And they all happily put their names to Darnley's paper justification for his conduct, which they agreed to be justified as a proper punishment by an aggrieved husband on a wife's seducer.

Bedford and Randolph set out Darnley's excuses.

We need not plainly describe the person. You have heard of the man whom to take away this occasion of slander, he is himself determined to be at the apprehension and execution of him, whom he is manifestly to charge with the crime, and to have done him the most dishonour that can be to any manwe mean.[44]

Seigneur Davie's many enemies had sharpened their dirks with a vengeance. The pity of it was that he was quite unaware of what was in store.

ELEVEN

Mary's Account

Most cruelly took him forth of our cabinet.
(Mary to the Archbishop of Glasgow, 15 March 1566)

It was an early spring night. All seemed calm, but murder was abroad in Edinburgh that evening. The conspirators had made their plans, but the victim was quite unaware of his fate. At about seven o'clock in the evening of 9 March, Mary was sitting in one of her small private chambers in Holyroodhouse at a quiet supper, with meat dishes on the menu, as allowed by the Church during the Lenten fast because of her pregnancy.

She had a small party of kinfolk, Janet Argyll and Lord Robert Stewart, with her at table. However, her husband was not with them. There was, of course, the usual retinue of servants in attendance, including a young page in Darnley's train, Anthony Standen. Mary described the scene afterwards in her own words:

> Upon the 9th day of March instant, We being at about 7 hours in our cabinet at our supper, accompanied by our sister, the Countess of Argyll, our brother the Commendator of Holyrood House, the Laird of Creich, Arthur Eskine, and certain others of our domestic servants, in quiet manner, especially of our ill disposition being counselled to sustain ourselves with flesh, having also then passed almost to the end of seven months in our birth.[1]

Of a sudden the assault began. There was no warning. Out of the night Lords Morton, Lindsay and Ruthven, with a troop of about 500 men, rushed into the old abbey and palace building, snatched the keys from the porters and secured the gate. The guards on duty were quickly overcome. With the entrance in their hands, the invaders 'would thole none to enter in the palace but were of their opinion'.[2] Armed with 'jacks, steel bonnets, guns, pistols, swords, bucklers, Jedburgh staffs, halberts, and other weapons', they soon secured their positions.[3] Ruthven then led a smaller squad of about eighty henchmen up to the Queen's private closet, where he knew he would find his victim. They included his young son Greysteil the Master of Ruthven, his nephew Andrew Kerr of Fawdonside, other Douglas borderers, various Scotts and Murrays, and other minor kinsmen, allies and border lairds, such as Adam Tweedie of Drava and William Tweedie of Drummelzier, so all in all the grim murder party was very much a family affair. Shouting their traditional war cry 'a Douglas, a Douglas', they then scattered the servants and knocked over the candles, as they hunted for their prey in the sudden darkness.

The commander, Patrick, Lord Ruthven, was about 45 years old, and a Protestant extremist. His reputation was poor. People whispered that he practised the black arts, which may just have meant that his mind was an enquiring one, with an interest in science. Scientist or not, he can certainly be held guilty of gross breach of faith. Only the previous summer he had entertained

Rizzio, with Mary and her train, in his castle by Perth, when they had stayed as his guests just before her wedding. Now his hospitality had curdled into something akin to Macbeth's.

Meanwhile the assault force had seized control of the rest of the property. 'The Earl of Morton and Lord Lindsay, with their assistants, boded in warlike manner, to the number of eightscore persons or thereby, kept and occupied the whole entry of our palace of Halyrudhouse, so that as they believed it was not possible to any person to escape forth of the same.'[4]

Darnley was with the assailants. He had joined them beforehand, knew the way and now led them up to his wife's little dinner party, where the elegant figure of David Rizzio was, as expected, among the guests. As Mary described it: 'The King our husband came to us in our cabinet, and placed himself beside us at our supper.'[5]

The spectral figure of Lord Ruthven, who had specially risen from his sick bed to lead the assault and wore full coat armour, then forced himself into the supper room past the terrified menials. He demanded to speak with 'our secretary'. Mary realised what was about to happen, did her best to negotiate a deal and offered to arrange for her favourite to be impeached before parliament, where any charges could be considered with due form of law. In the few moments left to him she tried desperately to save her friend. But Ruthven refused all her pleas for mercy.

'In the meantime the Lord Ruthven, bod [equipped] in like manner, with his complices, took entry perforce in our cabinet, and there seeing our secretary David Rizzio among others our servants, declared he had to speak with him.'[6] Mary then screamed at her husband. 'In this instant we required the King our husband, if he knew anything of that enterprise?'[7] It is easy to understand her indignation. Of course, he denied everything.

'Also we commanded the Lord Ruthven, under the pain of treason, to avoid him forth of our presence; declaring we should exhibit the said David before the Lords of Parliament, to be punished, if in any sorte he had offended.'[8] Ruthven scorned the offer.

'Notwithstanding the said Lord Ruthven attacked him [that is Rizzio] in our presence.'[9] Meanwhile Darnley 'biddeth her to be of

141

good courage for nothing was intended against her'.[10] But in his desperation the secretary tried to save himself, fumbled for his dagger, dropped it, shouted for help in Italian and then gripped Mary's waist tightly in vain hopes of safety. At the same time, Ruthven's nephew, Kerr of Fawdonside, held his pistol so close to her that it rubbed up against her stomach, as he bent Rizzio's fingers back grimly, 'so that for pain he was forced to forgo his grip'.[11] The King meanwhile yelled out to Mary, who was still trying to protect him: 'let him go, Madam, no harm is going to come to him.'[12]

She continues her description of the terrible events:

He then for refuge took safeguard, having retired behind our back, and with his complices cast down our table upon ourself, put violent hands in him, struck him over our shoulder with whinzeards [short swords or daggers], one part of them standing before our face with bended daggs [drawn swords], most cruelly took him forth of our cabinet, and at the entrance of our chamber gave him fifty-six strokes with whinzeards and swords. In doing whereof, we were not only struck with great dreadour [alarm], but also by sundry consideration was most justly induced to take extreme fear of our life.[13]

The wretched victim was then pulled from the room, all the time kicking and screaming, and dispatched. In all the turmoil the dining table was knocked over and the rapidly cooling cuts of meat on it were kicked to the floor. And, as soon as Kerr had dragged the terrified Italian out of her grasp, the murderers set to their butchery with a vengeance, inflicting more than fifty vicious wounds, as they stabbed away at their prize. Very soon his last words rang out: 'Madama, io son morto!' (Madame, I am dead!).[14] As she heard his lovely voice cry out in pain for that last time, she answered: 'Ah, poor David, my good and faithful servant, may the Lord have mercy on your soul.'[15]

142

Darnley's dagger was left in the corpse. Husband and wife then exchanged bitter words: 'There remained a long time with the Queen, her husband, and Ruthven.'[16] Mary then, and long after, blamed her weakling spouse for his part in the plot. 'She made great intercession that he should have no harm and blamed greatly her husband that was the author of so foul an act.'[17] He tried to justify himself by saying that Rizzio was having sex with her and that she had not allowed him to do so for the last two months. 'It is said that he did answer that David had more company of her body than he for the space of two months, and therefore for her honour and his own contentment he gave his consent that he should be taken away.'[18] This was the reason why he had joined the plot. Mary gave him the splendid reply: '"It is not," saith she, "the woman's part to seek the husband, and therefore, in that the fault was his own."'[19] He riposted that she had often refused him his marital rights, pleading a headache or whatever. 'He said that when he came, she either would not, or made herself sick.' '"Well," saith she, "you have taken your last of me, and your farewell."'[20]

Ruthven, having achieved his object and dispatched his prey, then tried to give the pair a little much-needed advice. He talked to them of their 'duty' to each other. '"That were a pity," saith Ruthven, "he is your Majesty's husband, and you must yield duty to each other."'[21] Yet even in this desperate crisis Mary was not to be bullied. She replied that he was in no position to talk to her about marriage reconciliation. If necessary she would leave her husband, as indeed, his own wife had just left him. '"Why may not I", saith she, "leave him as well as your wife did her husband? Others have done the like." Lord Ruthven then said she was lawfully divorced from her husband, and for no such cause as the King found himself aggrieved.'[22]

Then he came to the real objections the aristocracy and new reformed clergy had to the Italian. 'This man' was, he said, 'mean, base, enemy to the nobility, shame to herself, and destruction to her country', which effectively sums up why they wanted him dead.[23]

But still the drama went on. Mary tearfully defended her old friend, and at the same time threatened vengeance. '"Well," saith she, "it shall be dear blood to some of you if his be spilt." "God forbid," saith Ruthven, "for the more Your Grace shows yourself offended, the world will judge the worse."'[24] But she was never to forgive his behaviour.[25]

All the time she continued to sob out in distress. 'Her husband this time speaketh little. Her Grace continually weepeth.'[26] Ruthven then called for some wine, claiming that he felt tired by all this butchery. 'Lord Ruthven being evil at ease and weak, calleth for a drink, and saith, "This I must do with Your Majesty's pardon," and persuadeth her in the best sort he could that she would pacify herself.'[27]

Then he started again to try to justify himself. He railed at her, telling her that he, and his supporters, objected at her tyranny, which they feared, just as in Roman times Brutus had feared the tyranny of Julius Caesar. He claimed that Rizzio was her lover, and alleged that, under his malign influence, she had planned to restore the Roman Catholic faith and keep the rebel 'Protestant Lords' in permanent exile. He gave his views about her foreign policy, which was wholly misguided. As for her other advisers, by which he meant Lords Bothwell and Huntly, they were equally unsuitable and should not be on her council. Then he told her, with yet more callous impertinence, that her brother Moray and the other banished and rebel lords were newly arrived back to Edinburgh.

After this deed immediately the said Lord Ruthven coming again in our presence declared how they and their accomplices aforesaid were highly offended with our proceedings and tyranny, which was not to them tolerable; how we was abused by the said David, whom they had actually put to death, namely in taking his counsel for maintenance of the ancient religion, debarring of the lords which were fugitive, and entertaining of amity with foreign princes and nations with whom we were confederate; putting also upon council the Lords Bothwell and Huntly, who were traitors, and with whom he associated himself. That the Lords banished into England were in the morning to resort towards us, and would take plain part with them in our contrary [opposition]; and that the king was willing to remit them their offences.[28]

But even then the night's work was not over yet. The fanatics had further plans. David Rizzio was not to be the only victim. They also hoped to dispose of Bothwell and Huntly, who were still at large somewhere in the palace buildings, and execute condign punishment on Sir James Balfour. The zealots particularly loathed Balfour. He was a turncoat. As one of the 'Castilians', he had been on their side earlier and had even shared the rigours of life aboard the French slave galleys with Knox. Now instant justice was to be served. And so they had brought ropes with which they proposed to string him over the palace walls; but the wily lawyer was too quick on his feet for them. He got away first, to live into old age, become a respected Scots jurist, author the celebrated legal textbook known as *Balfour's Pratiques*, and die in his bed: 'We all this time took no less care of ourselves, than for our council and nobility, maintenance of our authority, being with us in our palace for the time; to wit, the Earls of Huntly, Bothwell, Atholl, Lords Fleming and Livingston, Sir James Balfour, and certain others our familiar servitors: against whom the enterprise was conspired as well as for David; and namely to have hanged the said Sir James in cords.'[29]

Bothwell and Huntly had managed to escape as well. Hearing the uproar, at first they tried to lead a counter-attack and mobilised some of the palace servants, cooks, scullions and other domestics, to defend their sovereign. But they soon realised they were heavily outnumbered and underarmed, and that any challenge was hopeless, so they fled the bloody scene and clambered out of a small window that overlooked a little garden where the lions and other beasts in the royal menagerie were kept. Then those sturdy representatives of municipal authority, the Provost and Baillies of Edinburgh, put in an appearance. Alarmed by all the tumult and turmoil, the Provost ordered that the great alarm bell in the Tolbooth, or town hall, be rung to rouse the townspeople.

Yet, by the providence of God, the earls of Huntly and Bothwell escaped forth of their chambers in our palace at a back window by some cords; wherein their conspirators took some fear, and thought themselves greatly disappointed in their interprise [enterprise]. The earl of Atholl and Sir James Balfour by some other means, with the Lords Fleming and Livingstone, obtained deliverance of their invasion.[30]

Yet again Mary was threatened with more brutality. The attackers told her that 'they should cut us in collops' – that is, into little pieces – should she try to get help from the townsfolk.

The provost and town of Edinburgh having understood this tumult in our palace, caused ring their common bell, came to us in great number, and desired to be seen in our presence, intercomone [to intercomune] with us, and to have known our welfare; to whom we was not permitted to give answer, being extremely bosted [controlled] by their lords, who, in our face declared, if we desired to have spoken with them, they should cut us in collops, and cast us over the walls.[31]

All that night they kept her in custody.

All that night we were detained in captivity within our chamber, not permitting us to have intercomoned scarcely with our servant women, nor domestick servitors. Upon the morn hereafter proclamation was made, in our husband's name, by our advice, commanding all prelates and other lords convened to Parliament, to retire themselves of our burgh of Edinburgh. That whole day we were kept in that condition, our familiar servitors and guard being debarred from our service, and we watched by the participants in these crimes; to whom a part of the community of Edinburgh, to the number of fourscore persons, assisted.[32]

By now Moray and the other banished Lords had made their way to the palace. Such was her obvious state of shock that even Moray's

146

austerely ambitious figure showed some traces of fraternal affection. His solicitude, however, was insufficient to stop his agreeing with the conspirators' suggestion that she be sent straight away under arrest to await the birth of her child behind the walls of Stirling Castle. Meanwhile, the necessary formalities could proceed to crown Darnley as King Regnant.

Darnley had promised the murderers that he would keep his wife for the night 'under sure guard'.

> The Earl of Moray that same day at even, accompanied by the earl of Rothes, Pitarrow, Grange, the tutor of Pitcurr, and others who were with him in England, came to them, and seeing our state and entertainment was moved with a natural affection towards us. Upon the morn he assembled the enterprisers of this late crime, and such of our rebels as came with him. In their council they thought it most expedient we should be warded in our castle of Stirling, there to remain while we approved in Parliament all their wicked enterprises, established their religion, and gave to the King, the Crown Matrimonial and the whole government of our realm; or else, by all appearance, they firmly purposed to have put us to death, or detain us in perpetual captivity. To avoid them of our palace with their guard and assistars, the King promised to keep us that night in sure guard, and that by compulsion he would cause us in Parliament to approve all their conspiracies. By this means he caused them to retire out of our palace.[33]

But during the night she managed to rekindle Darnley's affections. She persuaded him to stay beside her, pointing out that his own security was at risk if the conspiracy succeeded. They then decided to flee together as best they could, and managed to find an unguarded way out over the walls in the dark.

> This being granted, and the guards commanded to serve us in the customary manner (the fear and dreadour always remained with us) we declared our state to the King our husband, certifying him

how miserably he would be handled, in case he permitted these lords to prevail in our country; and how unacceptable it would be to the other princes, our confederates, in case they altered the religion. By this persuasion, he was induced to condescend to the purpose taken by us, and to retire him in our company to Dunbar; which we did under night, accompanied by the captain of our guard, Arthur Erskine, and two others only.[34]

Throughout the emergency Mary had depended very much on the redoubtable Bothwell, and on the quick thinking of Huntly. It was these two who crept back into the palace at night to organise her flight from the scene of horror, and helped to lower her heavily pregnant figure over the walls in a sort of bosun's chair.

Of before, we being of mind to have gotten ourselves relieved of this detention, desired in quiet manner the earls of Bothwell and Huntly to have prepared some way whereby they might have performed the same; who not doubting therein, at the least taking no regard to hazard their lives in that behalf, devised that we should have come over the walls of our palace in the night upon towes [ropes] and chairs, which they had in readiness to that effect.[35]

As they crept towards the stables looking for their horses in the dark, where they walked across an uneven pile of earth outside the entrance to the old abbey where Rizzio's corpse was temporarily interred, her contrite husband understandably looked more than a little embarrassed and uncomfortable. She asked him why. He replied: 'Madam, we are just now passing by the grave of poor David. In losing him I have lost a good and trusty servant, the like of whom I shall never see again. I shall regret him every day of my life.'[36]

Then came the gallop through the night. Once the King and Queen were safe in Dunbar, the people soon rallied to their sovereign. The Italian secretary may not have been widely popular, and was not greatly mourned, but public opinion still supported the legitimate monarch. Armed levies were quickly mobilised to uphold the Crown authority, and very soon many – Hepburns, Hamiltons, Gordons, with other good fighting men from the borders – came forward to defend her cause.

> Soon after our coming to Dunbar, sundry of our nobility zealous of our well-being, such as the earls of Huntly, Bothwell, Marshall, Atholl, Caithness, the Bishop of St Andrews, with his kin and friends; Lords Hume, Yester, Sempil and infinite others, assembled to us; by whose advice, proclamations being made for convening our lieges to attend to us and our service; the lords conspirators conceiving the same, the earl of Glencairn as innocent of this last crime, resorted towards us, by our tolerance, and hath taken his remission, and in similar fashion the earl of Rothes.[37]

With the Queen safely out of reach, the insurrection soon collapsed. 'We remained in Dunbar five days, and after returned to Edinburgh well accampanied with our subjects.'[38] So then she led her army back in triumph. In the face of the successful counter-revolution Moray swallowed his pride and tried to make his peace, while his old ally, Argyll, retreated back to his Campbell clan lands in the west. Most of the other conspirators had already escaped by the time the Crown officers initiated proceedings for treason against them. The Queen had commanded they be pressed 'with all vigour', and Sir James Balfour doubtless enjoyed drafting the indictments. This was no mean threat, since conviction meant forfeiture of the property of anyone found guilty.

> The Earl of Moray and Argyll sent diverse messages to procure our favour, to whom in likewise, for certain respects, by advice of our nobility and Council being with us, we have granted remission, under condition they in no way apply themselves to their last conspirators, but retire themselves in Argyll during our will; thinking it very difficult to have so many bent at once in our contrare, and knowing the promises which had passed already between the King and them; and our force not sufficient, through

inhability of our person to resist the same, and put the matter in so great hazard.[39]

Two minor participants in the plot, Thomas Scott and Henry Yair, were caught, tried, convicted, duly hanged drawn and quartered, and their severed parts put on display around the town by way of deterrent.

> The last conspirators, with their assisters [helpers], having removed themselves forth of the same before, and being presently fugitive from our laws, we have caused by our charges their whole fortunes, strengths, and houses to be rendered to us; have caused an inventory to be made of their goods and gear, and intend further to pursue them with all rigour.[40]

The business was then spun so that 'King Henry', that is Darnley, was then forced to make an abject apology to the Privy Council. He defended himself there by saying that he had known nothing of the plot, and explained that he had only agreed to join it to bring about the recall of Moray and his friends. But his public humiliation was complete when the Lord Lyon made another announcement at the Mercat Cross, to be repeated at all other market crosses throughout the realm. With all due ceremony the heralds bellowed out that, by order of the Queen's Grace:

> Whereunto we are assured to have the assistance of our husband, who hath declared to us, and in presence of the Lords of our Privy Council, his innocence of this last conspiracy; how he never counselled, commanded, consented, assisted, nor approved the same. Thus far only he oversaw himself, that at the enticement and persuasion of the late conspirators, he, without our advice or knowledge, consented to the bringing home forth of England, of the earls of Moray, Glencairn, Rothes, and other persons with whom we were offended. This you will consider by his declaration made hereupon; which at his desire hath been published at all the mercat crosses of this our realm.[41]

This is much the best account of the events of 9 March, and it comes from Mary herself. She sent it to her ambassador in Paris, James Beaton – 'that proud prelate', as Knox called him – who was another of her loyal and 'special servants'.[42] The nephew of the Cardinal Beaton, murdered by Knox's friends at St Andrews twenty years before, Beaton was a determined foe of the Calvinists. Consecrated Archbishop of Glasgow in 1552, he fled to France on the outbreak of the Reformation. And there as best he could for the rest of his long life he worked for and cherished the cause of the Queen of Scots. Her dispatch, which was dated 15 March 1566, was effectively an exercise in public relations, designed to bring Catholic opinion to her side, in Spain and at the Vatican, but above all to mobilise her friends in France.

Whether designed for publication, or not, her letter still gives a vivid description of the murder, in her own words, as she remembered and dictated them just a few days later.

But by then she had not even yet quite plumbed the depth of Darnley's treachery, or realised that he was to betray her, and so was happily ignorant of all that the leaders of the coup had done to bind him to their side.

> as we suppose because of his facility, and the subtle means of the lords aforesaid, he condescended to advance the pretended religion published here, to put the rebels in their homes and possessions which they had of before, and but our knowledge, grant to them a remit of all their trespasses. The said rebels and their favorites promised they would further him to the crown matrimonial, give him the succession thereof, and ware their lives in all his affairs; and if any would usurp contrary to his authority, they should defend the same to their uttermost power, not excepting our own person.[43]

Nevertheless, these legal niceties to justify the murder were to do him little good.

Mary told Beaton to circulate her account as widely as possible, and wrote a personal postscript to the letter in her own hand.[44] He recognised the importance of the news, and arranged for it to be translated into Latin. It was then published at Louvain in the Netherlands, so that soon most of literate Europe could read the extraordinary story.

TWELVE

The English Exult

David is Dispatched and Dead.

(Bedford to Cecil, 11 March 1566)

Sir William Cecil knew all about the plot to kill Rizzio. A list of the conspirators lingered in his papers and ended up in the Salisbury archives at Hatfield House, where it is headed by the names of the Scots lords concerned, Morton, Lindsay and Ruthven. Both the English military commander in the north, and his agent, Randolph, had kept him in the picture. And they both knew that the fatal contracts were now subscribed, the Italian interloper was to be struck down, and approximately when the coup d'état was to erupt.

Francis Russell, the Earl of Bedford, commanded the English garrison in the formidable border fortress town of Berwick. The

Russells were a family who had prospered greatly under King Henry VIII, and Bedford, a doughty Elizabethan soldier, was now responsible for the defence of the Anglo-Scottish frontier as Warden of the East March. Thomas Randolph had just joined him in Berwick after his expulsion from Edinburgh in disgrace. It was a useful place from which to stay in contact with the network of agents who kept him (and his alter ego 'Mr Barnaby') in touch with events as they unfolded in the Scottish capital. Now they both sent word south that the insurrection was about to explode. This is the precise language these high officials used on 8 March – that is, only twenty-four hours before the assassination.

Touching the attempts and enterprises to be done in Scotland of which we wrote to you in our last, we see them now grow near unto that point that they that are the entreprisers intend to bring them unto.

The Earl of Argyll and Morton have accorded unto all, and subscribed with the other: Morton is presently at Edinburgh, and Argyll will be there tomorrow.

My Lord of Moray is written for, and his whole company, safe conduct sent unto them, and commandment to the Lord Home and his friends to receive them and convey them to the King [that is Darnley], which he hath accepted.

Tomorrow my Lord of Moray, and his men, will be in this town; upon Sunday at night in Edinburgh; but that which is intended shall be executed before his coming there – We mean upon him whom you know – and so will there proceed to the rest, as time and opportunity will serve.

We advertise your honours thereof to communicate to Her Majesty as seems most convenient.[1]

So by then they knew most of the facts. They were aware there were 'attempts or enterprises to be done in Scotland', and were well briefed on the movements of the leading conspirators, in particular that Morton would be mustering his Douglas kinsmen in Edinburgh, and that Argyll and the Campbells were to gather there on the morrow. And at the same time, 'My Lord of Moray', the ambitious bastard brother of the Queen of Scots, who had long ago pledged his loyalty to the English state, was on his way north from Newcastle. Before he left, he wrote to Cecil, to tell him that he and his men expected 'to find ourselves at home shortly', and that his friendship had always been 'a special leaning stick' to him.[2] An English cavalry squadron escorted Moray to the border, and then handed him over to the Scots Warden of the East March, Lord Home. Home, hitherto a loyal servant to the Queen of Scots, was now in opposition too, perhaps jealous of Bothwell's growing influence near his ancestral lands.

Both Bedford and Randolph knew the storm was about to burst. This was to be just before Moray reached Edinburgh; and they used the ambiguous words 'to be executed before his coming there. We mean upon him whom you know' to describe Rizzio's approaching doom. What is not so clear is whether Queen Elizabeth herself knew about the plot. She may have been told there was 'a matter of no small consequence intended in Scotland', but Cecil was far too clever to force the details on her,[3] even though Randolph and Russell gave him discretion to do so, in their advice that 'we advertise your honours to communicate all this to Her Majesty, as seems most expedient to your wisdom'.[4]

In a another letter dated 11 March, Bedford also said that Moray was well aware of the various combinations in hand to dispose of the Italian adventurer, and that he knew where his loyalties lay, for he had 'acknowledged Her Majesty's great goodness, which he will never forget, but requite as best he may'.[5]

When the news of the coup's success reached him three days later, he wrote gleefully that Rizzio was indeed 'dispatched, and dead'.[6] And he showed no false sorrow at the information, since he considered Rizzio to be an 'enemy' to his faith, and a threat to 'the amity of these two realms'.[7]

So, David Rizzio was to die, as a sacrifice on the altar of the new Protestant religion, as a danger to peace on the Anglo-Scottish Border, and as a threat to the incipient 'amity', or *entente cordiale*, between the two kingdoms. Moray and his friends, 'the Protestant

Lords', in combination with Morton and his Douglas kinsmen, shared these sentiments to the full. The happy outcome was to be a puppet kingdom whereby Scotland was preserved free from hostile control, be it French, Spanish or Papal, and blessed with a Reformed church.

These then are the very words, which Bedford used on 11 March to give news of the murder. The language is a little diffuse, and full of Tudor circumlocution, but there is no doubting the meaning of the chilling phrase he used to confirm that 'certain advertisement is come that David is dispatched, and dead'. He said that Moray and the other 'Protestant Lords' had reached Edinburgh safely, that the operation was successful and that it had been put into effect without overt English assistance. And he promised more news in his next letter: 'The manner, and circumstances I hope to report in my next.' He went on to say that he hoped the removal of the Rizzio threat would bring peace to the borders. Conscious of a job well done, he also asked to be relieved of his post as Warden by St George's Day, so he could come and pay his respects at Court.

Yesterday morning Moray and the other lords entered Scotland, and went that night to Edinburgh. They were met not far from hence by Lord Home and so conveyed thither.

Moray at his departing, acknowledged Her Majesty's great goodness, which he will never forget, but requite as best he may. They count to find great aid, and so things will fall out in more open sort than as yet.

So, if you there handle things well, now therefore is the time to step in foot, if it please Her Majesty. . . .

Since the writing hitherto, certain advertisement is come that David is dispatched, and dead.

That it should so be you have heard before.

The manner, and circumstances I hope to report in my next.

In the meantime, since so great an enemy to religion, and the amity of these two realms is now taken away, I have greater hope of peace on these borders, and heartily pray that you will mean that I will be spared from this charge against St George's Day to come up, and do my duty to Her Majesty.

I sent Her Majesty's letter to Edinburgh, two or three days since by a captain here, but these broils I think have letted the answer.[8]

Once further and better particulars of the assassination crossed the border two days later, Bedford, ever the realist, immediately sent them on to his masters. He confirmed that 'David [that is, Rizzio], as I wrote to you in my last letters, is slain'; and that he was not the only victim.[9] And Darnley, whom he scornfully refers to as 'that King', had duly welcomed Moray home. There was to be no more talk of forfeiture proceedings against the property and estates of the rebel lords. Moray was now safe, both in his faith and in his lands.

And Rizzio was not the only victim. At least two other prominent Catholics perished in the sectarian violence that struck Edinburgh that night.

One of those killed with him was the Dominican priest Friar John Black, who was now back in Edinburgh and in high favour at court. Now he was assaulted again, but this time not openly in the High Street as in January, nor at Holyrood Palace among the Queen and her entourage, but asleep in his lodgings, where he was found in bed with a mistress – 'his woman', as Randolph complacently reported in a separate dispatch.[10] When Rizzio was killed, 'that same night one Friar Black was slain in his bed. This is he that was caught in the Castle chapel with his woman.'[11] Bedford confirmed it: 'at the same time was also slain by like order, one Friar Black, a rank Papist, and a man of evil life, whose death was attempted by another before, and he stricken and sore hurt.'[12]

William Kerr, the Abbot of Kelso, was the other Catholic priest murdered that evening. Unlike Fr Black, Knox, Buchanan and the other Protestant historians found little evil to say of him.

The English ambassador was also delighted to confirm on 13 March that Rizzio was really dead: 'Since the last act committed upon David, which now I am able to verify to be certain.'[13]

His testimony is unequivocal, but, of course, he wrote as a committed Protestant. And his correspondence about the business only proves yet again the belligerent faith that permeated the higher ranks of the Elizabethan administration.

Her ministers hated Rizzio, and so too did John Knox. Knox's detestation ran even deeper. He wrote up the story two or three years later in his *History of the Reformation in Scotland*, where he depicted the murder with rude enthusiasm.[14] He justified the killing, insulted poor Davie as a 'poltroon and vile knave' and heaped praise on the participants with his usual vigorous language. This is what he said:

> To let the world understand in plain terms what we mean, that great abuser of this Commonwealth, that poltroon and vile knave Davie, was justly punished, the ninth day of March in the year of God 1566 for abusing the Commonwealth, and for his other villainies, which we list not to express, by the counsel and hands of James Douglas, Earl of Morton; Patrick, Lord Lindsay; and the Lord Ruthven, with others, assisters in their company. Who all, for their just acts and most worthy of all praise, are now unworthily left of their brethren, and suffer the bitterness of banishment and exile.[15]

What other motives were there for the killing? Darnley was jealous, the Protestants were outraged by the Italian's ascendancy, and the English just wanted him out of the way. Simple envy of his new wealth was yet another reason for him to be disposed of. Darnley, in particular, was driven by private demons, which intermingled with his own ambitions. He thought himself deceived by his wife, had little interest in the unborn child growing in her womb, and was easily led on by Rizzio's rivals, men more intelligent than himself, to revenge his imagined wrongs by this brutal deed. The pressures behind the rest are more interesting.

The first and most obvious beneficiaries who stood to gain from the murder were Moray and his colleagues, 'the Protestant Lords'.

They saved their estates from confiscation, and put an end to impoverished exile. Now they could come back to enjoy their rents, and also profit from their belief that they had saved the new faith from Catholic reaction. The Church reformers, and those nobles who had embraced religious reform, or secured grants of the old Church lands, also supported the revolution, which ended any threat to their new possessions. Family and clan loyalties ran deep. Many of the lesser barons, vassals and other followers of the great houses, such as Douglas or Hamilton, were glad to help their chiefs remove 'Seigneur Davie', a man not of their class, foreign in every sense, an immigrant Catholic and a person who lacked the skills necessary to incorporate himself into their clan structures. He deserved his violent end.

Ruthven's justification was significant. 'This man, Rizzio, was mean, base, an enemy to the nobility, and a shame to herself, and destruction to her country.'[16]

The cold hand of death, when it touched the secretary, came quickly and unexpectedly. Surprise, a brief moment of terror, pain, shock and then finis. We have already seen Mary's account of the murder as she told it to her ambassador in France. We are lucky to have another account of it, in a letter she dictated just six days later to her 'cousin and good sister', Elizabeth of England.[17]

By then she had fled the scene of horror and ridden hard for almost twenty miles to safe haven in Dunbar; across the rich and fertile lands that lie between the Lothian coast and the rising flanks of the Lammermuir Hills. Today Dunbar is only a brief stop on the main east-coast rail link between Edinburgh and London, but to the fugitive Queen it then represented security. It must have been an uneasy journey for a 24-year-old mother-to-be after such a trauma, but, once safe in Bothwell's castle, she was able to regroup her forces and discuss counter-measures. Once again, Bothwell had proved his loyalty and been a tower of strength throughout the crisis – so unlike Darnley. And there, early in the morning, hungry after the long ride through the night, she ordered fresh eggs to be brought to her, which she proceeded to scramble herself for breakfast. Refreshed, she then dictated her letter to the English Queen. It starts quietly, but then her increasing indignation begins to show through. Although sometimes naive, and not a little overtrusting in her judgements, she knew the arguments to use with her cousin. Moreover, she had still not appreciated quite how deeply her sister Queen and ministers were involved in the murder plot. But she did know that Elizabeth disliked any hint of rebellion against duly constituted authority, and shrewdly played on that sentiment.

She started with a complaint about 'the Protestant Lords', who had supported her elder brother, Moray, in last summer's rising. This had failed because the promised English support had never appeared. Nonetheless she expressed surprise that Elizabeth had even contemplated support for the 'wicked and mischievous enterprises' of these people, who were 'unworthy to be called subjects'.[18]

Yet even with all the strain and stress she kept to the usual diplomatic courtesies. So she addressed her sister Queen as her 'Good Sister', and then went on to complain how her enemies always misrepresented her actions. She was irritated by the brutal message Elizabeth had just sent, in the form of a 'strangely devised letter, which we lately had of you by your servant', which asked her to pardon Moray and his friends. She had been gravely misrepresented.

> After our earlier communications, we thought you knew the power of the evil and wrong reports and false narrations made unto you of us, by our rebels and such as have extremely offended us in this realm . . . Marvelling greatly how you can be so inclined rather to believe and credit the false speakings of those unworthy to be called subjects than of us, who are of your own blood.[19]

She had 'never sought nor made you occasion to use such rigour and menacing of us as you do'.[20] Though England might have seen fit to support her treacherous brother, she rejected Elizabeth's call to show him mercy, and explained why she had not done so as she reminded her sister sovereign of his crimes. And she defended her actions with honesty and candour. She was not a person who 'thinks one thing and does another', for, as she told Elizabeth: 'You will find us to be exactly as we say.' Their shared status as rulers meant they must always keep solidarity with each other.[21]

> But I would never do it, and marvel at you wanting us to forgive their offences, that no prince of the world should do, but rather offer us help to their punishment. Whereas you wrote to us that we, in our former letters, blamed them that keeps not their promises, but thinks one thing and does another, we would you should remember the same; for you will find us to be exactly as we say, whom we have always done as we have spoken and they to us the contrary.[22]

She then gave a brief account of the murder; how a body of armed men, led by Ruthven, had broken into the palace and killed her personal secretary, David Rizzio, in her very presence; 'slain our most special servant'.[23] And how afterwards she was held 'captive treasonably'.[24] Happily she succeeded in escaping to find shelter with the faithful Bothwell. As a result: 'We were constrained to escape straitlie about midnight out of our Palace of Holyroodhouse to the place where we are for the present, in the greatest fear of our life, and the evilest state that ever a prince on earth stood in.'[25]

All this while she was expecting a child, and suffering 'with frequent sicknesses and ill dispositions', because of the pregnancy. And now, waxing very indignant, she expressed her outrage that Elizabeth should even contemplate sending 'rescue for such traitors as have taken our house, slain our most special servant in our own presence, and thereafter held our proper person captive treasonably'.[26] Elizabeth herself never lacked fortitude, but even her hard Tudor heart could not but admire her cousin's courage in the crisis. Mary also suggested that the other great powers might 'help and support' her to defend 'us and our realm', and gave a broad hint that rebellion can be catching. The English Queen's own subjects might in their turn be tempted to copy the example of the rebellious Scots.

Here is what she said in full:

As your servant can show and report you the whole at length, which handling, and cruel using no Christian prince will allow, neither yourself as we believe.

Desiring you earnestly to let us understand if you be of mind to help and support them against us as you boist to do; for we are assured and not so far disproved, that other princes that will hear of our estate, considering the same, will favour us sameikle as to help and support us (if needs be) to defend us, and our realm, against all and quhatumsoever our said rebels, and them that treacherously maintain or assist them against us. Were it but only for your own example that the like offences be not committed by your own subjects likewise, in your realms.

Praying you therefore to remember your own honour, and how near of blood we are to you.

Thinking upon the word of God which commands, that all princes should favour and defend the just actions of other princes as well as their own, which we doubt not but you will do unto us, knowing you to be so just, as all the world may testify.

We thought to have written you this letter with our own hand, that thereby you might have better understand all our meaning and take more familiarity therewith; but of truth we are so tired and ill at ease, quhat throw riding of twenty miles in five hours of the night, as with the frequent sicknesses and ill dispositions by the occasion of our child, that we could not at this time, as we was willing to have done.

And thus, right excellent, right Mighty Princess, and our good Sister, We commit you to the protection of Almighty God.

Of our castle of Dunbar, the 15 day of March. and of our Reign the 14th year, 1566. Your right good sister, and cousin, Marie R.[27]

But within three weeks of her loyal servant's death she was back in Edinburgh in triumph. The ubiquitous Thomas Randolph had also managed to make his way back to the capital too. He soon learnt she was safe there, and described how she, 'who was wont to be carried in a chair by four of her guard, was yet able to ride a horse, though by her own account within six weeks of her time'.[28] Yet even now, despite all the bloodletting and horrors, she kept enough presence of mind to try to salvage any of her confidential papers left behind in the secretary's rooms. His jewellery and money had, of course, long gone, but she did manage to stop his valuable stable of horses being stolen by the Douglases. And she gave the small boy sent with orders to lead them off to a place of safety nine shillings for his trouble.

Shortly afterwards Morton and Ruthven, who were now themselves in turn fugitives from justice across the border, sent Cecil what his filing clerk called a 'discourse touching the killing of David' in which they did their best to explain their behaviour. They claimed that taking 'God to witness, they had no quarrel against David, but seeing his extreme dealing against their brethren, his counsel to suppress religion, break amity, etc, and finding the King to have so heich a quarrel with him', their conduct was fully justified.[29] Ruthven himself, despite mortal illness, found the strength to dictate a paper from his sick bed in Newcastle, which defended his actions, and in which he said that 'Davie never received a stroke in Her Majesty's presence'.[30] This was an attempt to rebut Mary's claim of 13 March that the murderers' pistols were pressed so hard against her pregnant stomach during the assassination, and their daggers were held so close to her body, that 'she felt the coldness of the iron'.[31] He also challenged other parts of Mary's story, but overall his account sounds a little implausible, and may be largely discounted.

But in the meantime official England could exult in the pleasing outcome of the murder of the Italian secretary.

THIRTEEN

The Queen's Lover?

He reproved her more sharply than her own husband would
dare.

(George Buchanan, *History of Scotland*, 1572)

Meanwhile Mary stayed in melancholy mood as winter gave
way to spring, despite all her courage just after the killing.
Her coming motherhood gave her some comfort, but she still missed
her Italian and mourned him greatly. And her conscience pricked her
that perhaps the tragedy was in part her fault, caused by her
treatment of her husband, which had driven him to such desperate
measures. Perhaps this explained the frenzied rage that made him
putty in the hands of Morton and Ruthven, devious and grim
personages, only too glad to encourage his jealous imaginings for

their own purposes. Yet such speculations can take us only so far; what is clear is that Darnley envied Rizzio's affectionate links with the Queen and, in turn, was made miserable by her neglect. In consequence, his suspicions began to fester that she really was deceiving him, and having a passionate affair with his friend. On at least one occasion he was said to have found her bedroom door bolted against him. His fierce hammerings and loud demands to be let in resulted, when the door was at last unlocked, in the emergence of a sheepish looking Rizzio, wearing only a shirt with a fur robe thrown over it, muttering excuses about state business that required Her Grace's urgent attention.[1]

Is there any truth in these charges? What is certain is that Darnley's paranoid fantasies affected them all, and in due time led on to catastrophe.

Rizzio was a powerful figure who reassured Mary by his presence. She may well have found him attractive. But did they become lovers? She enjoyed his company and counsel, and found in his proximity a reminder of her happy childhood at the Valois court. After the defeat of Moray, political business often brought them together. His position as private secretary called for constant close contact on official business, and the time they spent together unchaperoned meant in turn that gossip ran riot of a love affair between them.

At informal council meetings he marshalled his arguments well, and his views counted. (The story of how he debated policy in his deep and eloquent bass voice has already been told.) There he argued forcibly with the Queen and other councillors, and occasionally 'he reproved her more sharply than her husband would dare'.[2]

The suggestion that Mary seduced and took him as her lover was, of course, sensational. It certainly damaged her reputation then, and continues to interest us today. And the innuendoes were, of course, a godsend to her enemies. All the tittle-tattle enabled a clear comparison to be made between 'the Scottish Queen', with her rampant sexual promiscuity, and her chaste cousin Elizabeth, 'the Virgin Queen'. But the propaganda battle that opened then has never really closed down. Of course the talk of illicit romance soon reached Randolph and lost nothing in the telling. He made mention of it as early as October 1565, when he suggested that Mary's dislike for her elder brother Moray was because 'he understandeth some such secret part (not to be named for reverence sake) that standeth not well with her honour, which he so much detesteth being her brother'.[3] Later he even claimed that she had done her best to persuade Moray to make his wife give herself to Bothwell. And, of course, the rumours of all this royal debauchery beside the Forth did not take long to reach the inquisitive French ambassador in London, Paul de Foix.

Such assaults on Mary's reputation were nothing new. She was already something of a fashion icon during the brief months of her reign as Queen of France in 1559–60. Reports of her Parisian dress sense had soon crossed the Channel and were thought such a threat to the Elizabethan state that the ladies of England were specifically warned not to model themselves on her magical sense of flair and style.

It was yet another Protestant preacher, John Aylmer, who spun the official line against her. He wrote an attack on Knox, which was published in Strasbourg in 1559 and dedicated to Bedford and Leicester (then just Lord Robert Dudley). He may have disagreed with John Knox about the precise limits of female participation in government, but they were at one with each other on the wickedness of Mary Stewart's looks and the risk her tempting allure posed to a newly Protestant people. This particular cleric complained how English women were trying to ape her pretty haircuts and dress codes by 'setting up the attire of Scottish skirts'. Bowled over by her fashion sense, 'at the coming in of the Scottish Queen' they had begun 'to go unbridled, and with their hairs crowned, and curled, and double curled', whereas Elizabeth 'altered nothing, but to the shame of them all, kept her old maidenly sameness'.[4] The racy French foreigner, with her stylish cut and beautiful curled hair, represented danger. Surely Elizabeth, with her virginal certainty, was the better model to follow? Already the Boleyn's daughter was in the process of building up her icon as a Virgin, or Holy Maid, who was married only to her country.

The story that Mary took the Italian lover was embroidered and embellished by George Buchanan in his history of Scotland entitled *Rerum Scoticarum Historia*. This famous work was written sometime before 1582 and published soon after. In it he described in his rather flowery style how 'the Queen, not content with thus bringing David out from his obscurity, began in another way to ornament him with domestic favours'.[5] Buchanan was writing to blacken her reputation as woman and queen, and to justify her forced removal from her throne by Moray and his supporters.

Rizzio's good luck was not always in. It was his particular misfortune to have George Buchanan for an opponent.[6] Buchanan was a scholar of immense distinction whose reputation had crossed Europe. Academic institutions and universities as far apart as Bordeaux, Paris and Lisbon competed to share his learning. But the great humanist grew tired of life overseas and decided to come home to Scotland, where at first he was made much of at court and where he became a sort of unofficial poet laureate. The then unmarried young Queen got into the habit of reading Roman history with him after dinner while he corrected her Latin pronunciation. And he also penned the occasional laudatory ode in her honour, with the result that he soon enjoyed an annual income of £500 granted from the abbey estates at Crossraguel, Ayrshire.

However, Buchanan became steadily disenchanted by her lack of Protestant zeal. He formed a close association with Moray and his reform party, and so effectively went into opposition. Randolph, the English ambassador, was a former pupil and friend. He thought highly of his old tutor and encouraged him to switch his allegiance. And so, although Buchanan owed his clan loyalties to Lennox, he began to sympathise with Moray's views about his son's elevation to the throne, and Knox's concerns at the threat the Catholic resurgence posed to the Reformation settlement.

His political philosophy then advanced apace, so that he became a radical, if not a revolutionary. He claimed that Rizzio's administration was 'tyrannical' because Moray was forced into exile, and went on to argue that the people were always empowered to remove tyrants. Charges of tyranny were common in Italy, where the Machiavellian politics of city states like Florence provided many examples. It was an argument that was used to justify the Queen's forced abdication from the throne of Scotland a year later in 1567, and was a theory of sovereignty to be extended by Buchanan's disciples in later ages.

However, the evidence extant for the few brief months of Rizzio's ascendancy shows little sign of any real tyranny. There may have been the occasional difficulties about government finance, but there was no reign of terror. Even the forfeiture proceedings against Moray and his co-conspirators were undertaken with due parliamentary process. And there were no non-judicial murders or assassinations. The criminal law may seem barbaric to our modern eyes, but, at least in contrast to the Tower of London, when Rizzio was ascendant the rack master in Edinburgh Castle was not ever present to torment unhappy state prisoners with his instruments.

The accusations of misconduct by Mary sound particularly damaging when painted in Buchanan's vivid prose. The allegations, however, are not necessarily supported by the available facts, and may be briefly summarized: first, the close propinquity between the Queen and secretary; secondly, the late nights shared together; thirdly, the music and cards, and the intimate little suppers: all these gave the opportunity. Mutual sexual attraction did the rest. As Buchanan puts it:

> at last it came to this, that he, with only one or two others, was daily at her table. That the smallness of the place might in part lessen the scandal, the meals were sometimes served in a little chamber, and occasionally in David's own lodging. But this means of lessening scandal increased their ill fame, nourished suspicion, and furnished matter for unfavourable comment.[7]

Then there are the assertions by Lord Ruthven. He had tried to justify himself by saying the victim was being justly punished for having seduced Mary to his sexual pleasure. When afterwards she recalled the horrors of the night of the murder, she would say how Ruthven had told her to her face that the reason for his behaviour was because 'We was abused by the said David'.[8]

Buchanan used the arrangements to bury the favourite's body in the abbey at Holyrood to support his argument. These certainly infuriated the more militant Protestants. News of the so-called outrage speedily crossed Europe to the Calvinist citadel at Geneva, where the preachers revelled in the thought of an adulterous intimacy between the couple. Again, as Buchanan puts it:

> what stronger confession of adultery could be expected than that she should try to treat a base born villain, a man without principle or distinction in public service, as equal to her father and brothers in the final honour of burial. What was even more abominable, she placed the foul creature almost in the arms of Magdelene de Valois, so recently the Queen.[9]

The evidence against a fully consummated love affair between Queen and secretary is, however, even stronger. Perhaps the best testimony is from Seigneur Davie himself. In mortal agony, in fear of his life, as he was dragged from her side, he cried out in terror: 'Madama, io son morto!' (Madame, I am dead!).[10] This does not sound much like the cry of a lover, even an unrequited one. It sounds much more like a desperate, yet respectful, statement of his factual position, joined with a plea as from a servant to his employer, for protection – protection she was unable to give.

Then again there are the comments from Pietro Bizari. When the news of the murder reached him in France, he described to his readers how Rizzio was killed by men from the Douglas clan to protect their family honour; so on his analysis it was a *crime passionel* motivated by revenge. The allegation was that Rizzio was having an affair with a young Douglas lady, a royal maid of honour, and so a kinswoman of Morton, and with whom he 'had intimate amorous intercourse'.[11] Whatever the truth, it is clear the facts had become somewhat garbled on the way from Edinburgh to Lyons.

Finally, there is the statement by Mary herself after the birth of her son, Prince James. When the proud mother showed the child to her husband, the King, she said with all due solemnity: 'my Lord, here I protest to God, and as I shall answer to Him at the Great day of Judgement, this is your son, and no other man's son.'[12]

It is hard to believe in such a status-conscious society that the pregnant Queen, conscious of her royal position, keen to be accepted as heir to the English throne and well taught by her church, encouraged the embraces of any retainer – even this one, 'our most special servant'. Bothwell was to be different.

Rizzio never married. Perhaps the habit of celibacy enforced by his seminary days never left him so that he lived and died a virgin. The accounts of his sexual inclinations, as of his looks, are equally conflicting. It is also possible that he was homosexual, a way of life after all that was by no means unknown in Renaissance Italy.[13] The suggestion seems to be based on a comment by the early Scottish historian of the Presbyterian Church, David Calderwood. According to him, Rizzio became an intimate friend of Darnley very soon after the latter arrived in Scotland, when they were so close that 'they would lie sometimes in one bed together'.[14] Yet such nocturnal proximity does not necessarily prove Rizzio was gay, especially in the sixteenth century, when beds were rare and valuable items of furniture, and commonly shared, and even though it was not unusual for Protestant controversialists to accuse the Catholic clergy of homosexual behaviour.[15] Such information about his first sleeping arrangements that does survive, particularly Ruthven's sneer that he was so poor when he first reached Scotland that he had to sleep on a chest in the backstairs of Holyroodhouse, does not take the question forward either. And, even if he was gay, Mary still found his company amusing, unthreatening and a source of great comfort.

So the conclusion must be that it is unlikely Mary took him as her lover, let alone allowed him to father her son. Of course, if David Rizzio really did father the child she bore after her long and painful labour in the late morning of 19 June 1566, then all his descendants in the royal houses of Stewart, Hanover, Saxe Coburg Gotha and Windsor may claim him as an ancestor. Unfortunately, there is no available DNA evidence to prove the genetic case one way or the other.

Nonetheless the thesis seems a little tenuous. Only Kings Charles II and James VII and II among subsequent British monarchs have a slight Mediterranean appearance that might indicate Italian ancestry, but this may be more attributable to their undoubted descent from the Medicis of Florence, through their mother Queen Henrietta Maria, than to any links with the Rizzio family of Piedmont. However, the more bigoted Protestants remained unconvinced, and for long afterwards firmly believed that both these Stuart monarchs of the United Kingdom of Great Britain derived from Rizzio 'their Italian complexion and constitution, both of body and mind, spare and swarthy, cruel and crafty'.[16]

It appears much more likely that Darnley was the father of the infant Prince James. The calendar shows the baby must have been conceived, if carried to full term, around September 1565, when the crisis caused by Moray's rebellion was at its peak and her honeymoon was barely over. There was no reliable method of contraception in the sixteenth century, and she had made it quite clear during her wedding how keen she was to conceive and give Scotland an heir. The charge of a consummated affair between Queen and servant is based more on uncorroborated assertions and allegations from hostile sources than on strict proof.

The accusations of impassioned adultery by Mary with Rizzio seem to be based on attempts by his murderers to justify their actions, and were soon seized on by Protestant writers like Buchanan. And Cecil, of course, encouraged the propaganda, since it was very much in England's interest to belittle the Queen of Scots and her reputation. If they were true, then Rizzio's genetic legacy to the blood royal is extensive.

But the rumours continued to spread as the century drew to an end. It was this story about King James VI's paternity that led to the clamour of the Perth mob in the riots that followed the failure of yet another plot by the Ruthvens (now called Gowries) in August 1600.

Then the indignant crowd shouted that Rizzio was really the King's father, and shrieked at him disrespectfully, 'come down the Son of Seignor Davie, thou hast slain an honester man than thyself'. It led too to the French King Henry IV's famous joke a year or two later, when King James was trying to encourage an international reputation for wisdom, that he must indeed be the 'British Solomon', since he was the 'the Son of David' – that is, of David Rizzio.[17] James's many enemies among the extreme Presbyterian faithful went so far as to blame his strange and ugly features on his genetic inheritance from Rizzio. And so the legend continued into the later seventeenth century, when their preachers taught the poor persecuted Covenanters that the father of Mary's only son was 'her darling, Davie Rizzio, the Italian fiddler'. And 150 years later, well into the early years of young Queen Victoria's reign, historians were still arguing whether 'Mary, in her passion, avows and justifies her criminal connection with Rizzio', or whether, to the contrary, there was 'no evidence whatever of such an outrageous intercourse as that imputed to Queen Mary without the least foundation'.[18]

The murder of David Rizzio undoubtedly affected Mary's son, James. Whatever the truth about his paternity, it caused him long-term psychological damage, which is well evidenced by his notorious timidity in the face of cold steel. When at last he came to the English throne, on the death of Elizabeth thirty-seven years later, numerous old retainers appeared who clamoured to share in his good luck. One reminder of the past came in the form of a petition from an elderly knight, Sir Anthony Standen. He said that he had come to Scotland as a young cupbearer in Darnley's train of servants and supporters and had actually been present on that fatal evening when Ruthven and his men so rudely broke into Mary's supper party.

Standen sounds like a rather decayed Falstaffian figure. He claimed that he was actually standing beside the Queen when the assault began; as he put it, when she was 'very great bellied with the King's Majesty, now our sovereign lord'.[19] He also claimed to have saved her and the baby from harm when he wrested his dagger from one of the murderers, and that his services were recognised by an immediate knighthood, but sadly that he later fell on hard times.

King James certainly knew all about the Rizzio murder. A good Scot with a long memory, he hated the Rizzio conspirators and kept up a ferocious vendetta against the surviving members of Ruthven's family, the Gowries, to punish them for their part in the proceedings. When the Gunpowder Plot was discovered in November 1605, he referred to the assassination in the speech that he gave to the English Parliament. His words then echoed the pleadings in Standen's petition, as he gave thanks for having survived the many dangers that had beset him all his life, 'even as I may justly say, before my birth, and while I was in my mother's belly'.[20]

But Seigneur Davie's sad and dramatic end did not only affect King James. The shadow of his cruel murder lingered long over the Scots people.

And, in response to the delicate question as to whether there was an actual liaison between Queen and secretary, the answer must surely be that good old verdict that is well known to Scots criminal law, 'Not Proven'.

FOURTEEN

The Legend of Rizzio

Our most Special Servant.

(Mary to Elizabeth, March 1566)

News of the murder spread quickly. It did not take long for the French and Spanish emissaries in London to be on the scent. And, keen for more information, the French envoy, de Foix, was able to give Catherine de' Medici an early account.[1] Rather tongue in cheek, he told her that the English Secretary of State had sent him an official communication about it. He proposed to accept his explanation that the killing was just the usual sort of thing that went on in Scotland, a *crime passionel*, carried out by a jealous husband and supported by his friends. So he duly replied to Cecil that he 'was horrified by the content of his letter, as nothing could be more

175

dreadful than that a deformed, and base menial should be caught in the act of adultery, and slain by her husband'.[2]

A few days later the Spanish ambassador, Guzman de Silva, called for a boat. He wanted to be taken downstream to call on Elizabeth at her palace by the river in Greenwich. The ostensible purpose of the audience was to discuss the latest news from North America, where Spanish forces had just destroyed a French beachhead on the new-found land of Florida. During their talk Elizabeth showed her ready wit, and teased him about the success of the Spanish riposte. She joked that 'she intended to send to conquer Florida' herself, had not the Spaniards beaten her to it, but 'was greatly pleased at the success of the voyage'.[3]

After this exchange of pleasantries, they got down to business. De Silva said that he had heard affairs in Scotland were not going well. Elizabeth was in good form. She was never averse to tweaking King Philip's moustache, and replied that 'so many things had happened, it would take three hours to tell me. Mary was in great trouble.'[4] Mary had 'now sent an envoy with a very humble letter, and she was determined to help her'.[5] By now she knew all about Rizzio's murder, and enjoyed teasing the Spaniard about it. She said playfully that, if she had a husband who had attacked her as Mary's had, 'she would have taken his dagger, and stabbed him with it, but she did not want your Majesty to think she would do this to the Archduke, if he came'.[6] The reference was to the Archduke Charles of Austria, the current Hapsburg candidate for her hand.

She had dressed for the occasion with great care, and wore a rich gold chain that had on it a medallion portrait of Mary, which hung down to her waist. As she lowered her eyes to look at it sorrowfully, she asked the envoy what he thought of the likeness, 'saying she was very sorry for the Queen's troubles, and for the murder of the Secretary'. It was a bravura performance by a great actress, but de Silva was not taken in. As he told Philip, 'a good Catholic tells me the plot for the murder of the Secretary was ordered from here. The Queen [Elizabeth] helped the conspiracy to the extent of 8000 crowns.'[7]

The assassination was soon news throughout Europe. In Brussels, Philip's viceroy, the Cardinal de Granville, summed the business up succinctly when he learnt of the Scottish turmoil, and heard that the Queen of Scotland's secretary was dead. 'Il y a révolte nouvelle en Ecosse, ou l'on tué le secretaire de la Royne, qui estait pour l'ancienne religion, et dit on que le Roi se met à la nouvelle.'[8]

The leaders of the divided Christian churches were equally intrigued by the news, though this took some time to cross the Alps, so that it was not until May that the Pope, Pius V, could write to Mary and congratulate her on having survived the dreadful event. He was delighted that her devotion to the true faith enabled 'God to graciously deliver her from the hands of the wicked'.[9] He was also shrewd enough not to be taken in by Elizabeth's protestations of innocence, and was well aware of her part in the conspiracy. He described her as 'She, by whose endeavours these wicked plots against your life, and throne were contrived'.[10] By now the new Papal Legate to Scotland was on his way there, and he had already summed up the whole catastrophe with a shrewd assessment of Darnley's part in it. He was

> an ambitious inconstant youth, and would like to rule the realm, which was the object of the plot he hatched a few weeks back when he made the Rebels come secretly to court with the purpose of getting himself crowned King, as has been discovered from the last declaration of Lord Ruthven, who died lately in England. It was he who got the Rebels to murder poor David Rizzio, the Queen's Piedmontese Secretary. He wanted all his wife's officials to depend on himself.[11]

Pope Pius saw the Queen of Scots as a co-belligerent in the fight against heathen and heretic. And he would make what personal sacrifices he could to help her. He would even stint his table and household expenses 'in order to have the more wherewith to help the Queen', as he told her envoy to the Vatican, the Bishop of Dunblane.

He asked the bishop to tell Mary that 'we are resolved that we ourselves, and our household, should suffer want rather than you'.[12] It was a gracious gesture. From now on his wines would be of inferior growth and his household staff cut back, if by such economies more funds could be found to recover her kingdom to the faith.

On the other side of the religious divide, the Protestants were greatly cheered by the butchery. The Reformers hated Rizzio, since, rightly or wrongly, they saw in him one of the Scottish Queen's chief Catholic advisers. His overthrow was therefore a cause for celebration throughout Protestant Europe, and made for much joy within reformed circles, sentiments that were especially strong among Calvin's disciples. When the Swiss Reformer, Théodore de Bèze, heard the details, he wrote immediately to tell his brother Reformer, Bullinger, in Zurich all about it.[13] He returned to the subject three weeks later, by when they knew all about the popular protests at the interment of the secretary's body in the royal mausoleum at Holyrood.[14]

The honoured funeral and burial in the abbey precincts were arranged on the Queen's orders. How long his corpse rested there is uncertain. In due time her own mortal remains were removed from their first place of burial in Peterborough Cathedral to Westminster Abbey. And likewise with his. At some stage after her forced abdication on 26 July 1567 his bones were dug up and reinterred with due respect a little way up the Royal Mile in the town cemetery of the old Canongate kirk. The gravestone may still be seen near the south wall of the church there in Edinburgh, complete with a small inscription above, which states: 'Tradition says that this is the grave of David Rizzio 1533–1566 transported from Holyrood.' The present Canongate church was built in the reign of King James VII and II during the seventeenth century, long after Rizzio's murder, but the gravestone certainly predates the church. If the remains beneath are really those of David Rizzio, it is quite fitting that they should still rest here deep within Scottish soil in an ancient churchyard maintained by the Church of Scotland, and in the city of Edinburgh that he loved.

The Elizabethan bishops of the Church of England could also smile when they heard of the killings. The Anglican Bishop of Norwich, Parkhurst, enjoyed writing to Zurich to tell the Swiss Reformer Bullinger of the death of 'Signor Davie, skilled in necromancy, and in great favour with the Queen of Scots'.[15] Such accusations of necromancy, or witchcraft, were common forms of abuse then, when periodic waves of judicial paranoia meant that witches were routinely burnt. Mary herself once alleged that Ruthven had consorted with warlocks, but in Rizzio's case the charge seems quite unjustified, though the stigma lingered. A generation later one of his old servants was even prosecuted on a charge of witchcraft – the allegation being that he was that rare commodity, a male witch.[16]

The Bishop of Norwich included a rather bad piece of doggerel with his letter about the notorious Dominican priest, Friar John Black, another of the victims on 9 March. The Bishop played in a rather racist way with the friar's name and misspent past, saying how:

> He took a Black whore, to wash his Black socks,
> Committing with her Black fornication.[17]

But to be fair to the Bishop of Norwich, the unfortunate friar did have a reputation for loose living.

The Bishop of London, Edmund Grindal, was rather more dubious about the long-term effects of all the violence on the success of the Reformation in Scotland. On 27 August 1566 he also wrote to Bullinger to tell him:

> Things in Scotland are not so well established as we would wish. The churches indeed still retain the pure confession of the Gospel; but the Queen of Scotland seems to be doing all in her power to extirpate it. She has lately given orders that six or seven Popish masses should be celebrated daily in her Court, where all are admitted who choose to attend; whereas she was till now content with only one mass, and that a private one, no Scotsman being allowed to be present.[18]

When Pope Pius V at last lost patience with Elizabeth and excommunicated her with the papal bull *Regnans in Excelsis* in 1570, episcopal English indignation knew no bounds. It was yet another Anglican bishop, John Jewel of Salisbury, who preached, and later published, a powerful sermon on the effrontery, 'A View of a Seditious Bull', in which he emphasised Rizzio's political importance and claimed the Pope himself had arranged for him to come to power in Mary's kingdom. The bishop argued the Scots example was an awful warning for the English. They must 'look somewhat abroad, and see what worthy wights the Pope hath placed in the councils of kings, and so let us be advised by the harms of our neighbours. Did he not place one David Rizzio so high in Scotland that he took upon him to rule the Queen there, and sought all means to disgrace, and disquiet the nobles, and therefore was slain in the Queen's presence?'[19]

The answer to the bishop's rhetorical question should be a firm no. The Pope did not put Rizzio in power, but political sermons are never a place for strict historical accuracy.

The legend of Rizzio as a demon figure to the Protestants was already beginning to take shape. The Elizabethan ecclesiastical and political establishments feared his influence, thought his religious and political policies threatened their Anglican supremacy, and were overjoyed at his fate. So too did John Knox, but Knox's antipathy ran even deeper. The great preacher naturally had his views about the assassination. He did not actually participate in it, but he knew most of the conspirators, and on the evidence available must be considered to some degree an accessory thereto. Shortly afterwards he slipped away from Edinburgh, and took shelter with sympathisers over in Strathclyde, perhaps fearful he might suffer in any counter-revolution.

Like an Old Testament prophet, Knox was not a man who shirked confrontation. In his person were embodied the rights of the new Reformed Church to express God's opinions on the issues of the day. So it is little surprise that he was an enthusiastic supporter of Ruthven and his friends. And he pondered on the details with relish.

To Knox the murder was entirely justified. He saw it as a kind of holy sacrifice, sanctified by the special Lenten fast already ordered by the General Assembly of the Kirk. His belief that this was an entirely proper, almost quasi-judicial, punishment on an evildoer stayed with him for the rest of his life. And when, six years later, he sat down to compose yet another polemic against the Catholics, he refers to the incident in his history of the times as a 'judgement', in which he recalled returning to his manse in the High Street 'immediately after I was called back from exile by the Kirk of Edinburgh, after David's judgement'.[20]

The success of the Reformation in Scotland was now assured, notwithstanding the Bishop of London's reservations, although there were to be much more turmoil and civil war, involving such dramatic incidents as the murder of the King (that is, Darnley), Mary's abduction, rape and marriage to Bothwell, abdication, imprisonment, escape and final flight into England, before the position became clearer. In the meantime Rizzio was not forgotten, least of all by Mary.

The 'tortoise jewel' is the tangible evidence here, given to Mary as a token of his love and in appreciation for her support. The jewel was a rich mix of ten rubies intermingled with pearls, the whole sculpted in the form of a tortoise.[21] Mary was so fond of the piece that, when she came to make her will in anticipation of the dangers of childbirth, she included the tortoise jewel as a specific bequest. In the event that she, and her child, failed to survive, it was to pass to Joseph Rizzio, David Rizzio's 18-year-old younger brother, who had just reached Scotland. From Berwick Randolph had noted his arrival on 25 April 1566: 'David's brother Joseph, who came through this way with Mauvissière, unknown to any here, is become secretary in his brother's place.'[22] Three other jewels, together with the tortoise jewel, were also left to Joseph with a cryptic injunction, endorsed on the margin of the paper in the Queen's own hand, that he was to do with them as she had instructed.[23] This may suggest she hoped to establish some form of secret trust for the Rizzio family. And she also appointed the rather inexperienced Joseph to be secretary in his brother's place. He was not so clever as his older brother, and made little mark in state affairs, though he was later to be one of those accused of helping to kill the King at Kirk o'Fields.

Every mother-to-be in Elizabethan Britain inevitably faced great risks at delivery. Her will contained a long list of wishes for the disposal of her property and jewellery, among her family and retainers, should she, and her baby, both die. The testamentary document gives a good insight into her feelings just a few weeks after the murder, and as her pregnancy was close to term. It is interesting to see how she gave numerous bequests to Darnley, which may have meant that all was not quite lost between them. No less than twenty-six pretty pieces were left him, including a watch studded with diamonds and rubies, and the diamond ring that he had given her on their wedding day, which shows perhaps that by then they were to some degree reconciled. It certainly evidences her capacity to forgive.[24]

But she continued to be irritated by English claims to superiority. A rather bathetic example was the incident of the parrot – a present from an admirer in France. A disrespectful border official at Berwick had stolen the bird, and her correspondence was also rifled. Cecil pretended to take the theft seriously, and gave the new English ambassador, who was taking over from Randolph, detailed instructions on how to answer any complaints from the Queen about her loss.

But the birth of a son and heir, Prince James, was Mary's great triumph. Her shrewd and experienced courtier James Melville was waiting impatiently in Edinburgh Castle with instructions to bring the news to London post-haste immediately the baby arrived. He duly appeared between the hours of 10 and 11 on the summer's morning of 19 June 1566. Within the hour Melville was astride his mount and heading south. By nightfall he was at Berwick; four days'

hard riding saw him safely in London, where he put up with his brother Robert Melville, the Scots envoy at the English court. They told Cecil the good news and were asked down to Greenwich, where Elizabeth was at the revels, 'in great merriness, and dancing after supper', at the palace, when 'Cecil whispered in her ear the news of the prince's birth'. She immediately stopped the dance, and sighed sadly to her ladies 'that the Queen of Scotland was lighter of a fair son, while she was but a barren stock'.[25]

However, the Scottish Queen had the good sense not to crow too much to either Elizabeth or Darnley. She asked Elizabeth to be godmother to the child. The Duke of Savoy was also a godparent. And, when she introduced the baby to his putative father, she emphasised that the child was his, and did her best to make sure he accepted paternity. She may have cherished Rizzio's memory in her heart, but she was concerned to underline Darnley's responsibilities as the new father.

Her enemies were already circulating rumours about the child's provenance, and doubtless it was this slur on his legitimacy that she was trying to rebut. The suggestion that Rizzio was really the father of the royal baby was already current gossip among the Protestant faithful, and had been picked up by Randolph in the increasingly febrile atmosphere that pervaded Edinburgh. Some months before he had even written to Leicester, apparently to endorse the story, full of foreboding of a time of which he said: 'Woe is me for you, when David's son shall be a King of England'[26] – a forecast that was suprisingly accurate about the sex and bright future of the foetus Mary carried, but one that was open to challenge as to his parentage.

There was a pleasant irony too in the fact that de Moretto, with a strong delegation from Savoy, came back to represent the duke at the sumptuous baptism ceremonies held for Prince James in the chapel at Stirling Castle later that year, 1566. Rizzio might have been dead, but he was by no means forgotten. De Moretto arrived just too late for the service but was there for the later celebrations. And on his way back through London he stayed again with the Spanish ambassador, now Guzman de Silva, who described his visit to King Philip afterwards. 'Moretto has not yet left. He told me he asked Mary to let him see Darnley. She told him she would not. She did not think Darnley would be pleased to see Moretto in consequence of the Secretary's murder, he, the Secretary, having been a servant of Moretto.'[27]

But the final triumph for Savoyard diplomacy was the birth of that male heir to the royal mistress Seigneur Davie had so faithfully served.

Postscript

The legend of David Rizzio lingered long after his death. There are many Shakespearian echoes to his story that were kept alive long afterwards by most of the great arts – in opera, folk song, theatre and painting. The Romantic age gloried in his dramatic end and his love for the Queen of Scots. Charlotte Brontë, for one, knew the story well, and in *Jane Eyre* makes Mr Rochester flatter a female admirer, anxious to hear him sing, by asking, 'Who would not be the Rizzio to so divine a Mary?'

In many ways he was a classic royal favourite. He was petted, enriched and over-promoted. His achievements may seem small, and his promise unfulfilled, buried like his bones in the old abbey at Holyrood, and with his brief moment of glory lost to history. But the story of his rise, his intimate position so close to the Queen, the manner of his death and his exotic butterfly-like character live on, whether or not her son, King James VI, and her further posterity are really able to trace their descent from him.

Nevertheless, the treachery that caused his death, founded in the hostile propaganda of the Protestant reformers, obscures his services to Scotland.

A fair judgement about him might be that, though sometimes brave and always true to his mistress, he was promoted beyond the reach of his abilities and was soon out of his depth in the turbulent political currents of Elizabethan Britain. In particular, the stark pressures of the Reformation on individual issues of conscience were too much for him. His fatal charm combined with the treacherous political situation accounted for his fate.

But he died a Scottish patriot who in his short life stood up for the independence of his adopted country.

Notes

Prologue

1. George Buchanan, *History of Scotland*, vol. II (Edinburgh, 1752), p. 309.
2. *CSP Scotland*, vol. II, *1563–1569*, ed. Joseph Bain (Edinburgh, 1900), p. 222.

Chapter One

1. The poet Buchanan composed an elaborate poem, an epithalamium about the marriage, to advertise the delights of Scotland to the French. It has 283 sonorous Latin verses.
2. Sir James Melville, *The Memoirs of Sir James Melville of Halhill*, ed. Gordon Donaldson, Folio Society (London, 1969), p. 36.
3. Michel Duchein, at the Collogue IRIS, Institut du monde anglophone, Paris 75006, 21 June 2001.
4. Lord Herries, *Historical Memoirs of the Reign of Mary Queen of Scots, and a Portion of the Reign of King James VI* (Edinburgh, 1836), p. 54.
5. Prince A. Labanoff (ed.), *Lettres, instructions et mémoires de Marie Stuart, Reine d'Écosse* (London, 1844), vol. VII, p. 89: 'Primo bastardo di Scotia', as Mary described him in her dispatch to Cosimo, Grand Duke of Tuscany, dated 8 October 1566.
6. *CSP Simancas*, p. 222, Quadra to the Duchess of Parma, 3 January 1562.
7. David Calderwood, *History of the Kirk in Scotland*, vol. I, Woodrow Society (Edinburgh, 1843), p. 204.
8. *The Works of John Knox*, ed. David Laing, Woodrow Society (Edinburgh, 1848–64), vol. II, p. 285; 'The Devil, now finding his reins loosed, ran forward in his course; and the Queen took upon her greater boldness than she and Baal's bleating priests durst have attempted before. For upon All Hallows day they blended up their Mass with all mischievous solemnity' (*ibid.*).
9. *CSP Milan*, 22 May 1527. King Henry was away hunting near Windsor, but wanted 'the usual diligence shown with regard to the divorce' (p. 484).
10. Father J.H. Pollen, *Papal Negotiations with Mary Queen of Scots*, Scottish History Society (Edinburgh, 1901), 30 November 1561. Monsignor Commendone writing from Brussels to Cardinal Borromeo, with the latest news from the Spanish Ambassador in England. 'Monsieur de Foix, sent by the Queen Mother of France, and Monsignor Morretta from the Duke of Savoy, have reached London, and after visiting the Queen of England, desired to go on to Scotland, but separately' (p. 68).

11. *CSP Simancas*, p. 219.
12. *Ibid.*, p. 282.
13. *Ibid.*, p. 279.
14. *CSP Scotland*, vol. I, *1547–1563*, ed. Joseph Bain (Edinburgh, 1898), p. 579.
15. Randolph wrote copious secret dispatches from Edinburgh; not just to Sir William Cecil, the principal Secretary of State, but also to Lord Leicester and the other members of the English Privy Council, most of which survive and are printed in the Calendars of State Papers. They give a vivid picture of life at Mary's northern court.
16. Sir James Balfour Paul (ed.), *Accounts of the Lord High Treasurer of Scotland*, vol XI (Edinburgh, 1916), p. 94.
17. *CSP Scotland*, vol. I, p. 532.
18. *The Works of John Knox*, ed. Laing, vol. II, p. 294.
19. Joseph Robertson (ed.), *Inventaires de la Royne Descosse Douairiere de France*, Bannantyne Club (Edinburgh, 1863), p. 130.

Chapter Two

1. The works of Martin Luther when first printed had a German circulation of no less than 400,000 copies. Personal information given by Dr Gottfried Seebass of the Heidelberger Akademie der Wissenschaften, Conference of the Society for Reformation Studies, Cambridge, April 2001.
2. The Geneva Bible came to influence the consciences of both English Puritans and Scottish Covenanters alike. More than 140 editions were published in the eighty-four years between 1560 and 1644.
3. Iain Ross, *The Gude and Godlie Ballatis* (Edinburgh, 1939), p. 62.
4. *The Works of John Knox*, ed. David Laing, Woodrow Society (Edinburgh, 1848–64), vol. VI, p. xxi.
5. *Ibid.*, vol I, p. 149.
6. *Ibid.*, vol. II, p. 279.
7. T. Thomson and C. Innes (eds), *Acts of the Parliaments of Scotland* (Edinburgh, 1814–75), vol. II, p. 525; 'Long have we thirsted, dear Brethren to have notified unto the world for some of that doctrine which we professed, and for the which we have sustained infamy and danger. But such has been the rage of Satan against us, and against Christ Jesus his eternal verity lastly born amongst us which to this day and time has been granted unto us to clear our consciences as most gladly we would have done for, how we have been tossed a whole Serpent the most part of Europe (we suppose) does understand' (*ibid.*).
8. *Ibid.*, p. 527.
9. *Ibid.*, p. 534.
10. Prince A. Labanoff (ed.), *Lettres, instructions et mémoires de Marie Stuart, Reine d'Écosse* (London, 1844), vol. I, pp. 341 ff.
11. Historical Manuscripts Commission, *Calendar of the Manuscripts of the Most Hon. the Marquis of Salisbury KG etc. preserved at Hatfield House, Hertfordshire* (London, 1883), p. 262.
12. *Ibid.*

13. *The Works of John Knox*, ed. Laing, vol. II, p. 197.
14. *Ibid.*
15. Annie I. Cameron (ed.), *Warrender Papers*, vol. I, Scottish History Society (Edinburgh, 1931), p. 32.
16. *The Works of John Knox*, ed. Laing, vol. II, p. 277.

Chapter Three

1. Quoted in Conyers Read, *Mr Secretary Cecil and Queen Elizabeth* (London, 1955), p. 149.
2. *Ibid.*
3. *CSP Simancas*, p. 222, Quadra to the Duchess of Parma.
4. Read, *Mr Secretary Cecil and Queen Elizabeth*, p. 143.
5. Robert Keith, *History of the Affairs of Church and State in Scotland from the Beginning of the Reformation to 1568*, vol II, Spottiswoode Society (Edinburgh, 1845), p. 15.
6. Michael Lynch (ed.), *Mary Stewart, Queen in Three Kingdoms* (Oxford, 1988), p. xiii.
7. Historical Manuscripts Commission, *Calendar of the Manuscripts of the Most Hon. the Marquis of Salisbury KG etc. preserved at Hatfield House, Hertfordshire* (London, 1883), no. 595, p. 169, 11 January 1560.
8. *Ibid.*, no. 602, p. 173.
9. Quoted in Stephen Alford, *The Early Elizabethan Polity: William Cecil and the British Succession Crisis 1558–1569* (Cambridge, 1998), p. 75.
10. *CSP Scotland*, vol. II, *1563–1569*, ed. Joseph Bain (Edinburgh, 1900), p. 5, Randolph to Cecil, 10 April 1563.
11. Read, *Mr Secretary Cecil and Queen Elizabeth*, p. 184.

Chapter Four

1. David Calderwood, *History of the Kirk in Scotland*, vol. II, Woodrow Society (Edinburgh, 1843), p. 179.
2. *Ibid.*, p. 285.
3. *CSP Scotland*, vol. II, *1563–1569*, ed. Joseph Bain (Edinburgh, 1900), p. 144, Randolph to Cecil, 18 April 1565.
4. *The Works of John Knox*, ed. David Laing, Woodrow Society (Edinburgh, 1848–64), vol. II, p. 279.
5. *Ibid.*
6. *Ibid.*
7. John Aylmer (1521–94) was Bishop of London for eighteen years from 1576 to 1594. Preferment taught him to be a little more tactful on the subject of women rulers. Queen Elizabeth I once came to stay with him at Fulham Palace. She complained how the trees in the grounds had grown so high that they stopped her view of the River Thames flowing past her bedroom window. Much to the annoyance of the local residents, the Bishop immediately ordered the offending elms be cut down.

8. John Aylmer, *An harbour (Harborowe) for faithful and true subjects against the late blown blast concerning the Government of Women, wherein is confuted all such reasons as a Stranger of late made in that behalf, with a brief Exhortation to Obedience* (Strasbourg, 1559), [p. 52].

9. Sir James Balfour Paul (ed.), *Accounts of the Lord High Treasurer of Scotland*, vol. XI (Edinburgh, 1916), p. 102.

10. *Ibid.*, p. 158.

11. Mrs Agnes Strickland, *Life of Mary Queen of Scots*, vol. I (London, 1873), quoting A. Teulet, *Papiers d'état: Pieces et documents inédits ou peu connus relatifs à l'histoire d'Écosse au XVI siècle*, vol. II (Paris, 1859), p. 162.

12. 'The Queens potticarie gotte one of the Queens maydens, a Frenche woman in credyt and nere abowte Her Grace's self, with chylde. Thynkinge to have covered his fawlte with medicines, the child was slayne in the mother's bellie. They are both sent to prison' (*CSP Scotland*, vol. II, p. 30, Randolph to Cecil, 21 December 1563).

13. *Ibid.*, p. 33.

14. David Calderwood, *History of the Kirk in Scotland*, Woodrow Society (Edinburgh, 1843), vol. II, p. 164.

15. Ninian Winzet, included in *Certain Tractates for the Reformation of Doctrine and Manners in Scotland, together with the book of Fourscore Three Questions and a translation of Vincentius Lirensis*, Maitland Club (Edinburgh, 1835), p. 118.

16. Lady Antonia Fraser, 'The Religion of Mary, Queen of Scots', *Lambeth Palace Library Annual Review* (2000), pp. 55–64.

17. Winzet, in *Certain Tractates*, p. 118.

18. Calderwood, *History of the Kirk in Scotland*, vol. II, p. 266.

19. *The Works of John Knox*, ed. Laing, vol. II, p. 381.

20. *Ibid.*, p. 389.

21. *Ibid.*, p. 421.

22. Sir James Melville, *The Memoirs of Sir James Melville of Halhill*, ed. Gordon Donaldson (London, 1969), p. 43.

23. *Ibid.*

24. Lord Herries, *Historical Memoirs of the Reign of Mary Queen of Scots, and a Portion of the Reign of King James VI* (Edinburgh, 1836), p. 69.

Chapter Five

1. David Calderwood, *History of the Kirk in Scotland*, vol. II, Woodrow Society (Edinburgh, 1843), p. 248, 20 January 1564.

2. *CSP Scotland*, vol. II, *1563–1569*, ed. Joseph Bain (Edinburgh, 1900), p. 47, Randolph to Cecil, 21 February 1564.

3. Many thanks to Dr Rosalind Marshall for this information, given at the conference 'Enfers et délices à la Rennaissance', Université de la Sorbonne, Nouvelle, Paris III, 21 June 2001.

4. *CSP Scotland*, vol. II, p. 47.

5. Joseph Robertson (ed.), *Inventaires de la Royne Descosse Douairiere de France*, Bannantyne Club (Edinburgh, 1863), p. lxxxiii, n. 1.

6. 'Mon Oncle, ayant entendu votre arivée à Lions avec Madame ma Tante, je n'ay voullu failler par ce mot de vous dire combien j'eusse desiré d'avoir cest heur de vous y voir tous deus, et vous prier aussi de vous assurer d'avoir en moy une bien fort affectionnée et bonne niece, et qui vous sera telle toute sa vie. Je ne vous importunerays pour ce coup de plus long discours, me contentant que la présente serve de me ramantevoir à votre bonne grace; à la quelle, en cest endroit, je présenteray mes recommandions, aprés avoir prié Dieu qu'il vous doint mon oncle, en santé, trés heureuse et longue vie. De Dondi ce ix de septembre.

    Votre bien bonne niepce, MARIE R.'

('My Uncle, having heard of your arrival at Lyons, with Madame my Aunt, I could not let this moment pass without saying how much I would have wished to have this opportunity to see the two of you, and also to tell you that you have in me a very loving and good niece, who hopes to continue so all her life. I will not bother you at this time with a long speech, only contenting myself with reminding you how much I hope to stay in your good grace, and so, from this place, I send you my best wishes, first having prayed to God that he will keep you, my uncle, in good health with a happy and long life. From Dundee, this 9 September.

    Your very good niece, MARIE R.')

(Prince A. Labanoff (ed.), *Lettres, instructions et mémoires de Marie Stuart, Reine d'Écosse* (London, 1844), vol. I, p. 223.)

7. *CSP Simancas*, p. 361, Guzman de Silva to King Philip, 8 June 1564.
8. *CSP Scotland*, vol. II, p. 133, Randolph to Cecil, 1 March 1565.
9. Cardinal Granvelle and the Duchess of Aershot.
10. *CSP Scotland*, vol. II, p. 101, 15 December 1564.
11. *The Works of John Knox*, ed. David Laing, Woodrow Society (Edinburgh, 1848–64), vol II, p.335.
12. Annie I. Cameron (ed.), *Warrender Papers*, vol. I, Scottish History Society (Edinburgh, 1931), p. 36.
13. *CSP Scotland*, vol. II, p. 81, Cecil to Randolph and Bedford, 7 October 1564.
14. Cameron (ed.), *Warrender Papers*, vol. I, p. 41.
15. Historical Manuscripts Commission, *Calendar of the Manuscripts of the Most Hon. the Marquis of Salisbury KG etc. preserved at Hatfield House, Hertfordshire* (London, 1883), p. 158.
16. T. Thomson and C. Innes (eds), *Acts of the Parliaments of Scotland* (Edinburgh, 1814–75), vol. III, p. 541, 4 June 1563.
17. Cameron (ed.), *Warrender Papers*, vol. I, p. 41.
18. *Ibid.*, vol. I, p. 42.
19. A. Teulet, *Papiers d'état: Pieces et documents inédits ou peu connus relatifs a l'histoire d'Écosse au XVI siècle* (Paris, 1859), vol. II, p. 31.

Chapter Six

1. Simon Adams, 'The Release of Lord Darnley and the Failure of the Amity', in Michael Lynch (ed.), *Mary Stewart: Queen in Three Kingdoms* (Oxford, 1988), p. 132.

2. *CSP Scotland*, vol. II, *1563–1569*, ed. Joseph Bain (Edinburgh, 1900), p. 134.
3. *Ibid.*, p. 85, Randolph to Cecil, 24 October 1564.
4. *Ibid.*
5. Quoted in *ibid.*
6. Quoted in *ibid.*
7. *Ibid.*, p. 120, Randolph to Cecil, 5 February 5 1565.
8. *Ibid.*, p. 134.
9. 'One thing more. When Clenraure, the Frenchman departed, he took many of his countrymen's letters. The Queen (suspecting that some of them were about her, or hearing that they advertised her doings, and fashions of the country, which they misliked) caused a trusty couple to disguise themselves, and by the way riding, take and bring back all Clernaure's letters save her own.

   Among them was found by one of her own chamber to "Sipeer" containing many privy matters, full of doubtful words, that may be ill considered. It is yet dissembled, and I hear he goes shortly to France there to say what he likes, and shall not be so privy to our affairs as in time past.

   One Montenac and his brother will shortly pass by you to France. He brings a letter to the Queen's Majesty.

   Edinburgh, signed: Tho. Randolph' (*ibid.*, p. 101).
10. Robert Keith, *History of the Affairs of Church and State in Scotland from the Beginning of the Reformation to 1568*, vol. II, Spottiswoode Society (Edinburgh, 1845), p. 284.
11. *CSP Scotland*, vol. II, p. 133, Randolph to Cecil, 1 March 1565; 'When we parted, Moray said secretly to me, "Whatsoever you do with us, contend and strive as much as you can to bring us from our Papistry, for otherwise it will be worse for us than ever"' (*ibid.*).
12. *Ibid.*, p. 131, Randolph to Cecil, 1 March 1565.
13. Lady Antonia Fraser, 'The Religion of Mary Queen of Scots', *Lambeth Palace Library Annual Review* (2000), p. 62.
14. *CSP Scotland*, vol. II, p. 134, Randolph to Cecil, 1 March 1565.
15. *Ibid.*
16. *Ibid.*
17. *Ibid.*, p. 147, Cecil to Throgmorton, 24 April 1565.
18. A. Teulet, *Papiers d'état: Pieces et documents inédits ou peu connus relatifs a l'histoire d'Écosse au XVI siècle* (Paris, 1859), vol. II, p. 36, de Foix to Catherine de' Medici, 26 April 1565.
19. *CSP Scotland*, vol. II, p. 155, Randolph to Cecil, 3 Mary 1565.
20. Sir James Melville, *The Memoirs of Sir James of Halhill*, ed. Gordon Donaldson, Folio Society (London, 1969), p. 45.
21. *The Works of John Knox*, ed. David Laing, Woodrow Society (Edinburgh, 1848–64), vol. II, p. 483.
22. Calderwood, *History of the Kirk in Scotland*, vol. II, p. 285.
23. *CSP Scotland*, vol. II, p. 148, Randolph to Cecil, 29 April 1565.
24. Hatfield House, Calendar of Manuscripts, vol. 147, no. 25, and Revd Samuel Haynes (ed.), *Collection of State Papers Left by William Cecil, Lord Burghley* (London, 1740), p. 436. With grateful acknowledgements to Mr Robin

Harcourt Williams, librarian to the 6th & 7th Marquesses of Salisbury, for making the original letter from the archives at Hatfield House available. See also Historical Manuscripts Commission, *Calendar of the Manuscripts of the Most Hon. the Marquis of Salisbury KG etc. preserved at Hatfield House, Hertfordshire* (London, 1883), no. 1054, p. 321.

25. Quoted in Lord David Cecil, *The Cecils of Hatfield House* (London, 1973), p. 80.
26. *CSP Scotland*, vol. II, p. 155, Randolph to Cecil, 3 May 1565.
27. *Ibid.*, vol. II, p. 154, Randolph to Cecil, 3 May 1565.
28. Teulet, *Papiers d'état*, vol. II, p. 44, 15 May 1565.
29. *CSP Scotland*, vol. II, p. 171, Randolph to Leicester, 3 June 3 1565.
30. *Ibid.*, vol. II, p. 171, Randolph to Leicester, 3 June 1565.
31. *Ibid.*
32. *Ibid.*
33. *Ibid.*, vol. II, p. 172, Randolph to Leicester, 3 June 1565.
34. Robert Keith, *History of the Affairs of Church and State in Scotland from the Beginning of the Reformation to 1568*, vol. II, Spottiswoode Society (Edinburgh, 1845), p. 302.
35. John Bruce (ed.), *Papers relating to William first Earl of Gowrie and Patrick Ruthven his Fifth and Last Surviving Son* (London 1867), p. 101.
36. Teulet, *Papiers d'état*, vol. II, p. 48, de Foix to Catherine de' Medici, 3 June 1565.
37. Keith, *History of the Affairs of Church and State*, vol. II, p. 337.

Chapter Seven

1. David Chalmers (*Chronicles of the Kings of Scotland from Fergus I to James VI*, Maitland Club (Edinburgh, 1830), p. 102) records that one reform-minded laird, Andrew Stewart of Ochiltree, went so far as to grumble 'that he would never consent that there should be a Papist King in Scotland'.
2. Adam Blackwood, *History of Mary Queen of Scots: A Fragment*, ed. Alexander Macdonald, Maitland Club (Edinburgh, 1834), p. 3.
3. Quoted in Caroline Bingham, *A Life of Henry Stewart Lord Darnley Consort of Mary Queen of Scots* (London, 1995), p. 102.
4. 'Redshanks' means Campbells, so called because their bare knees were said to go red with cold when away fighting.
5. Thomas Thomson (ed.), *A Diurnal of Remarkable Occurents . . .*, Bannantyne Club (Edinburgh, 1833), p. 80.
6. Prince A. Labanoff (ed.), *Lettres, instructions et mémoires de Marie Stuart, Reine d'Écosse* (London, 1844), vol. VII, p. 90.
7. Joseph Robertson (ed.), *Inventaires de la Royne Descosse Douairiere de France*, Bannantyne Club (Edinburgh, 1863), p. lxxxiv.
8. W. Drummond, *An Enquiry Historical and Critical with the evidence against Mary Queen of Scots, and an examination of the histories of Dr Robertson and Mr Hume with regard therto . . .* (Edinburgh, 1767), p. 193, Randolph to Cecil.
9. James Taylor, *The Great Historic Families of Scotland*, vol. I (London, 1889), p. 13.
10. Thomson (ed.), *A Diurnal of Remarkable Occurents . . .*, p. 81.

11. *CSP Scotland*, vol. II, *1563–1569*, ed. Joseph Bain (Edinburgh, 1900), p. 198, Randolph to Cecil, 27 August 1565.
12. *The Works of John Knox*, ed. David Laing, Woodrow Society (Edinburgh, 1848–64), vol. VI, p. 233. Knox published the sermon in 1566. The text comes from the Old Testament and is based on Isaiah 26: 13–21.
13. *CSP Scotland*, vol. II, p. 185, 29 July 1565.
14. Labanoff (ed.), *Lettres, instructions et mémoires*, vol. I, p. 279: 'True friend. We greet you well. That which we suspected has now declared itself in deed, for our Rebels have retired to the country and We mind, God willing, in proper person to pass for their pursuit, whereunto it is needful that we be well and substantially accompanied.'
15. *CSP Scotland*, vol. II, p. 198, Randolph to Cecil, 27 August 1565.
16. *The Works of John Knox*, ed. Laing, vol. II, p. 501.
17. Although one Johnston and his partner, two prominent Edinburgh lawyers, were sufficiently tempted by Moray's appeal to leave their chambers and flee to his camp.
18. *The Works of John Knox*, ed. Laing, vol. VI, p. 273.

Chapter Eight

1. A. Teulet, *Papiers d'état: Pieces et documents inédits ou peu connus relatifs a l'histoire d'Écosse au XVI siècle* (Paris, 1859), vol. II, p. 78.
2. 'against those who wish to establish their unhappy errors. There was a danger I might lose my crown unless Philip, as one of the greatest Christian princes, sent aid' (*ibid.*).
3. Prince A. Labanoff (ed.), *Lettres, instructions et mémoires de Marie Stuart, Reine d'Écosse* (London, 1844), vol. I, p. 281.
4. *CSP Scotland*, vol. II, *1563–1569*, ed. Joseph Bain (Edinburgh, 1900), p. 221, Randolph to Cecil, 8 October 1565.
5. *Ibid.*, p. 218, Randolph to Leicester, 4 October 1565: 'With the Regent of Flanders she has daily to do. I wot not what, but am assured of a very dispiteful letter written to her not long since by this Queen, and perchance may get some of the contents.'
6. Teulet, *Papiers d'état*, vol. II, p. 85.
7. *Ibid.*, vol. II, p. 67.
8. David Calderwood, *History of the Kirk in Scotland*, Woodrow Society (Edinburgh, 1843), vol. II, pp. 569–76.
9. *Ibid.*, p. 570.
10. *Ibid.*, p. 573.
11. Elizabeth's candidate was Robert Dudley, Earl of Leicester.
12. Thomas Thomson (ed.), *A Diurnal of Remarkable Occurents . . .*, Bannantyne Club (Edinburgh, 1833), p. 83.
13. *CSP Scotland*, vol. I, *1547–1563*, ed. Joseph Bain (Edinburgh, 1898), p. 679, Randolph to Cecil, 22 January 1563.
14. *CSP Scotland*, vol. II, p. 219, Randolph to Cecil, 4 October 1565.
15. *Ibid.*, p. 213.

16. *Ibid.*
17. *Ibid.*, p. 219.
18. *Ibid.*, p. 217.
19. Teulet, *Papiers d'état*, vol. II, p. 104.
20. *The Works of John Knox*, ed. David Laing, Woodrow Society (Edinburgh, 1848–64), vol. II, p. 510.
21. R.V. Hannay, *History of the Society of Writers to the Signet* (Edinburgh, 1936), p. 43.
22. *The Works of John Knox*, ed. Laing, vol. II, p. 516.

Chapter Nine

1. Joseph Robertson (ed.), *Inventaires de la Royne Descosse Douairiere de France*, Bannantyne Club (Edinburgh, 1863), pp. 155, 159, 161.
2. Adam Blackwood, *History of Mary Queen of Scots: A Fragment*, ed. Alexander Macdonald, Maitland Club (Edinburgh, 1834), p. 9.
3. Bizari arrived in England in 1549 during the Edwardian Reformation at the same time as the great Protestant theologian Martin Bucer. Like Bucer he was given a university post at Cambridge, a fellowship at St John's College. Four years later he also received a small living in Wiltshire, at Alton Parva, near Salisbury, worth £20 a year.
4. See also *The Chronicles of Savoy*, p. cxiii, quoted in Robertson (ed.), *Inventaires de la Royne Descosse*, p. cii.
5. Pietro Bizari, *Historia di Pietro Bizari della guerra fatta in Hungaria contra de quello de Turchi* (Lyons, 1569), p. 168; BL 1054.a28 (1): 'Haveva la Reina in corta sua, un gentil'huomo Piemontese, chiamato S. David, C'haveva preso al servivtio sua di Camerieo mentre ch'effa era in Francia. Era questo gentil'huomo, oltr L cognitione c' haveva della belle lettere, di cosigrato aspetto, & dicosi cortesi costume, che sforzava ogni huomo ad amarlo, & haverlo caro, si come io molto ben conobri intrinsicamente l'anno 1564, che sui in quelle corte, & seco hebbi famigliar converzatione.' See also G.F. Barwick, 'A Sidelight on the Mystery of Mary Stuart', *Scottish History Review*, 221 (1929), 116.
6. Quoted in Mrs Agnes Strickland, *Life of Mary Queen of Scots*, vol. I (London, 1873), p. 268.
7. A. Teulet, *Papiers d'état: Pieces et documents inédits ou peu connus relatifs a l'histoire d'Écosse au XVI siècle*, vol. II (Paris, 1859), p. 67.
8. Personal information kindly given by Professor Ian Hazlett at the Society of Reformation Studies Conference, Cambridge, April 2001.
9. Alma B. Calderwood (ed.), *Buik of the Kirk of Canagait 1564–1567*, Scottish Record Society (Edinburgh, 1967), pp. 74, 75, 109.
10. George Buchanan, *The Tyrannous Reign of Mary Stewart (Rerum Scoticarum Historia)*, ed. W.A. Gatherer (Edinburgh, 1958), p. 87.
11. Cecil preserved an example of his verse at Burghley, and endorsed on the cover 'Fowler, a ballad.1565' (Hatfield MSS, Part XIII (addenda). BL p.70.233. 10 (London, 1915)).

What time apells learned hand, the famous shape of Venus drew,
Her hue, her limbs so lively wrought, thou needest but for her have sought,
if Time play the tomboy and go where she will,
now laughing, now quaffing, with company still,
And he will thee ever safe, keep, and defend,
in quiet state of life, world without end.

12. Revd Samuel Haynes (ed.), *Collection of State Papers Left by William Cecil, Lord Burghley* (London, 1740), p. 443, 19 December 1565.
13. Father J.H. Pollen, *Papal Negotiations with Mary Queen of Scots*, Scottish History Society (Edinburgh, 1901), p. 299.
14. *CSP Scotland*, vol. II, *1563–1569*, ed. Joseph Bain (Edinburgh, 1900), p. 221, Anthony Jenkinson to the Privy Council.
15. *Ibid.*, p. 218, 4 October 1565.
16. *Ibid.*, p. 225, 18 October 1565.
17. Private information kindly given by Lord Stewartby, May 2001. See further Ian Halley Stewart (Lord Stewartby), *The Scottish Coinage* (London, 1955), p. 89.
18. V.J. Parry, 'The Ottoman Empire 1520–1566', in G.R. Elton (ed.), *The New Cambridge Modern History*, vol. II, *The Reformation 1520–1566* (Cambridge, 1990), p. 593. The Ottoman fleet was commanded by one of Sulaiman the Magnificent's greatest admirals, Piyale. He sailed from Istanbul in April 1565. Despite much support from the corsairs of Algiers and Tripoli, his attack on Malta was over by September of that year.
19. Pollen, *Papal Negotiations*, p. 489, Father John Polanco to Father Simon Beclost, 13 November 1565.
20. Robertson (ed.), *Inventaires de la Royne Descosse*, p. 123.
21. David Calderwood, *History of the Kirk in Scotland*, vol. II, Woodrow Society (Edinburgh, 1843), p. 311.
22. George Brunton and David Haig, *An Historical Account of the Senators of the College of Justice from its Institution in MDXXXII* (Edinburgh, 1832), p. 132.
23. 'Et eidem in octuagiinta libus per solutionem facte David Rizzio servitori Domine Regine, pro sua pensione, de terminus computi, ut patet perssuam acquittantiam, ostensam super computum, £80' (G.P. McNeil (ed.), *The Exchequer Rolls of Scotland*, vol. XIX (Edinburgh, 1898), p. 236).
24. Sir James Balfour Paul (ed.), *Accounts of the Lord High Treasurer of Scotland*, vol. XI (Edinburgh, 1916), p. 475.
25. See Historical Manuscripts Commission, *Calendar of the Manuscripts of the Most Hon. the Marquis of Salisbury KG etc. preserved at Hatfield House, Hertfordshire* (London, 1883), no. 1105, p. 336.
26. *Ibid.*
27. *Ibid.*
28. David Chalmers, *Chronicles of the Kings of Scotland from Fergus I to James VI*, Maitland Club (Edinburgh, 1830). He had 'been well brought up in learning' (p. 101).
29. Although in later years many celebrated eighteenth-century painters, such as John Opie and George Romney, enjoyed depicting the grim scene of the Rizzio murder.

30. Lord Seaforth gave the picture to the Palace of Holyroodhouse in 1953. Rizzio is shown here in seventeenth-century dress. The portrait has been attributed to George Jameson.
31. Calderwood, *History of the Kirk in Scotland*, vol. II, p. 311.
32. *Ibid.*, p. 312.
33. Historical Manuscripts Commission, *Calendar of the Manuscripts of the Most Hon. the Marquis of Salisbury*, no. 1105, p. 338.

Chapter Ten

1. Ian Halley Stewart (Lord Stewartby), *The Scottish Coinage* (London, 1955), p. 86.
2. Historical Manuscripts Commission, *Calendar of the Manuscripts of the Most Hon. the Marquis of Salisbury KG etc. preserved at Hatfield House, Hertfordshire* (London, 1883), p. 336, Bedford and Randolph to the Privy Council of England, 27 March 1566.
3. John Hill Burton (ed.), *Register of the Privy Council of Scotland*, vol. I (Edinburgh, 1877), p. 388.
4. *CSP Scotland*, vol. II, *1563–1569*, ed. Joseph Bain (Edinburgh, 1900), p. 240.
5. *Ibid.*, pp. 245–6, Randolph to Cecil, 23 December 1565.
6. *Ibid.*, p. 247, Randolph to Cecil, 25 December 1565.
7. *Ibid.*
8. *Ibid.*, p. 254.
9. *Ibid.*, p. 267, Randolph to Cecil, 13 March 1566.
10. *Ibid.*, p. 254, Randolph to Cecil, 7 February 1566.
11. Father J.H. Pollen, *Papal Negotiations with Mary Queen of Scots*, Scottish History Society (Edinburgh, 1901), p. cviii.
12. Joseph Robertson (ed.), *Inventaires de la Royne Descosse Douairiere de France*, Bannatyne Club (Edinburgh, 1863), p. lxxxvi.
13. *CSP Simancas*, p. 527.
14. W. Drummond, *An Enquiry Historical and Critical with the evidence against Mary Queen of Scots, and an examination of the histories of Dr Robertson and Mr Hume with regard therto* . . . (Edinburgh, 1767), p. 193.
15. Adam Blackwood, *History of Mary Queen of Scots: A Fragment*, ed. Alexander Macdonald, Maitland Club (Edinburgh, 1834), p. 9.
16. David Calderwood, *History of the Kirk in Scotland*, vol. II, Woodrow Society (Edinburgh, 1843), p. 311.
17. George Buchanan, *The Tyrannous Reign of Mary Stewart (Rerum Scoticarum Historia)*, ed. W.A. Gatherer (Edinburgh, 1958), pp. 93–6.
18. Personal information from Mr Peter Hay, Melville Castle Hotel, March 2004.
19. *CSP Scotland*, vol. II, p. 264, Randolph to Cecil, 6 March 1566.
20. Sir James Melville, *The Memoirs of Sir James of Halhill*, ed. Gordon Donaldson, Folio Society (London, 1969), p. 44.
21. Quoted in Mrs Agnes Strickland, *Life of Mary Queen of Scots*, vol. 1 (London, 1873), p. 272.
22. Buchanan, *The Tyrannous Reign of Mary Stewart*, ed. Gatherer, p. 98.
23. Quoted in Strickland, *Life of Mary Queen of Scots*, vol. I, p. 272.

24. *Ibid.*
25. *Ibid.*
26. *Ibid.*
27. Melville, *The Memoirs of Sir James of Halhill*, ed. Donaldson, p. 49.
28. Calderwood, *History of the Kirk in Scotland*, vol. I, p. 315.
29. *Ibid.*
30. *CSP Scotland*, vol. II, p. 235.
31. *Ibid.*, p. 257, Mary to Elizabeth.
32. Strickland, *Life of Mary Queen of Scots*, vol. I, p. 263.
33. *The Works of John Knox*, ed. David Laing, Woodrow Society (Edinburgh, 1848–64), vol. II, p. 521.
34. *CSP Scotland*, vol. II, p. 242, Randolph to Cecil, 1 December 1565.
35. Calderwood, *History of the Kirk in Scotland*, vol. II, p. 311.
36. *CSP Scotland*, vol. II, p. 255, Maitland to Cecil, 9 February 1566.
37. *Ibid.*, p. 254, Randolph to Cecil, 7 February 1566.
38. *Ibid.*, p. 258, Randolph to Cecil, 25 February 1566.
39. *Ibid.*, p. 259, Elizabeth to Mary, 3 March 1566.
40. *Ibid.*, p. 259, Bedford and Randolph to Cecil, 6 March 1566.
41. Robert Keith, *History of the Affairs of Church and State in Scotland from the Beginning of the Reformation to 1568*, vol. II, Spottiswoode Society (Edinburgh, 1845), p. 399.
42. Gordon Donaldson, *All the Queen's Men* (London, 1983), p. 78.
43. *CSP Scotland*, vol. II, p. 260, Bedford and Randolph to Cecil, 6 March 1566.
44. *Ibid.*, vol. II, p. 260, Bedford and Randolph to Cecil, 6 March 1566.

Chapter Eleven

1. Prince A. Labanoff (ed.), *Lettres, instructions et mémoires de Marie Stuart, Reine d'Écosse* (London, 1844), vol. I, p. 344.
2. Thomas Thomson (ed.), *A Diurnal of Remarkable Occurents . . .*, Bannantyne Club (Edinburgh, 1833), p. 89.
3. R. Pitcairn (ed.), *Ancient Criminal Trials in Scotland*, Bannantyne Club (Edinburgh, 1833), vol. I, p. 481.
4. Labanoff (ed.), *Lettres, instructions et mémoires*, vol. I, p. 344.
5. *Ibid.*
6. *Ibid.*
7. *Ibid.*
8. *Ibid.*
9. *Ibid.*
10. David Calderwood, *History of the Kirk in Scotland*, vol. II, Woodrow Society (Edinburgh, 1843), p. 314.
11. *Ibid.*
12. Labanoff (ed.), *Lettres, instructions et mémoires*, vol. VII, p. 93: 'Lasciatelo andare, Madama, disse, che non lisara fatto alcun male.'
13. *Ibid.*, vol. I, p. 345.
14. *Ibid.*, vol. VII, p. 74.

15. *Ibid.*, vol. VII, p. 93: 'Ah povero David, mio buono et fidel servitore, Dio habbi misericordia di vostra anima!'

16. Historical Manuscripts Commission, *Calendar of the Manuscripts of the Most Hon. the Marquis of Salisbury KG etc. Preserved at Hatfield House, Hertfordshire* (London, 1883), no. 1105, p. 334.

17. *Ibid.*

18. *Ibid.*

19. *Ibid.*

20. *Ibid.*

21. *Ibid.*

22. *Ibid.*

23. *Ibid.*

24. *Ibid.*

25. Her understandable hatred for the Ruthven family and name was inherited by her son, King James VI & I. He kept on the vendetta to exact fierce revenge. Ruthven wrote a defence and explanation for his part in the murder just before he died.

26. Historical Manuscripts Commission, *Calendar of the Manuscripts of the Most Hon the Marquis of Salisbury KG*, no. 1105, p. 334.

27. *Ibid.*

28. Labanoff (ed.), *Lettres, instructions et mémoires*, vol. I, p. 345.

29. *Ibid.*, vol. I, pp. 345–6.

30. *Ibid.*, p. 349.

31. *Ibid.*

32. *Ibid.*, p. 346.

33. *Ibid.*, vol. I, p. 347.

34. *Ibid.*, vol. I, p. 348.

35. *Ibid.*

36. Claude Nau, *The History of Mary Stewart* (Edinburgh, 1883), p. xcvi.

37. Labanoff (ed.), *Lettres, instructions et mémoires*, vol. I, p. 348.

38. *Ibid.*

39. *Ibid.*, pp. 348–9.

40. *Ibid.*, vol. I, p. 349.

41. *Ibid.*

42. *Ibid.*

43. *Ibid.*, vol. I, p. 343.

44. 'Je vous prie ne faillez, incontinant ces lettres vues, aller a la Cour, afin que vous puissiez empescher les bruits faux d'estre creus; et faites en un discours a l'ambassadeur d'Espagne et autres etrangers. Votre bien bonne maistresse et amie, Marie R.' (*ibid.*).

Chapter Twelve

1. *CSP Scotland*, vol. II, *1563–1569*, ed. Joseph Bain (Edinburgh, 1900), pp. 264–5.

2. *Ibid.*, p. 265.

3. *Ibid.*, p. 259.

4. *Ibid.*, p. 265.
5. *Ibid.*, p. 265.
6. *Ibid.*, p. 266
7. *Ibid.*
8. *Ibid.*, pp. 265–6.
9. *Ibid.*, p. 266.
10 *Ibid.*, p. 267.
11. *Ibid.*
12. *Ibid.*, pp. 265–6.
13. *Ibid.*, p. 267.
14. John Knox, *History of the Reformation in Scotland*, bk 1, ch. V, p. 101, in *The Works of John Knox*, ed. David Laing (Edinburgh, 1848–64), vol. I, p. 235.
15. *Ibid.*
16. Historical Manuscripts Commission, *Calendar of the Manuscripts of the Most Hon. the Marquis of Salisbury KG etc. preserved at Hatfield House, Hertfordshire* (London, 1883), p. 334.
17. Prince A. Labanoff (ed.), *Lettres, instructions et mémoires de Marie Stuart, Reine d'Écosse* (London, 1844), vol. I, pp. 335–8.
18. *Ibid.*, p. 335.
19. *Ibid.*
20. *Ibid.*
21. *Ibid.*, p. 336.
22. *Ibid.*
23. *Ibid.*
24. *Ibid.*
25. *Ibid.*
26. *Ibid.*
27. *Ibid.*, pp. 337–8.
28. *CSP Scotland*, vol. II, p. 269.
29. *Ibid.*, p. 274.
30. John Bruce (ed.), *Papers relating to William First Earl of Gowrie and Patrick Ruthven his Fifth and Last Surviving Son* (London, 1867), p. 7.
31. *Ibid.*

Chapter Thirteen

1. A. Teulet, *Papiers d'état: Pieces et documents inédits ou peu connus relatifs a l'histoire d'Écosse au XVI siècle*, vol. II (Paris, 1859), p. 119.
2. George Buchanan, *The Tyrannous Reign of Mary Stewart (Rerum Scoticarum Historia)*, ed. W.A. Gatherer (Edinburgh, 1958), p. 95. This is the best modern translation of this work first published c. 1582, but see also the earlier edition: George Buchanan, *History of Scotland*, vol. II (Edinburgh, 1752), p. 309.
3. *CSP Scotland*, vol. II, *1563–1569*, ed. Joseph Bain (Edinburgh, 1900), vol. II, p. 222, Randolph to Cecil, 13 October 1565.
4. John Aylmer, *An harbour (Harvorowe) for faithful and true subjects against the late blown blast concerning the Government of Women, wherein is confuted all*

such reasons as a Stranger of late made in that behalf, with a brief Exhortation to Obedience (Strasbourg, 1559), [p. 96]; BL C.38.c1.1–2.

5. Buchanan, *The Tyrannous Reign of Mary Stewart*, ed. Gatherer, p. 92.
6. Buchanan was one of the most brilliant Latin scholars of the northern renaissance. He was also a gifted poet who wrote a long ode in Latin, an epithalamium, to tell the French a little more about the glories of Scots civilisation when Mary married their Dauphin, François.
7. Buchanan, *The Tyrannous Reign of Mary Stewart*, ed. Gatherer, p. 93.
8. Prince A. Labanoff (ed.), *Lettres, instructions et mémoires de Marie Stuart, Reine d'Écosse* (London, 1844), vol. I, p. 345.
9. Buchanan, *The Tyrannous Reign of Mary Stewart*, ed. Gatherer, p. 100.
10. Labanoff (ed.), *Lettres, instructions et mémoires*, vol. VII, p. 74.
11. G.F. Barwick, 'A Sidelight on the Mystery of Mary Stuart', *Scottish History Review*, 221 (1924), p. 118.
12. David Hay Fleming, *Mary Queen of Scots from her Birth to her Flight into England* (London, 1898), p. 399.
13. Tamar Herzig, 'The Demons' Reaction to Sodomy: Witchcraft and Homosexuality in Gianfrancesco Pico della Mirandola's Strix', *Sixteenth Century Journal*, 34/1 (2003), p. 65.
14. David Calderwood, *History of the Kirk in Scotland*, vol. II, Woodrow Society (Edinburgh, 1843), p. 286.
15. Tony Betteridge, 'Staging Reformation Authority: John Bale's "King Johan" and Nicholas Udall's "Respublica"', *Reformation and Renaissance Review*, 3 (June 2000), p. 54.
16. Hay Fleming, *Mary Queen of Scots*, p. 400.
17. James Taylor, *The Great Historic Families of Scotland*, vol. I (London, 1889), p. 161.
18. Robert Keith, *History of the Affairs of Church and State in Scotland from the Beginning of the Reformation to 1568*, vol II, Spottiswoode Society (Edinburgh, 1845), p. vi.
19. Claude Nau, *The History of Mary Stewart* (Edinburgh, 1883), p. cii.
20. Alan Stewart, *The Cradle King: A Life of James VI & I* (London, 2003), p. 222.

Chapter Fourteen

1. A. Teulet, *Papiers d'état: Pieces et documents inédits ou peu connus relatifs a l'histoire d'Écosse au XVI siècle* (Paris, 1859), vol. II, p. 119, 20 March 1566.
2. *CSP Foreign, 1566–1568*, ed. A.J. Crosby (London, 1871), p. 37.
3. *CSP Simincas*, vol. I, p. 537.
4. *Ibid.*
5. *Ibid.*
6. *Ibid.*
7. *Ibid.*
8. M. Edmond Poulett (ed.), *Correspondence du Cardinal de Granvelle* (Brussels, 1877), vol. I, p. 194, Le Prévôt Mouillon au Cardinal de Granville, Brussels, 31 March 1566.

9. Father J.H. Pollen, *Papal Negotiations with Mary Queen of Scots*, Scottish History Society (Edinburgh, 1901), p. 239.

10. *Ibid.*

11. Bishop of Mondovi to Cardinal of Alessandria, 21 August 1566, in *ibid.*, p. 277.

12. *Ibid.*, p. 239.

13. Théodore de Bèze, *Correspondence*, vol. VII, Librarie Droz (Geneva, 1973), p. 86, 15 May 1566: 'Anderisse te opinor in Scotiae res omnes satia bonis conditionibus transactus si modo satis firmae fuerent.' The editors to the published edition underline the point by heading the commentary 'assez bonnes nouvelles d'Ecosse'. With grateful acknowledgements to the Director and staff of the Institut d'Histoire de la Réformation at the Université de Genève.

14. 'In Scotia post secretarium Davidem interfectum eo usque regina insinisse dicitur ut eius etiam ossa curavit paterno sepulcra inferanda. Hinc novae exortae turbae, Sed in summa nunc erunt composita esse omnia non iniquis conditionibus modo satis sint firmae' (*ibid.*, vol. VII, p. 124).

15. Quoted in *The Works of John Knox*, ed. David Laing, Woodrow Society (Edinburgh, 1848–64), vol. II, p. 595, 21 August 1566.

16. With grateful acknowledgements to Dr Julian Goodares (University of Edinburgh) for this information, given at the conference 'King James VI & I Quarter Centenary Perspectives', University of Reading, July 2003.

17. Quoted in *The Works of John Knox*, ed. Laing, vol. II, p. 594.

18. Quoted in *ibid.*, vol. VI, p. 542.

19. *Works of John Jewel, Bishop of Salisbury*, ed. John Ayre, vol. IV (Parker Society (Cambridge, 1850), p. 114.

20. *An Answer to a Jesuit named Tyrie*, printed at St Andrew's by Robert Lekprevik, 1572, in *The Works of John Knox*, ed. Laing, vol. VI, p. 481.

21. 'un aultre enseigne garnye de dix rubiz en tortue avec une perle pendante au bout' (June 1566), in Joseph Robertson (ed.), *Inventaires de la Royne Descosse Douairiere de France*, Bannantyne Club (Edinburgh, 1863), p. 123.

22. *CSP Scotland*, vol. II, *1563–1569*, ed. Joseph Bain (Edinburgh, 1900), vol. II, p. 278, Randolph to Cecil, 25 April 1566.

23. A jewel containing ten rubies and pearls that Rizzio gave Mary, an emerald ring enamelled in white, and a 21-diamond jewel.

24. Robertson (ed.), *Inventaires de la Royne Descosse*, p. 122.

25. Sir James Melville, *The Memoirs of Sir James Melville of Halhill*, ed. Gordon Donaldson, Folio Society (London, 1969), p. 56.

26. *CSP Foreign, Elizabeth I*, p. 13; see also David Hay Fleming, *Mary Queen of Scots from her Birth to her Flight into England* (London, 1898), p. 399.

27. *CSP Simancas*, p. 622.

Note on Principal Sources

The main sources consulted were *Calendar of the State Papers relating to Scotland and Mary, Queen of Scots*, vol. I, 1547–1563, ed. Joseph Bain (Edinburgh, 1898), and *Calendar of the State Papers relating to Scotland and Mary, Queen of Scots*, vol. II, *1563–1569*, ed. Joseph Bain (Edinburgh, 1900). They are referred to as *CSP Scotland* in the endnotes. See also *Calendar of State Papers, Foreign Series, Elizabeth I, 1566–1568*, ed. A.J. Crosby (London, 1871), referred to as *CSP Foreign, Elizabeth I*; *Calendar of State Papers and Manuscripts Existing in the Archives and Collections of Milan*, ed. Allen B. Hinds (London, 1912), referred to as *CSP Milan*; and *Calendar of State Papers relating to English Affairs Preserved Principally in the Archives of Simancas, Elizabeth, 1558–1567*, ed. Martin A.S. Hume, vol. I (London, 1892), referred to as *CSP Simancas*.

Prince A. Labanoff, *Lettres, instructions et mémoires de Marie Stuart, Reine d'Écosse* (London, 1844), vols I–VII, is essential, as it has much of Mary's contemporary correspondence.

I have used Gordon Donaldson's edition of *The Memoirs of Sir James Melville of Halhill*, Folio Society (London, 1969), as the best available edition of Sir James Melville's memoirs, which were first published in 1683. Also W.A. Gatherer's edition (Edinburgh, 1958) of George Buchanan, *The Tyrannous Reign of Mary Stewart*, in Latin, *Rerum Scoticarum Historia, or History of Scotland*, which was originally written and first published in 1571/2.

David Laing's edition of *The Works of John Knox*, Woodrow Society (Edinburgh 1848–64), especially vols I, II, IV and VI, contains the writings of the great reformer, in particular his *History of the Reformation in Scotland*, which (except the last volume) were written in his lifetime, and first published in 1586–7. David Calderwood, *History of the Kirk in Scotland*, vols I and II, Woodrow Society (Edinburgh, 1843), and Robert Keith, *History of the Affairs of Church and State in Scotland from the Beginning of the Reformation to 1568*, vol. II, Spottiswoode Society (Edinburgh, 1845), first published in 1734, have earlier materials, and expand on other church records that are not in Knox.

Bibliography

MANUSCRIPT AND ARCHIVAL SOURCES

British Library

Aylmer, John, *An harbour (Harborowe) for faithful and true subjects against the late blown blast concerning the Government of Women, wherein is confuted all such reasons as a Stranger of late made in that behalf, with a brief Exhortation to Obedience* (Strasbourg, 1559), unpaginated; BL C.38.e2 (1)

Bizari, Pietro, *Historia di Pietro Bizari della guerra fatta in Hungaria contra de quello de Turchi* (Lyons, 1569); BL 1054.a28 (1)

——, *Rerum Persicarum Historia initia Gentis Moris* (Frankfurt, 1601); BL c75.g7

Hatfield House

Calendar of Manuscripts, vol. 147, no. 25 (but see also Hatfield MSS, Part XIII (addenda), BL p.70.233.10 (London, 1915))

PRINTED PRIMARY SOURCES

Balfour Paul, Sir James (ed.), *Accounts of the Lord High Treasurer of Scotland, vol. XI* (Edinburgh, 1916)

Bèze, Théodore de, *Correspondence*, vol. VII, Librarie Droz (Geneva, 1973)

Blackwood, Adam, *History of Mary Queen of Scots: A Fragment*, ed. Alexander Macdonald, Maitland Club (Edinburgh, 1834)

Bruce, John (ed.), *Papers relating to William First Earl of Gowrie and Patrick Ruthven his Fifth and Last Surviving Son* (London, 1867)

Brunton, George, and Haig, David, *An Historical Account of the Senators of the College of Justice from its Institution in MDXXXII* (Edinburgh, 1832)

Buchanan, George, *History of Scotland*, vol. II (Edinburgh, 1752)

——, *The Tyrannous Reign of Mary Stewart (Rerum Scoticarum Historia)*, ed. W.A. Gatherer (Edinburgh, 1958)

Burton, John Hill (ed.), *Register of the Privy Council of Scotland*, vol. I (Edinburgh, 1877)

Calderwood, Alma B. (ed.), *Buik of the Kirk of Canagait 1564–1567*, Scottish Record Society (Edinburgh, 1967)

Bibliography

Calderwood, David, *History of the Kirk in Scotland*, vols I and II, Woodrow Society (Edinburgh, 1843)

Calendar of State Papers, Foreign Series, Edward VI, 1547–1553, ed. William B. Turnbull (London, 1861)

Calendar of State Papers, Foreign Series, Elizabeth I, 1566–1568, ed. A.J. Crosby (London, 1871)

Calendar of State Papers and Manuscripts Existing in the Archives and Collections of Milan, ed. Allen B. Hinds (London, 1912)

Calendar of the State Papers relating to Scotland and Mary, Queen of Scots, vol. I, *1547–1563*, ed. Joseph Bain (Edinburgh, 1898)

Calendar of the State Papers relating to Scotland and Mary, Queen of Scots, vol. II, *1563–1569*, ed. Joseph Bain (Edinburgh, 1900)

Calendar of State Papers relating to English Affairs Preserved Principally in the Archives of Simancas, Elizabeth, 1558–1567, ed. Martin A.S. Hume, vol. I (London, 1892)

Cameron, Annie I. (ed.), *Warrender Papers*, vol. I, Scottish History Society (Edinburgh, 1931)

Chalmers, David, *Chronicles of the Kings of Scotland from Fergus I to James VI*, Maitland Club (Edinburgh, 1830)

Drummond, W, *An Enquiry Historical and Critical with the evidence against Mary Queen of Scots, and an examination of the histories of Dr Robertson and Mr Hume with regard therto . . .* (Edinburgh, 1767)

Haynes, Revd Samuel (ed.), *Collection of State Papers left by William Cecil, Lord Burghley* (London, 1740)

Herries, Lord, *Historical Memoirs of the Reign of Mary Queen of Scots, and a Portion of the Reign of King James VI* (Edinburgh, 1836)

Historical Manuscripts Commission, *Calendar of the Manuscripts of the Most Hon. the Marquis of Salisbury KG etc. Preserved at Hatfield House, Hertfordshire* (London, 1883)

Jewel, John, *Works of John Jewel, Bishop of Salisbury*, ed. John Ayre, vol. IV, Parker Society (Cambridge, 1850)

Keith, Robert, *History of the Affairs of Church and State in Scotland from the Beginning of the Reformation to 1568*, vol. II, Spottiswoode Society (Edinburgh, 1845)

Knox, John, *The Works of John Knox*, ed. David Laing, Woodrow Society (Edinburgh, 1848–64), vols I, II, IV and VI

Labanoff, Prince A. (ed.) *Lettres, instructions et mémoires de Marie Stuart, Reine d'Écosse* (London, 1844), vols I–VII

McNeil, G.P. (ed.), *The Exchequer Rolls of Scotland*, vol. XIX (Edinburgh, 1898)

Melville, Sir James, *The Memoirs of Sir James Melville of Halhill*, ed. Gordon Donaldson, Folio Society (London, 1969), which is a later edition of the original work first edited by George Scott of Pitlochie (London, 1683)

Nau, Claude, *The History of Mary Stewart from the Murder of Riccio until her Flight into England* (Edinburgh, 1883)

Pitcairn, R. (ed.), *Ancient Criminal Trials in Scotland*, vol. I, Bannantyne Club (Edinburgh, 1833)

Pollen, Father J.H., *Papal Negotiations with Mary Queen of Scots during her Reign in Scotland* (Edinburgh, 1901)

Poulett, M. Edmond (ed.), *Correspondence du Cardinal de Granvelle*, vol. I (Brussels, 1877)

Robertson, Joseph (ed.), *Inventaires de la Royne Descosse Douairiere de France*, Bannantyne Club (Edinburgh, 1863)

Robinson, Revd Hastings (ed.), *The Zurich Letters . . . Correspondence of Several English Bishops with the Helvetian Reformers*, Parker Society (Cambridge, 1842)

—— (ed.), *Original Letter relative to the English Reformation*, Parker Society (Cambridge, 1846)

Stewart, Ian Halley (Lord Stewartby), *The Scottish Coinage* (London, 1955)

Teulet, Jean Baptiste Alexandre Théodore, *Papiers d'état: Pièces et documents inédits ou peu connus relatifs à l'histoire d'Écosse au XVI siècle*, vol. II (Paris, 1859)

Thomson, Thomas (ed.), *A Diurnal of Remarkable Occurents . . .*, Bannantyne Club (Edinburgh, 1833)

Thomson, T., and Innes, C. (eds), *Acts of the Parliaments of Scotland* (Edinburgh, 1814–75)

Tweedie, Michael Forbes, *The History of the Tweedie, or Tweedy, Family: A Record of Scottish Lowland Life and Character* (London, 1902)

Tytler, Patrick Fraser, *History of Scotland*, vols vi, vii (Edinburgh, 1842)

Winzet, Ninian, included in *Certain Tractates for the Reformation of Doctrine and Manners in Scotland, together with the book of Fourscore Three Questions and a translation of Vincentius Lirensis*, Maitland Club (Edinburgh, 1835)

PRINTED SECONDARY WORKS

Alford, Steven, *The Early Elizabethan Polity: William Cecil and the British Succession Crisis 1558–1569* (Cambridge, 1998)

Betteridge, Tom, 'Staging Reformation Authority: John Bale's "King Johan" and Nicholas Udall's "Respublica"', *Reformation and Renaissance Review*, 3 (June 2000), 34–58

Barwick, G.F., 'A Sidelight on the Mystery of Mary Stuart', *Scottish Historical Review*, 21 (1924), 115–27

Bingham, Caroline, *Darnley: A Life of Henry Stuart Lord Darnley, Consort of Mary Queen of Scots* (London, 1995)

Carpenter, Sarah, 'Performing Diplomacy: The 1560s Court Entertainments of Mary, Queen of Scots', *Scottish Historical Review*, 82 (October 2003), 194–225

Cecil, Lord David, *The Cecils of Hatfield House* (London, 1973)

Coventry, Martin, *The Castles of Scotland* (Musselburgh 2001)

Croft, Pauline (ed.), *Patronage, Culture and Power: The Early Cecils* (New Haven and London, 2002)

Dawson, Jane E.A., *The Politics of Religion in the Age of Mary Queen of Scots: The Earl of Argyll and the Struggle for Britain and Ireland* (Cambridge, 2002)

Donaldson, Gordon, *All the Queen's Men* (London, 1983)

Dunn, Jane, *Elizabeth and Mary, Cousins, Rivals, Queens* (London, 2003)

Duchein, Michel, *Marie Stuart* (Paris, 1987)

Elton, G.R. (ed.), *New Cambridge Modern History*, vol. II, *The Reformation 1520–1559* (Cambridge, 1990)

Fraser, Antonia, *Mary Queen of Scots* (London, 1969)

——, 'The Religion of Mary Queen of Scots', *Lambeth Palace Library Annual Review* (2000), 55–64

Gore-Browne, Lt-Col Robert F., *Lord Bothwell* (London, 1937)

Guthrie, C.J. (ed.), *The History of the Reformation of Religion within the Realm of Scotland, Written by John Knox* (Edinburgh, 1898; Pennsylvania, 1982)

Guy, John, *My Heart is my Own: The Life of Mary Queen of Scots* (London, 2004)

Hannay, R.V., *History of the Society of Writers to the Signet* (Edinburgh, 1936)

Hay Fleming, David, *Mary Queen of Scots from her Birth to her Flight into England* (London, 1898)

Herzig, Tamar, 'The Demons' Reaction to Sodomy: Witchcraft and Homosexuality in Gianfrancesco Pico della Mirandola's Strix', *Sixteenth Century Journal*, 34/1 (2003), 53–72

Hollingsworth, Mary, *The Cardinal's Hat: Money, Ambition and Housekeeping in a Renaissance Court* (London, 2004)

Hume Brown, P., *Scotland in the Time of Queen Mary* (London, 1904)

Lee, Maurice, Jr, *James Stewart, Earl of Murray: A Political Study of the Reformation in Scotland* (New York, 1966)

Lynch, Michael (ed.), *Mary Stewart: Queen in Three Kingdoms* (Oxford, 1988)

MacGregor, Geddes, *The Thundering Scot: A Portrait of John Knox* (London, 1958)

Macnalty, Sir Arthur S., *Mary Queen of Scots, the Daughter of Debate* (London, 1960)

Mahon, Major-General R.H., *The Tragedy of Kirk o' Field* (Cambridge, 1930)

——, *Mary Queen of Scots: A Study of the Lennox Narrative* (Cambridge, 1924)

Marshall, Rosalind K., *Mary of Guise* (London, 1977)

——, *Queen of Scots* (Edinburgh, 2000)

Mason, Roger A. (ed.), *John Knox and the British Reformation* (Aldershot, 1998)

Merriman, Marcus, *The Rough Wooings: Mary Queen of Scots 1542–1551* (East Linton, 2000)

Parry, V.J., 'The Ottoman Empire 1520–1566', in G.R. Elton (ed.), *The New Cambridge Modern History*, vol. II, *The Reformation 1520–1566* (Cambridge, 1990), 570–94

Percy, Lord Eustace, *John Knox* (London, n.d.)

Pollard, A.F., *Tudor Tracts* (London, 1903)

Read, Conyers, *Mr Secretary Cecil and Queen Elizabeth* (London, 1955)

Ridley, Jasper, *John Knox* (Oxford, 1968)

Ross, Iain, *The Gude and Godlie Ballatis* (Edinburgh, 1939)

Ryrie, Alec, 'Reform without Frontiers in the Last Years of Catholic Scotland', *English Historical Review*, 119 (2004), 27–56

Sanderson, Margaret H.B., *Mary Stewart's People* (Edinburgh, 1987)

Smailes, Helen, and Thomson, Duncan, *The Queen's Image: A Celebration of Mary Queen of Scots* (Edinburgh, 1987)

Bibliography

Smout, T.C., *A History of the Scottish People* (London, 1969)

Steuart, A Francis, *Seigneur Davie: A Sketch Life of David Riccio (Rizzio)* (London and Edinburgh, 1922)

Stewart, Alan, *The Cradle King: A Life of James VI & I* (London, 2003)

Strickland, Mrs Agnes, *Life of Mary Queen of Scots*, vol. I (London, 1873)

Taylor, James, *The Great Historic Families of Scotland*, vol. I (London, 1889)

Weir, Alison, *Mary Queen of Scots and the Murder of Lord Darnley* (London, 2003)

Woolfson, Jonathan, *Padua and the Tudors: English Students in Italy 1485–1603* (Cambridge, 1998)

Wormald, Jenny, *Court, Kirk, and Community, Scotland 1470–1625* (Edinburgh, 1981)

——, *Mary, Queen of Scots, Politics, Passion, and a Kingdom Lost* (London, 1988)

Index

208